THE NIHILISM OF JOHN DEWEY

PAUL K. CROSSER

THE NIHILISM OF JOHN DEWEY

PHILOSOPHICAL LIBRARY
NEW YORK

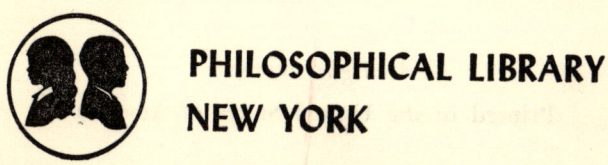

Copyright, 1955,
by Philosophical Library, Inc.
15 East 40th Street, New York 16, N. Y.

All rights reseved
Printed in the United States of America

TO F. S. C., AN AMERICAN TEACHER

CONTENTS

CHAPTER   **PAGE**

Part A - In Place of Science

1. The Dissolution of the Subject Matter of Natural Science.   3
2. The Disassembling of the Subject Matter of Social Science.   39
3. The Degradation of Knowledge.   73

Part B - In Lieu of Art

4. and 5. The Removal of the Art Object followed by a Disposal of the Artist.   97
6. The Dissipation of the Sense of Beauty.   151

Part C - Instead of Education

7. The Suspension of Learning and Teaching.   175
8. The Exclusion of Schools.   209

PREFACE

[Dewey's philosophy in all its major aspects constitutes an attempt to destroy all philosophy. In that sense, Dewey undertook a monumental task. The success of his undertaking, however, was to leave the many Americans who came under his influence without any generalized outlook on life. It left the American intellectual at large, as well as the American artist, with a fragmentary view of things, it left, in particular, the American teacher enmeshed in unrelated details.

Dewey has deprived those Americans who have come under his influence of a general framework within which they could place their everyday activities. Dewey has made America lose its perspective and has thus greatly weakened the intellectual potential of American leadership at home and abroad.]

With these factors in mind, the author of this volume undertakes to demonstrate the cognitive untenability of Dewey's position. In commenting upon Dewey's reasoning, this author uncovers the utter meaninglessness of Dewey's philosophy of science, the utter emptiness of his philosophy of art and the utter sterility of his philosophy of education.

In advancing his criticism of the basic parts of Dewey's fundamental writings, this author is guided by the objective of stating what should not be done, as far as the devising of a philosophy for a great and an intellectually resourceful America is concerned. It is not within the purview of this critical inquiry to develop a specific way of American philosophical thinking. [The author limits himself to the task of clearing away the conceptual shambles which have been left by Dewey's destructive philosophy.] This author is but trying to set the sights for a constructive cognitive ground on which a philosophical rebirth of an intellectually mature and self-confident America could be based.

This is not to say that Dewey and Deweyism had no legitimate place in America, it had. Dewey and Deweyism cleared away the conceptual road-blocks against rational thinking which had been erected in America by preceding philosophic schools. Dewey and Deweyism swept away much of the conceptual dead wood which blocked the progress of American science and education, as well as the advance of American art. Dewey and Deweyism were, however, by the very nature of its conceptions, unable to provide a constructive program for thought and action. A constructive American philosophy, to take the place of the intellectually defeatist philosophy of John Dewey, has yet to be evolved.

Contrary to the claim of the Deweyites, Dewey was not an American Socrates, he is to be more properly regarded as the foremost American sophist. The American Socrates, who will be called upon to undertake a reintegration of American thought, has yet to appear on the American cultural scene.

As far as his relation to Western European philosophy is concerned, John Dewey, it should be noted, had left the broad highways of reasoning which had been charted by Descartes, Spinoza and Locke. He has chosen to tread on the slippery cognitive paths of radical empiricism and extreme subjectivism which bear the imprint of John Stuart Mill.

Dewey has descended to a position of *extreme relativism* which constitutes the ultimate destination on the road to cognitive indeterminableness.

This inquiry evaluates those aspects of Dewey's thinking which have found the most systematic correlation in his writings. The critical essays which form the body of this exposition present a reappraisal of the works of John Dewey in which his *extreme relativistic* position had come to a full turn. Not until the later part of his literary career, it should be noted, did Dewey's *extreme relativistic* position come to be expressed in a fully systematic manner in his writngs. A number of Dewey's works, which predate those which are dealt with in this exposition. constitute for the most part but preliminary exercises and present but fragmentary statements, as far as his ultimate cognitive position of *extreme relativism* is concerned. Some of his later writings present, in turn, but restatements and reformulations of his *extreme relativistic* position.

Various other writings of John Dewey, regardless of the period of his literary career to which they belong, deal with matter which is extraneous with regard to his *extreme relativistic* position and have thus little relevance, as far as his standing as a systematic philosopher is concerned.

The idea of writing this tract had taken hold of the author in the course of conversations which he had with Dr. Robert M. MacIver, Professor Emeritus of Political Philosophy and Sociology and recently Director of the American Academic Freedom Project at Columbia University, as well as with Dr. Joseph Lauwerys, Professor of Comparative Education at the University of London, England and Chairman of the International New Education Fellowship. Professor Robert M. MacIver, Professor Harold D. Lasswell of the Yale University Law School, Mr. Brian Holmes of the Institute of Education, University of London, England, as well as the American author and lecturer Miss Dorothy Thompson have read various parts of this exposition and have communicated their incisive comments to the author.

Permission has been granted by the following publishers to refer to excerpts:

Henry Holt & Company, Inc. from Chapters II, III and IV of John Dewey, *Logic, the Theory of Inquiry,* Henry Holt & Company, Inc. New York, 1938.

G.P. Putnam's Sons, from Chapters I and III of John Dewey, *Art as Experience,* Minton Balch & Co., New York, 1934.

The MacMillan Company, from Chapters II-VII of John Dewey, *Experience and Education,* MacMillan Company, New York, 1938, the author gratefully acknowledges.

PAUL K. CROSSER

A — IN PLACE OF SCIENCE

Chapter One

THE DISSOLUTION OF THE SUBJECT MATTER OF NATURAL SCIENCE

From the very start of his magnum opus, Dewey becomes absorbed with the propagation of nothingness. From the very onset of his *"Logic, the Theory of Inquiry,"* Dewey becomes engaged in the task of furnishing nihilistic devices. He opens the chapter on what he chooses to name "The existential matrix of inquiry: biological" with the proclamation that he is about to develop a statement on naturalistic logic. He then proceeds to evolve what he postulates as "the biological natural foundations of inquiry" (*"Logic the Theory of Inquiry"* p. 23). Though he is willing to admit that "biological operations and structures are not sufficient conditions of inquiry," he wants to have it taken for granted that they are "necessary conditions" (p. 23 op. cit.). In the discussion which follows, he aims at showing, so he declares, the way in which "biological functions and structures prepare the way for deliberate inquiry," (p. 23 op. cit.).

As his primary postulate of what he terms the naturalistic theory of logic, he introduces the notion of "continuity of the lower (less complex) and the higher (more complex) activities and forms" (p. 23 op. cit.). The idea of continuity, he is willing to explain, refers to the exclusion of a "complete rupture of one side and mere repetition of identities on the other; it precludes reduction of the "higher" to the "lower" just as it precludes complete breaks and gaps" (p. 23 op. cit.). Continuity, Dewey inadvertently admits by this explanation, is to be used by him as a major device for defying determinability and denying differentiation.

His subsequent assurance that "the growth and development

of any living organism from seed to maturity illustrates the meaning of continuity" (p. 23 op. cit.) but underscores the purpose of disorientation to which he intends to put his key formulation.

"The method by which development takes place is something to be determined by a study of what actually occurs" (p. 23, 24 op. cit.), he insists. He then goes on to elaborate by stating that it is impossible to "say in advance that development proceeds by minute increments or by abrupt mutations; that it proceeds from the part to the whole by means of compounding of elements or that it proceeds by differentiation of gross wholes into definite related parts" (p. 24 op. cit.).

Though he concedes that "none of these possibilities are excluded as *hypotheses* to be tested by the results of investigation" (p. 24 op. cit.), he does not make any conceptual provisions for the evolvement of a hypothesis. He does not care to go into the question raised by Newton, as to whether a hypothesis has to base itself on something definite, on something which is admittedly definitely attained and determined. The inconclusiveness to which he commits himself by elevating continuity to an all embracing principle compels him to abstain from saying anything about the conceptual requirements for the laying down of a hypothesis.

Within the range of indefiniteness and indeterminableness which the rule of the principle of continuity requires, a hypothetical proposition can hardly be evolved. Within the range of the indefinite and indeterminable a hypothetical proposition can at best become an unsubstantiated guess.

"What is excluded by the postulate of continuity is the appearance upon the scene of a totally outside force as a cause of changes" (p. 24 op. cit.), Dewey protests. Though he ostensibly refers to an outside force, Dewey actually invokes the principle of continuity, in order to deny the feasibility of the specifiability of any definite and determinable causal factor.

"Perhaps," he states as an example, "from mutations that are due to some form of radio-activity a strikingly new form emerges" (p. 24 op. cit.). "But radio-activity," he amplifies, "is not invented *ad hoc* and introduced from without in order to account for such transformation" (p. 24 op. cit.). What he does not state in this connection, is that the principle of continuity, which he considers all pervading, is bound to prevent the realization of anything definite and determinable. He conveniently forgets mentioning at this juncture, that his principle of continuity is so devised as to prevent cognitive recognition of any phenomenon whether new or old. The principle of continuity is so conceived by Dewey, as to make a correlation of two established factors inconceivable. According to the principle of continuity which he propounds, Dewey does not care to be reminded at this instance, nothing can ever be considered established.

Dewey, it can be understood, does not want it to be known at this early stage of his exposition that evolvement of scientific propositions is incompatible with his promulgation of the principle of continuity. By obscuring the implication of his major postulate, he is able to maintain the appearance that he has yet something pertinent to say on the subject. In leaving things unsaid when he touches upon causal specification, he can continue to claim high significance for his contribution to scientific inquiry.

Dewey proceeds to implement his relativistic approach by incorporating the factor of environment. "Whatever else organic life is or is not, it is a process of activity that involves an environment. It is a transaction extending beyond the spatial limits of the organism" (p. 25 op. cit.). In the same breath he insists that "an organism does not live *in* an environment; it lives by means of an environment" (p. 25 op. cit.). By insisting that an organism does not live in an environment, that it lives by means of an environment, Dewey disestablishes the feasibility of any contrasting of what constitutes environment and what does not constitute environment.

In his effort to erase a conceptual distinguishability of environment and organism, Dewey introduces another terminological vehicle. With his declaration that "every organic function is an interaction of intra-organic and extra-organic energies, either directly or indirectly" (p. 25 op. cit.), he makes another attempt to obstruct any conceivable cause and effect relation between organism and environment.

"Not even a hibernating animal can live indefinitely upon itself" (p. 25 op cit.), Dewey protests. "The energy that is drawn is not forced in from without; it is a consequence of energy expended" (p. 25 op. cit.), i.e., Dewey wants the life process to be regarded as a continuous flow of a flow, of a flow and so on ad infinitum of something unfathomable.

The conceptual undifferentiation of organism and environment is, in turn, used by Dewey as a basis for undifferentiating the comprehension of organic functions. In stating that with every differentiation of structure, the environment expands, he wants to bring it out that any manifestation of the life process is characterized by an undifferentiation of organism and environment.

"The difference," as Dewey puts it himself, "is not just that a fish lives *in* the water and a bird *in* the air, but that the characteristic functions of these animals are what they are because of the special way in which water and air enter into their respective activities" (p. 25, 26 op. cit.). He invokes the principle of continuum in this instance to prevent the distinction of organic and non-organic factors in any analysis of a life function. Beyond that, the invocation of the principle of continuum is to make it conceptually impossible to determine what does, and what does not constitute a life function.

Though he has committed himself most fully to have the organism and the environment presented in an undifferentiated form, Dewey, nonetheless, continues to talk about the "differentiation of interactions" and the "need of maintaining a balance among them" (p. 26 op. cit.). He speaks of "unified environment in objective terms" or "a fairly uniform integration with the environment" (p. 26 op. cit.), when he actually refers to the undifferentiation of organic function and the means for its operation. He but reemphasizes the aspect of undifferentiation in arguing that "the balance (between organic and non-organic factors P.C.) has to be maintained by a mechanism that responds both (without any qualification P.C.) to variations that occur within the organism and in surroundings" (p. 26 op. cit.).

In stressing that such an "apparently self-contained function as that of respiration is kept constant by means of active exchanges between the alkaline and carbon dioxide contents of changing pressures exerted by blood and carbon dioxide in the lungs" (p. 26 op. cit.) Dewey is trying to make all over again the point that the organic function and the means for making it function are indistinguishable. In describing the lungs, in turn, as "dependent upon interactions effected by kidneys and liver, which effect the interactions of the circulating blood with materials of the digestive tract" (p. 26 op. cit.), he is but underlining the indeterminableness of the functions of specific organs in terms of specific cause and effect relations.

Though he concludes that "this whole system of accurately timed interchanges is regulated by changes in the nervous system" (p. 26 op. cit.), he does not care to reveal how he expects to analyze that system without making due allowance for a comprehension of the parts which form the system, nor does he care to disclose how "accurate timing" and "regulation" are to be assessed in "an interchange" without making a cognitive provision for the identification of the factors of interchange.

Dewey reinforces the extremity of his position in the matter of indefiniteness by launching another attack on the cause effect correlation. "Each particular activity prepares a way for the activity that follows" (p. 27 op. cit.), he seems to be willing to admit. He is quick to warn, however, that "these" (activities P.C.) "form not a mere succession but a series" (p. 27 op. cit.). "This seriated quality of life activities," he hastens to explain, "is effected through the delicate balance of the complex factors in each particular activity" (p. 27 op. cit.). What he is actually saying here amounts to a negation of any particularity. By introducing the terms "delicate balance" and 'complex factors," he absolves himself from the considerations of any specific sequence with reference to life processes.

Though he asserts that 'if there is a surplus balance, growth occurs" and "if there is a deficit balance, degeneration commences" (p. 25 op. cit.), he does not provide any conceptual means for distinguishing a biological balance from an imbalance. He leaves the words growth and degeneration unexplained. His reference to growth as surplus balance remains as indeterminate as his reference to degeneration as deficit imbalance.

Balance Dewey wants to be understood as the balance "within a given activity" (p. 27 op. cit.), meaning balance not between two determinable factors but a balance within one indeterminable factor. In that sense he argues that when a balance within a given activity is disturbed "when . . . there is a proportionate excess or deficit in some factor (he means again some indeterminable factor, P.C.)—then there is exhibited need, search and fulfillment (or satisfaction) in the objective meaning of those terms" (p. 27 op. cit.). The stated argument might have some plausibility in the absence of the principle of continuum. In the presence of the principle of continuum to which Dewey continues to subscribe, the question logically arises, how the need of an organism which is considered indeterminable as such and the fulfillment or, more exact, satisfaction of an organic function considered unspecifiable as such, can ever be established.

In his subsequent treatment of the subject-matter of natural science, Dewey indulges in the propagation of paradoxes. He appears to be fascinated by the prospect of startling his readers by the use of commonly used terms in a rather uncommon fashion. He substitutes the term tension for the term need. He does not concede that the term tension refers exclusively to emotions and feelings. He wants the term tension to be regarded as all inclusive. The term tension is to be used in a manner which is supposed to give an account of the factor which causes the tension as well as the factor which the tension effects.

"A state of tension," Dewey declares, "is an actual state (not mere feeling) of organic uneasiness and restlessness" (p. 27 op. cit.). "This state of tension (which defines need)," Dewey proclaims, "passes into search for material that will restore the condition of balance" (p. 27 op. cit.). The substitution of tension for need is closely connected with his unwillingness to concede the cognitive identifiability of the subject-matter under discussion, either in the material or the ideal sense. The word tension is to serve as a kind of protective device for any conceivable intrusion of subject-matter in any determinable form. The subject-matter in question is not to be allowed to play the role of either a determining factor or a determined factor.

Indeterminableness to which the word tension is supposed to give added support is further enhanced by the substitution of the word satisfaction. Sensing that the word satisfaction in its common use requires a more or less distinct answer to the question what is to be satisfied and with what that satisfaction is to be attained, Dewey prefers to have the established denotation of satisfaction replaced by the rather innocuous term adaptation.

Should the question of adaptation of what to what arise, Dewey makes it sure, that a definite answer is not to be forthcoming. To provide himself with an alibi for keeping the word adaptation within the range of indefiniteness, Dewey starts an ad hoc discussion with the author of *"The Psychology of Reasoning,"* Rignano. Dewey disapproves of Rignano's postulation according to which "every organism strives to stay in a stationary state" (p. 27 op. cit.). He takes objection to Rignano's statement that "a prior physiological state cannot be perfectly reestablished and made to persist in normal activity until an animal by its movements has succeeded in getting again into an environment identical with its old one" (p. 28 op. cit.).

He takes issue with Rignano on the latter's insistence on "the *restoration* of the previous *state* of the *organism*" (p. 28 op. cit.). Dewey is apparently trying to make a point for the recognition of the factor of change. He argues against Rignano's inference of a return to a previous condition. His argument however, remains strictly formal. Instead of Rignano's emphasis on the "restoration of a previous state of the organism" Dewey insists on what he calls "the institution of an integrated relation" (p. 28 op. cit.). The institution of an integrated relation Dewey asserts "is compatible with definite changes in both the organism and the environment; it does not require that old and new states of either the organism or the environments be identical with one another" (p. 28 op. cit.).

Though he uses the words "definite changes" and "old and new states of organism and environment," Dewey does not lift his ban with the just cited assertion on a separate identification of either organism and environment. Since environment as well as organism continue to be denied cognitive identifiability, Dewey's references to "definite changes" and "old and new states of organism and environment" are to be taken as lacking any specification. No matter what issue one takes with Rignano, in regard to his stand "on the restoration of the previous state of organism," his utterance has one advantage over that of Dewey; he, Rignano, definitely means what he says in the stated connection. No matter what objections one might have against principal Rignano's contention, he cannot be accused of a deliberate attempt to discount any evidence.

The amplification Dewey proffers restresses his tendency of saying nothing in so many words. In bringing up as an example the search for food found in connection with the higher organisms, Dewey considers "it appears clear that the very search often leads the organism into an environment that differs from the old one, and that the appropriation of food under new conditions involves a modified state of the organism" (p. 28 op. cit.). When, however, he is called upon to specify his description of "an environment that differs from the old one" and the "modified state of the organism," he becomes as usual, evasive. He evades the issue of identification of "old and new" as far as the environment is concerned as well as the issue of specification of the "old and new" in regard to the organism, by having it implied that the question of old and new is of no relevance as far as either the environment, or the organism is concerned.

What is involved, according to Dewey, is solely a matter of *"interaction."* In the defining of "interaction" the question of the identifiability of either the organism or the environment is not supposed to be raised. The interaction refers in Dewey's own words, to *"form* of the relationship" (p. 28 op. cit.). The substance of such relationship is not to be subject of any inquiry.

Change, Dewey engages in a terminological fence ride, is supposed to refer to a qualitative change. A quantitative change, a gradual change, a change which can be observed, is not to be recognized as a change. Only a change for which no observable reason can be accounted is to be rated as a change. Only a change which is unaccountable is to be regarded as a change.

What Dewey terms as qualitative change is in turn not supplied by him with any such attributes which could make it recognizable as such. In describing what he regards as qualitative change, he but discloses that he is playing with words.

Qualitative change, Dewey elaborates, refers to a change of the *connection* between organism and environment. He is not, however, willing to allow any specification either of the organism or the environment the connection of which is supposed to be manifested in a qualitative change. In the sense in which Dewey applies the word connection, it is cognitively as unfeasible to determine what specifically constitutes the qualitative change and how specifically is a qualitatively changed connection to be distinguished from a qualitatively unchanged connection.

His high-sounding phrase which refers to "the ability to make and retain a changed mode of adaptation in response to new conditions" as the "source of that more extensive development called organic evolution" (p. 28 op. cit.) does not make his denotation of qualitative change any more meaningful. His reference to "the changed mode of adaptation in response to new conditions" constitutes but a rephrasing of his general reference to adaptation as a correlation of an organism, which is not supposed to be determinable to an environment, which is not supposed to be specifiable.

What exactly, one is prone to ask, is adaptation in the sense of unaccountable satisfaction to an indeterminable need to mean? What meaning can there be attached to a definition which describes organic evolution as something the evolvement and establishment of which is not supposed to submit to any concrete observation of the specific substances which are involved in the process.

Apparently to be sure, Dewey allows for a distinctive characterization of "lower and higher" organism. On its face value Dewey concedes a cognitive differentiation between those organisms in which "the interaction between organic and environ-energies takes place for the most part through direct contact" (p. 28, 29 op. cit.), and those organisms "that have distance receptors and special organs of locomotion" (p. 29 op. cit.). When, however, he is called upon to provide cognitive rules by which a lower organism can be set apart from a higher organism, Dewey falters.

Though he admits that the "serial nature of life behavior demands that earlier acts in the series be such as to prepare the way for the later" (p. 29 op. cit.), he does not furnish any cognitive medium by means of which a series can be determined as such. Though he states that "the time between the occurrence of need and the occurrence of its satisfaction inevitably becomes longer when the interaction is not one of direct contact" (p. 29 op. cit.), he fails to proffer any means for a cognitive determination of either need or satisfaction. Though he relates that "the attainment of an integral relation is . . . dependent upon establishing connections with the things at a distance" (p. 29 op. cit.), he continues to refer to integral relation as something highly ephemeral.

How time and distance of something indeterminable are to be determined as Dewey suggests, has to remain anybody's guess. Time and distance in the stated connection can be regarded only as declaratory terms.

Though Dewey professes to see "a definite order of initial, of intermediate, and of final or closing activities" (p. 29 op. cit.) in which the integration of the higher organism with the environment takes place, he makes a supreme effort to have the respective stages confounded. He is out to limit causal specification to what he calls "excitation-reaction." He exemplifies excitation-reaction by reciting that "an animal at rest is moved to sniff, say, by a sensory excitation. If this special relation is isolated and complete in itself or is taken to be such," Dewey elaborates, "there is simply excitation reaction, as when a person jumps, but does nothing else when he hears a sudden noise" (p. 29 op. cit.).

"The excitation," Dewey continues, "is specific and so is the reaction" (p. 29 op. cit.) as a specific case of cause and effect relation, to interpret Dewey at this point.

"Now suppose an excitation comes from a remote object through a distance receptor, as, the eye" (p. 29 op. cit.): Dewey expands his demonstration. "There is also excitation reaction" (p. 29 op. cit.). "But," Dewey becomes emphatic, "if the animal is aroused to an act of pursuit, the situation is quite different" (p. 29 op. cit.). "The particular sensory excitation occurs," Dewey asserts, "but it is coordinated with a larger number of other organic processes—those of its digestive and circulatory organs and its neuro-muscular system, autonomic, proprioceptor and central" (p. 29, 30 op. cit.).

Dewey undertakes here to sidetrack the issue of cause effect relation in this instance by making reference to coordination of an indeterminable number of factors.

By referring to coordination, Dewey provides himself with a catch-all device. When he calls "this coordination . . . a state of the total organism" (p. 30 op. cit.), Dewey says everything and nothing. The reference to "coordination" as "a state of the total organism" relates but one unexplained term to another.

When he in turn suggests that the "coordination" termed as a "state of the total organism" is on its part to be labeled as a stimulus, he but adds another term the specific explanation of which he is out to dodge.

Dewey himself does not feel in any way hesitant to proclaim that the term stimulus is supposed to refer to as nebulous a situation as could be conceived of.

"The so-called stimulus being a total state of the organism, moves of itself" (p. 30 op. cit.), Dewey declares. "Though the stimulus moves of itself," he amplifies, "it moves because of the tensions contained" (p. 30 op. cit.).

Though he refers to a causal aspect at this point, he does not care to state how a respective causal link can be established in the stated connection. He does not care to proffer any device as to how a causal relation to a kind of tension can ever be established which by itself is to be considered as something highly elusive.

Tension to Dewey presents "such a condition of imbalance in the organism that integration of organic factors cannot be attained by any material with which the organism is in direct contact" (p. 29 op. cit.). "Certain of its (the organism's, P.C.) activities," Dewey elaborates, "tend into one direction; others move in a different direction" (p. 29 op. cit.). "More particularly," he continues, "its existing contact-activities and those aroused by its distance-receptors, are at odds with each other, and the outcome of this tension is that the latter activities dominate" (p. 29 op. cit.).

So far so good, but by what is the organism ever to be prompted to effect a change from a tense to a tenseless condition and vice-versa, should the specific appraisal of its organismic needs and satisfactions to be denied to the organism on Dewey's insistence.

Dewey, to be sure, continues with his description in which he relates that "a satiated animal is not stirred by the sight or smell of the prey that moves him when he is hungry" (p. 29 op. cit.). He refuses, however, to give a specific account and is moreover unwilling to admit the very conceivability of a specific account in regard to the satiation of the animal.

Dewey upholds his ban against specifiability when he goes on to describe the unsatiated animal. "In the hungry creature," he states, "activities of search become a definite intervening or intermediate series" (p. 29 op. cit.). Since "series" presents in Dewey's formulation a reference to indefiniteness, the citation of "definite intervening" in the stated connection can mean little, if anything.

The aspect of indefiniteness comes to be underscored in Dewey's subsequent statement which relates that "at each intermediate stage there is still tension between contact activities and those responsive to stimuli through distance receptors" (p. 29 op. cit.).

The pale of indefiniteness is not lifted by Dewey's concluding statement on this point. His assertion that "movement continues until integration is established between contact and visual and motor activities" (p. 29 op. cit.) places the emphasis on the term integration in an effort to screen off causal explanation.

Instead of a causal explanation Dewey proffers a teleological interpretation. By insisting that the stimulus be recognized as the driving force of the total activity Dewey leaves the sphere of empirical observation. He places the predetermined in the place of the determined.

In asserting that the "stimulus in its *relationship* to special activities persists throughout the entire pursuit" (p. 30 op. cit.) Dewey but underscores that he is unwilling to recognize the causal relevance of the special activities. By further elaborating that the "relationship to special activities persists throughout the entire pursuit, although it changes its actual content at each stage of the chase" (p. 30 op. cit.), Dewey once more underscores the factor of causal irrelevance in the operation of the stimulus.

The causal disqualification of observable factors with regard to the operation of the stimulus is brought out in detail by Dewey. He admits that "as the animal runs, specific sensory excitations, those of contact and those that are olfactory and visual, alter with every change of position; with every change in the character of the ground; with changing objects (like bushes and rocks) that progressively intervene; and they also change in intensity with every change in distance from the hunted object" (p. 30 op. cit.). He does not consider, however, that the respective changes might be made accountable to specifiable stimuli.

"The changing excitations" are to be viewed as being "integrated into a single stimulus by the total state of the organism" (p. 30 op. cit.). In considering that in Dewey's vocabulary the words "integration" and "total state of the organism" lack any definiteness, the direction they are supposed to provide for the accountability of "the changing excitations" assumes a rather doubtful nature.

Dewey insists that "the theory that identifies stimuli with a

15

succession of specific sensory excitations cannot possibly account for such unified and continuous response as hunting and stalking prey" (p. 30 op. cit.). "On that theory," he protests, "the animal would have to make at each stage a new and isolated "response" (reaction) to everything that came across his path" (p. 30 op. cit.). He then unscrupulously dismisses the very factor of causative sense reaction since it interferes with his preconceived notion of the "stimulus" as the expression of the "state of totality of the organism."

Dewey demonstrates his cognitive arbitrariness in this case by relating that "he" (the animal, P.C.) "would be reacting to stones, bushes and to changes in the levels and character of the ground in so many independent acts that there would be no continuity of behavior" (p. 30, 31 op. cit.). Why specific acts are not compatible with a "continuity of behavior," Dewey does not care to explain. Nor is he willing to consider that specific sense reactions can either have the effect of having the animal deviate or abandon a course, he, the animal, has set upon.

Dewey's assertion that "he" (the animal, P.C.) "would forget, as we say, what he was after in the multitude of separate reactions he would have to make to independent excitations" (p. 31 op. cit.) constitutes but another tour de force in Dewey's drive to dismiss causal specification. Dewey uses a figure of speech to make the critical observer forget or overlook the bearing of specific hurdles which are likely to arise in the path of an animal which is being saddled with the task of carrying out a premeditated notion of an odd logician.

Dewey's reassurance that "because behavior is in fact a function of the total state of the organism in relation to environment, stimuli are functionally constant in spite of changes in specific content" (p. 31 op. cit.) is not based on any proof. His concluding remark, therefore, that "because of this fact, behavior is sequential, one act growing out of another and leading cumulatively to a further act until the consummatory fully integrated activity occurs" (p. 31 op. cit.) cannot be rated as more than an oratorical pronouncement.

Dewey's further elaborations on the subject of integrated

activity are not in any way designed to have the matter submitted to any specific analysis. His contention that "what exists in normal behavior—development is thus a circuit of which the earlier or 'open' phase is the tension of various elements of organic energy, while the final and 'closed' phase is the institution of integrated interaction of organism and environment" (p. 31 op. cit.) constitutes but a rephrasing of earlier unsubstantiated statements.

Neither does Dewey's declaration that "this integration is represented upon the organic side by equilibration of organic energies, and upon the environmental side by the existence of satisfying conditions" (p. 31 op. cit.), convey anything which Dewey had not previously stated in a rather indefinite form.

Little analytical ground is recovered by Dewey's statement that "in the behavior of higher organisms, the close of the circuit is not identical with the state out of which disequilibration and tension emerged" (p. 31 op. cit.). The territory he allots to inquiry is hardly enlarged by his relation that "a certain modification of environment has also occurred, though it may be only a change in the conditions which future behavior must meet" (p. 31 op. cit.).

Nothing is added in the analytical sense by his subsequent recitation that "on the other hand, there is change in the organic structure that conditions further behavior" (p. 31 op. cit.).

His claim, therefore, that "this modification constitutes what is termed habit" (p. 31 op. cit.), forms but a plea for a terminological changeover without any attendant change in the range of analysis.

Dewey explicitly rejects "the theory of independent successive units of excitation-reaction," according to which, "habit-formation can mean only the increasing fixation of certain ways of behavior through repetition, and an attendant weakening of other behavioral activities" (p. 31, 32 op. cit.).

Though grudgingly, he admits that "the effect of terminal success or consummatory satisfaction in determining habit has always been a stumbling block to those who hold that there are excitation-reaction "bonds" (p. 32 op. cit. footnote). He thus is forced to acknowledge that a view which does not accept the feasibility of a conception of habit which excludes the causal relevance of habit-formation in its specific elements is incompatible with his own approach to habit.

In answer to the stated oppositionist view Dewey reiterates that the "terminal success or consummatory satisfaction in determining habit" "is just what should be expected on the ground of the view expounded in the text, since it is an expression of the fact that the stimulus-response relation is a function of the state of the organism as a whole" (p. 32 op. cit. footnote). He thus but reemphasizes his unwillingness to consider habit as a gradual development the evolvement of which can be sequentially traced from step to step.

He makes it a point to stress that "developmental behavior shows . . . that in the higher organisms excitations are so diffusely linked with reactions that the sequel is affected by the state of the organism in relation to environment" (p. 32 op. cit.). He thus redismisses the causal relevance of excitations with regard to reaction by insisting that they are so diffusely linked as to make them wholly ineffective as compared with the sequel which comes to be effected by the "state of organism in relation to the environment."

In a further elaboration of his organismic view on habit Dewey emphasizes that "in habit and learning the linkage is tightened up not by sheer repetition but by the institution of effective integrated interaction of organic-environing energies—the consummatory close of activities of exploration and search" (p. 32 op. cit.).

By referring to "an integrated interaction of organic and environing energies" Dewey furnishes himself with a cognitive escape clause. Since in his (Dewey's) conception "integrated interaction" refers to an indeterminable correlation of "organic environing energies," he can well use this aspect of indefiniteness in his formulation to disclaim the factor of rigidity in habit within the range of the definition which he is trying to advance.

He cites the interrelation of factors in a behavior pattern to support his claim that "in organisms of the higher order, the special and more definite pattern of recurrent behavior thus formed, does not become completely rigid" (p. 32 op. cit.). "There is for example," he relates, "reciprocal excitation between hand and eye activity; a movement of the hand is aroused by visual activity, then the movement of the hand is followed by a change in visual activity, and so on" (p. 32 op. cit.).

Dewey is concerned in this citation with demonstrating the relativity of the specific activities; he has no intention of providing a conceptual means by which one activity can be causally traced to another activity. He brings into the picture the aspect of multiplicity, in an obvious effort to disqualify a specified cause-effect relation still further.

"If the hand never did but one thing, say reach," Dewey states, "then this habit pattern might become rigidly set" (p. 32 op. cit.). "But," Dewey consoles himself, "the hand also grabs, pushes, draws and manipulates" (p. 32 op. cit.).

"Visual behavior," Dewey continues his venture into multiplicity, "has to be responsive to the performance of a great variety of manual activities" (p. 32 op. cit.). He then reaches the desired conclusion to the effect that through a multiplicity which is so elusive as to defy any concrete cause and effect correlation, the habit pattern comes to maintain a "flexibility and readaptability."

The elusiveness of the concrete thus comes to be wedded to the evasiveness of the general in the conceptualization of Dewey.

The only matter about which Dewey remains very definite in his formulation of habit is his insistence that habit is something which constitutes an organismic attribute. Only under the presumption that habit refers to an organic function can Dewey's assertion that "the view that habits are formed by sheer repetition puts the cart before the horse" (p. 32 op. cit.) be left unchallenged.

Dewey makes it quite clear that his formulation of habit is based on an asocial preconception by stating that "ability to repeat is a result of a formation of a habit through the organic redispositions effected by attainment of a consummatory close" (p. 32 op. cit.). It is the organic predisposition which to Dewey predetermines habit. He insists that environing conditions have to be made to conform to the organic dictation of habit.

Habit as a social factor is prevented by Dewey to play any effective role in the conceptualization of habit. The social aspect of habit is made to submit itself by Dewey, without any reservation, to an organically conceived habit.

"Sheer repetition," Dewey states, "is, in the case of the human organism, the product of conditions that are uniform because they have been made so mechanically—as in much school and factory 'work.'" (p. 33 op. cit.). "Such habits," Dewey continues, "are limited in their manifestation to the rather artificial conditions in which they operate." (p. 32, 33 op. cit.).

"Mechanistic artificial" stand for social in the just cited quotation. Non-mechanistic conditions, by the same token, are such conditions in which social factors in forming habits are overruled in favor of asocial factors. The non-artificial conditions for forming habits are, moreover, by the same token, conditions which are being preconditioned by a submerging of human in non-human nature.

It is in this last connection in which the placing of the word work in quotation marks in the just cited quote can be properly understood.

Dewey's insistence on the subordination to the point of merging of the social and human aspects of habit in the organic is not in any way followed by any strict delineation of the sphere of the organic, on his, Dewey's, part. Organic continues to be presented as ephemeral a factor as ever.

Though Dewey insists that the "ability to repeat is a result of a formation of habit through organic redisposition effected by attainment of a consummatory close" (p. 32 op. cit.), he is utterly unwilling to proffer a cognitive means by which the factor of "consummatory close" could be ascertained.

Though he in turn asserts that this unascertainable modification which is involved in "the attainment of a consummatory close" is equivalent to giving "some definite directions of future actions" (p. 32 op. cit.) he does not provide any cognitive basis by which any kind of direction, not to speak of a "definite direction," could ever be determined. He does not in the slightest recede from his addiction to the indeterminable and indefinite in approaching what he chooses to call an organic habit.

The indeterminableness to which Dewey is committed in his preconceptions is being further emphasized by the general conclusions he wants to be drawn from his addiction to indefiniteness. The extreme relativism to which Dewey descends in his deconceptualization of organism and environment is being carried over by him into further ranges of natural science.

Without any hesitation, Dewey proceeds to invalidate the methods by which nature can be made to yield to man.

"Environmental conditions and energies," Dewey unabashedly proclaims, "are inherent in inquiry as a special mode of organic behavior" (p. 33 op. cit.). No cognitive distinction, i.e., is to be made between organism and environment in making them subject to an inquiry.

In the following sentence Dewey wars against the cognitive distinction between the subject-matter and the subject who comes to be engaged in conducting the inquiry. He ostensibly declares that in "any account of inquiry that supposes the factors involved in it, say, doubt, belief, observed qualities and ideas, to be referable to an isolated organism (subject, self, mind) is bound to destroy all ties between inquiry as reflective thought and as scientific method" (p. 33 op. cit.) and thus is supplying himself with a prescription for the elimination of all reflective thought.

In using the term "isolated organism" and citing in parenthesis subject, self, mind, he is doubtlessly aiming at an interdiction of any conceptual separation of subjective and objective factors in inquiry. It is therefore logical on his part to discount in the same breath doubt, belief, observed qualities and ideas, as means by which the subject tries to orient himself in facing nature.

When he expresses opposition against making doubt, belief, observed qualities and ideas referable to an "isolated organism" (read in this context the subject who is engaged in conducting the inquiry, P.C.) he but voices disapproval of any conceivable comprehension of nature by the human.

In disallowing doubt, belief, observed qualities and ideas, to serve as means for the ascertainability of the object by the subject, Dewey renders the categories of doubt, belief, observed qualities and ideas inoperative as mediums of thought.

Though he recognizes that "such isolation" (meaning cognitive separation of the object and the subject, P.C.) "logically entails a view of inquiry which renders absurd the idea that there is a necessary connection between inquiry and logical theory" (p. 33 op. cit.), he is quick to retort that "the absurdity rests upon the acceptance of an unexamined premise which is the product of a local "subjectivistic" phase of European philosophy" (p. 33 op. cit.).

In voicing such wholesale condemnation he fails to allow for any distinction between the philosophy of extreme subjectivism, which is as much European as non-European, and the philosophy which, in its turn, without any geographical limitations, tries to strike a balance between the conceptualization of an object and a subject.

Dewey's reference to "subjectivistic" phase in quotation marks constitutes an indirect admission on the part of the author of "Logic, the Theory of Inquiry" that he is throwing subjective philosophy, the premises of which warrant that label, together with the philosophy, the premises of which do not warrant a consigning of it to the subjectivistic fold.

In protesting his opposition to what he wants to be regarded as subjectivistic philosophy, Dewey is but throwing a screen over what he undertakes to refer to as objective. His breast beating declaration in which he contends "if what is designated by such terms as doubt, belief, idea, conception, is to have any objective meaning, to say nothing of public verifiability, it must be located and described as behavior in which organism and environment act together, or *inter*-act" (p. 33 op. cit.), is but aimed to conceal his cognitive inability to present "any objective meaning to say nothing of public verifiability," on his terms.

Dewey himself reveals his utter cognitive helplessness in the course of subsequent qualifications with which he supplies the just quoted pronouncement. He but underscores that he has no intention to allow such terms as doubt, belief, idea acquire any meaning at all, not to speak of any definite meaning.

"The earlier discussion," Dewey recounts, "set out with the familiar common sense distinction of organism and environment, and went on to speak of their interaction" (p. 33 op. cit.). "Unfortunately," Dewey expresses regret, "a special philosophical interpretation may be unconsciously read into the common sense distinction" (p. 33 op. cit.). "It will then be supposed," Dewey is horrified, "that organism and environment are 'given' as independent things and interaction is a third independent thing which finally intervenes." (p. 33 op. cit.).

To Dewey, nothing is supposed to be given, since he does not recognize the organism as such and the environment as such; he cannot possibly recognize within the ultra-relativistic cognitive frame which he sets anything but a correlation, as far as organism and environment are concerned.

"In fact," Dewey insists, "the distinction is a practical and temporal one, arising out of the state of tension in which the organism at a given time, in a given phase of life-activity, is set over against the environment as it then and there exists" (p. 33 op. cit.).

In fact, to rephrase Dewey's just cited quote, organism and environment do not manifest themselves in any other recognizable way than by arousing each other. The arousing, or in Dewey's terminology, tension, is the only relevant manifestation of the organism and the environment which Dewey conceives of in the stated context.

Though he refers to "an organism at a given time in a given phase of life activity" and the "environment as it then and there exists," he does not make any cognitive concessions which would permit the identification of any of those aspects. His reference to "the organism at a given time" is not supposed to provide a cognitive lead for answering the question what time, nor is his reference to "a given phase of life activity" supposed to furnish any cognitive indication of how a particular phase of life activity is to be determined, nor is his reference to the "environment as it then and there exists" supposed to provide any cognitive hint of how the then and there is to be ascertained.

He does concede, to be sure, that "there is, of course, a natural world that exists independently of the organism" (p. 33), "but this world," he immediately makes his concession nominal, "is *environment* only as it enters directly and indirectly into life functions" (p. 33 op. cit.).

Organism, i.e., is something which is also environment and environment is something which is also organism in the conceptualization offered by Dewey.

Within such a conceptual framework an interaction cannot be comprehended since it is inconceivable that something should interact with itself.

Conscious of the cognitive impasse to which his postulation of organism as environment and environment as organism leads with regard to the determination of an interaction, Dewey reinvokes the conception of integration in the sense of merging.

"Integration," Dewey asserts, "is more fundamental than is the distinction designated by interaction of organism *and* environment" (p. 34 op. cit.).

He wants the *and* eliminated in any cognitive attempt to comprehend organism and environment, in the just stated pronouncement.

In taking recourse to integration, Dewey compresses organism and environment in the cognitive sense into one single indeterminable factor.

"The latter" (meaning interaction, P.C.), Dewey underscores, "is indicative of a partial disintegration of a prior integration, but one which is of such a dynamic nature that it moves (as long as life continues) toward redintegration" (p. 34 op. cit.).

Instead of interaction of organism and environment, Dewey

proffers a continuous flow of "integration, disintegration" and "redintegration" in which neither organism nor environment are to be cognitively recognized as such. For interaction of organism and environment, Dewey, i.e., wants to substitute an intermixture of indeterminable components.

A respective reference to interaction, Dewey has come to admit in his just cited terminological about face, is not incompatible with the proposition that organism can be cognitively set apart from environment. On that ground, he commits himself to having interaction confined to the same range of indefinite correlation to which he has confined organism and environment by having all three cognitive propositions—interaction, organism and environment—referred to as integration.

By leaving it all to integration, disintegration and redintegration, Dewey presumes he has succeeded in banning the very thought of a cognitive recognition of a given interaction, in which organism and environment could conceivably be identified as factors which react upon each other in any specifiable form.

Dewey's subsequent assertion that "the structure and course of life-behavior has a definite pattern, spatial and temporal" (p. 34 op. cit.) can only be taken to mean, in the light of his preceding pronouncements, that the structure of life behavior has a definitely indeterminable pattern, spatial and temporal.

Dewey himself is obliging in referring back to what he has previously stated, by reminding the reader that "inquiry grows out of an earlier state of settled adjustment, which, because of disturbance, is indeterminate or problematic (corresponding to the first phase of tensional activity)" (p. 34 op. cit.).

While Dewey has failed to provide any conceptual means for the determination of "an earlier state of settled adjustment," he has made plenty of provisions for having the indeterminable placed in the position of serving as the cognitive frame of reference of any inquiry.

His insistence that the first phase of inquiry "passes into inquiry proper, (corresponding to the searching and exploring activities of an organism)" (p. 34 op. cit.), does not add much of a note of definiteness. The "searching and exploring activities" of an organism, which Dewey cites, do not signify anything specifiable within his conceptual framework.

"Searching and exploring activities" of an organism within Dewey's cognitive range, one has to remember, refer to a situation in which neither a need nor a satisfaction are permitted to be comprehended as such. "Searching and exploring activities" of an organism, one is to recall Dewey's previously cited strictures, refer to a condition in which the means are not supposed to be cognitively distinguishable from the ends.

When he calls for assent to his observation that "when the search is successful, belief or assertion is the counterpart upon this level, of redintegration upon the organic level" (p. 34 op. cit.), he remains true to himself. When he solicits approval of his contention that the goal of searching and exploring activities of an organism has been successfully reached with "redintegration upon the organic level," he but reiterates his appeal for a recognition that the goal consists in the reaching of a higher and higher state of indefiniteness. When he elicits acceptance in turn for his postulation that belief and assertion is the counterpart of "redintegration upon the organic level," he but reemphasizes his exposition of belief and assertion as instrumentalities for the determining of the indeterminable.

Unconcerned about the sterility of his propositions, Dewey proceeds to link what he calls the life behavior to the pattern of inquiry.

"There is no inquiry," he is prepared to concede, "that does not involve the making of *some* change in environing conditions" (p. 34 op. cit.). This admission is not followed, however, by a reversal of his stand on the determinability of the environment. How is a change of environment to be comprehended, one is prone to ask, in the face of Dewey's cognitive prohibition to have the organism considered apart from environment.

On the subject how a change of environment is to be determined in the face of the cognitive ban on anything but an unspecifiable interaction in the relation of organism and environment Dewey prefers to remain silent.

His subsequent reference in which he cites "the indispensable place of experiment in inquiry" (p. 34 op. cit.) is not followed by any cognitive concessions which would make the setting up of such experiments feasible. How in the face of his drive to have the subject made cognitively indistinguishable from the object, one is bound to ask, is Dewey to have the objects of demonstration cognitively distinguished from the demonstrator.

His subsequent reference to "experimentation" as "deliberate modification of prior conditions" (p. 34 op. cit.) is not, in turn, followed by a recantation of his insistence on the inconceivability of assessing any specific conditions. His decree against the postulating of a condition, in terms of specific cause and effect relations of organism and environment, remains in force; so does his ban against having the conception of time express itself in any such definite form in which the present can be cognitively distinguished from the past.

In recalling that "even in the pre-scientific stage, an individual moves head, eyes, often the entire body, in order to determine the conditions to be taken account of in forming a judgment" (p. 34 op. cit.), Dewey furnishes an inadvertent characterization of the limited power of observation which he himself is granting the individual.

The kind of individual which Dewey has come to expound does, to be sure, retain the capacity to move his head, eyes, or entire body. The individual cast in the image of Dewey's conceptions can hardly be credited, however, with the capacity to determine the conditions to be taken account of in forming a judgment.

Determination and taking account of, lies beyond the range of comprehensibility which Dewey is willing to grant the kind of individual which he espouses.

Should the movement of the head, the eyes, or the entire body by the type of individual conceived by Dewey "effect a change in environmental relations" (p. 34 op. cit.), the Dewey type of individual could hardly claim that such a change has been brought about by his, the individual's, determined action. Nor could the individual whose mental and physical capacity is being restricted by Dewey ever be credited with gaining any definite knowledge about the change in environment, should that change actually have taken place.

By ending his sentence in which he states that the movements of the individual effect changes in environment with the word *relations,* Dewey himself indicates that he has no intention of abandoning a previously taken cognitive position in the just stated context. In using the word *relations* with reference to environmental changes, Dewey but reaffirms his cognitive stand that all movements of the individual are supposed to be contained within the range of an indeterminable reaction of the organism to environment.

In relating that "active pressure by touch, the acts of pushing, pulling, pounding and manipulating to find out what things 'are like' is an even more overt approach to scientific experimentation" (p. 34 op. cit.), Dewey comes as near as he conceivably could, in placing the scientific experiment within the range of his deconceptualization effort.

The individual who is denied the capacity to determine why he moves and where he moves, can hardly undertake any acts which in their cause and effect relation are more definite than the acts of pushing, pulling, pounding and manipulating.

The instinctive acts of pushing, pulling and pounding, along with intuitive manipulation could well serve as instrumentalities for furnishing some hints of what things "are like," as Dewey suggests. Those instinctive and intuitive individual acts could not conceivably lead to the determination of how things really are, as Dewey probably realized.

The instinctive acts of pushing, pulling, pounding and the intuitive acts of manipulation could, i.e., conceivably provide an inkling of the most immediate reaction to such acts in the sense of psychophysiological reflexes, they could hardly, however, furnish any basis for linking specific environmental results with a premeditated action of the organism.

The instinctive acts of pushing, pulling, pounding and the

intuitive acts of manipulation are not devices by which an organism can gain control over environment.

The instinctive acts of pushing, pulling, pounding along with the intuitiveacts of manipulation to find out what things "are like" do not constitute an overt approach to scientific experimentation, as Dewey would have it, since such acts are in no way conducive to provide any conclusive evidence as to either the qualities of the object under investigation, or the capacities of the individual observer.

The instinctive acts of pushing, pulling, pounding along with the intuitive acts of manipulating can at best be termed as an "overt approach" to the kind of scientific experimentation which can be conducted under the provisions of Dewey's cognitive strictures, which do not provide for a contradistinction between the imaginary and non-imaginary.

Dewey, on his part, wants to maintain the appearance that a regression towards greater indefiniteness presents a more advanced pattern of scientific inquiry. He holds up the pattern "which is serial or sequential" (p. 34 op. cit.), as the more adequate scientific instrument.

He does not care to mention in this connection that he has introduced the aspect of the "serial" in an effort to exclude precision in the kind of scientific observation which he suggests. He apparently does not want to be reminded at this intersection that he has invoked the denotation of "serial" as a means to bar exactness in the presentation of scientific data.

Dewey would like to avoid the embarrassment of being reminded that he uses the term serial in as loose a manner as he is applying the terms integration and redintegration. Dewey does not cherish the prospect of having it called to his attention that in relying on the term serial he provides himself with a terminological means for having the range of his conception of interaction extended ad infinitum.

Dewey does not at all welcome the prospect of having it made clear to him that the using of the term serial in connection with life behavior makes it feasible for him to relate an indeterminable number of synthetically conceived life manifestations to each other, under the presumption that those serial manifestations are unanalyzable.

"It has already been noted," Dewey remarks nonchalantly, "that this trait of life-behavior (i.e. the serial and sequential) becomes more marked with the emergence of distance-receptors and of the neural apparatus necessary for coordinating their excitation with contact-receptors and with the muscular, circulatory and respiratory mechanisms which are involved in behavior" (p. 34 op. cit.).

He is not at all prepared to have the implication spelled out that his relegation of mechanisms of life behavior to a serial pattern amounts to a denial of a specification of the coordination of "the excitations with contact receptors and with the muscular, circulatory and respiratory mechanisms" and any other factors involved in the stated coordination.

In presenting coordination as a "serial pattern" Dewey disowns the relevance of any of the factors of "excitation" as well as the factor "contact receptors." In fashioning coordination in a "serial pattern" Dewey, in turn, deprives the "muscular, circulatory, and respiratory mechanisms" of any specifiable role in his formulation of life behavior.

His subsequent declaration that "in the human organism, organic retention (or habit-patterns) give rise to recollection" (p. 34 op. cit.) is not followed by any device which could lead to a specification of such recollections.

By reciting that "goals or consequences that are even more remote in time and space are then set up" (p. 34, 35 op. cit.) Dewey himself testifies to the confounding of indeterminableness, if such were cognitively possible, in any attempt to ascertain the goal or the consequences of life behavior within his relativistic approach.

Dewey but underscores that he has an ever progressing unspecifiability in mind in his reference to the goals or consequences when he relates "the intervening process of search becomes more seriated in temporal span and in connecting links than in the case of the simple presence of distance-stimuli" (p. 35 op. cit.).

"More seriated" definitely stands for more indefinite in the just cited reference.

In his subsequent formulation Dewey undertakes to reduce the organic cause and effect relation in the evolvement of a life-pattern to an all but unrecognizable factor.

In making the statement that the "formation of an end-in-view, or consequence to be brought about, is conditioned by recollection" (p. 35 op. cit.), Dewey places the emphasis on the word conditioned.

Conditioned in the stated context, means preconditioned. Conditioned, in the sense in which Dewey uses the word, refers to the mere reflexive.

Since he keeps the factors of conditioning within a non-reflective scope, Dewey absolves himself from the logical requirement of having to provide any definite accounting for the factor of recollections.

In keeping conditioning within the range of an instinctive reaction, Dewey frees himself from the necessity to furnish any answer to the questions:

first, what the recollections to which he refers really are,
second, by what specifically are those recollections caused,
third, what in particular do those recollections effect.

Dewey, to be sure, continues to refer to recollections as if he regards them as being reflective. His statement that "it requires making plans in conjunction with selection and ordering of the consecutive means by which the plan may become an actuality" (p. 35 op. cit.), it should be noted, does make a reference to a reflective chain reaction.

Plans, it should be admitted, cannot be made and actualized, without the selection and ordering of consecutive means.

Dewey, however, does not regard his statement on planning as being more than of declaratory import. Dewey considers it superfluous to explain how a selection and ordering of consecutive means in any definite form is to be squared with his notion of serial unspecifiability.

Dewey admits that "the serially connected processes and operations by means of which a consummatory close is brought into being are, by description, intermediate and instrumental" (p. 35 op. cit.), or are, i.e., indefinite.

He is even willing to concede that "this distinctive characteristic" (i.e. the characteristic of indistinctiveness, P.C.) "prefigures, on the biological level, the interpretation that must be given, upon the level of inquiry, to operations of inference and discourse in their relation to final judgment as the consummation of inquiry" (p. 35 op. cit.).

He holds it to be entirely unnecessary to proffer any device by means of which the operations of inference and discourse in their relation to final judgment as the consummation of inquiry could be ascertained in any specifiable form.

To Dewey logic presents as indefinite a factor as the subject-matter to which he refers. He fits logic into the indefiniteness to which he commits the subject under investigation by qualifying both as serial. To use Dewey's own phraseology, "the basic importance of the serial relation in logic is rooted in the conditions of life itself" (p. 35 op. cit.).

In life itself, the serial quality refers to, in Dewey's words, to "the modification of both organic and environmental energies . . . involved in life activity" (p. 35 op. cit.).

The serial quality in life activity is termed by Dewey as "organic fact." Fact, in this connection, comes to refer to something which cannot be properly identified.

Fact, in the stated context, does not refer to anything which can be specifically observed. Organic fact means something indeterminable to Dewey. Organic fact signifies to Dewey an interaction of an organism, which is not supposed to be comprehended as such, with an environment, which is not supposed to be considered a factor sui generis.

"This organic fact," (i.e. a fact in which nothing factual can be really determined, P.C.), "foreshadows" to Dewey "learning and discovery" (p. 35 op. cit.).

How the indeterminable situation as which he presents the organic fact can ever be interpreted as leading to learning and discovery in the sense of something determinable, is difficult to see.

Indeterminableness assigned to the role of an overriding factor in an inquiry does, to be sure, throw its shadow upon the whole subsequent course of inquiry in Dewey's exposition.

Indeterminableness as a major premise of inquiry can logically foreshadow nothing but indeterminableness or, i.e., inconclusiveness of the inquiry as its result.

The application of indeterminableness as a major cognitive device can lead but to the discovery and learning that the object of inquiry is indeterminable.

Dewey's insistence that the unfactual organic fact "foreshadows learning and discovery, with the consequent outgrowth of new needs and new problematic situations" (p. 35 op. cit.) has but oratorical significance.

Since his cognitive prohibition on having needs identified as such and problematic situations specifically delineated remains in force, he has deprived himself of the cognitive means of contrasting new and old needs and differentiating between new and old problematic situations.

Indeterminableness as an overriding cognitive factor is being reinforced by Dewey's treatment of what he calls experience.

He first objects to the use of the word experience in the sense "that a certain conclusion or theory is experientially verified, and is thereby marked off from a wild fancy, a happy guess and from a *merely* theoretical construction" (p. 37 op. cit.).

Dewey is bent on having the word experience used in a manner in which experiential verification of a certain conclusion or theory does not mark it off from a wild fancy or a happy guess or from a *"merely* theoretical construction" which can be more adequately defined as a concoction.

In proceeding to make the term experience mean anything and nothing, Dewey complains that "because of the influence of psychological epistemology of a subjective, private type, 'experience' has been limited to conscious states and processes" (p. 37 op. cit.).

He does not object at this crucial turn to psychological

epistemology as such, but the use of psychological epistemology or, to say it in plainer language, the use of subjective preconceptions for the marking off of conscious from unconscious statuses and processes.

He is determined, he leaves little doubt about it, to make it cognitively unfeasible to mark off the conscious in the experience of the individual.

To clear the way for having experience rated as a factor in which consciousness is granted the same validity as unconsciousness, Dewey equates experiential and empirical.

"When it is said," he asserts, "that certain conclusions are experientially or empirically confirmed, a scientist means anything but that they rest upon mental and personal states of mind" (p. 38 op. cit.). He implies in the stated assertion that empirical and experiential in the scientific sense does not involve the relation of object to subject.

He goes as far as to attack the positing of the word empirical against the word rational. He cites with approval that the word empirical has lost what he regards as the early meaning in which the word was applied "to conclusions that rest upon accumulation of past experiences to exclusion of insight into principles" (p. 37 op. cit.).

Dewey remains true to his postulate of relativistic continuity with its prime corollary that "inquiry is a development out of organic-environment integration and interaction" (p. 35 op. cit.) in which, let us add, psychology as a factor in the individual's orientation has no place.

Since he employs logic as an instrument of disorientation, he cannot, logically, do otherwise than to have psychology applied as a disorienting device.

He complains of "the divorce between logic and scientific methodology" which, to him, has its "basis largely in the belief that since inquiry involves doubt, suggestion, observation, conjecture, sagacious discernment, etc., and since it is assumed that all these things are 'mentalistic' there is a gulf between inquiry (or reflective thinking) and logic" (p. 36 op. cit.).

He makes no effort to wrest the just stated cognitive instrumentalities of doubt, observation, conjecture and sagacious discernment from the fold of subjectivistic extremity into which they have allegedly fallen. He is but speaking of a "gulf between inquiry (or reflective thinking) and logic," in order to provide himself with a talking point from which he can argue in favor of an emphasis of the non-reflective at the exclusion of the reflective.

To exemplify what he means by "an accumulation of past experience to the exclusion of insight into principles" (p. 37 op. cit.), Dewey cites the case of "a medical practitioner" who "may have skill in recognizing the symptoms of disease and skill in their treatment because of repeated past observations and customary modes of treatment, without understanding the etiology of disease and the reasons for the kind of treatment employed" (p. 37 op. cit.).

"The same thing," Dewey asserts, "holds of the skills of many mechanics and artisans" (p. 37 op. cit.).

He wants " 'empirical' in this sense" to be regarded as describing "an actual fact," which "is justly distinguished from 'rational' activity meaning by that word, conduct grounded in the understanding of principles" (p. 37 op. cit.).

He thus posits habitual as non-reasoned.

"It is evident," he asserts, "that when a scientific conclusion is said to be empirically established, no such conclusion of rationality or reasoning is intended or involved" (p. 37 op. cit.).

"On the contrary," he relates, in positing the habitual as against the reasoned, "every conclusion scientifically reached as to matters of fact involves reasoning with and from principles, usually mathematically expressed" (p. 37 op. cit.).

He thus comes to talk of two modes of empirical, empirical in the sense of the non-reasoned habitual and empirical in the sense of the reasoned non-habitual, in an obvious effort to have the two meanings of empiricism rendered indistinguishable.

"To say then," he declares, "that it is empirically established is to say the opposite of what is said when 'empirical' means only observations and habitual response to what is observed" (p. 37 op. cit.).

Such contradistinction, he then proclaims, is to be considered unacceptable. "The conversion of a justifiable distinction," he insists, "between empirical as defined in terms of the knowledge and actions of artisans and rational as defined in terms of scientific understanding, into something absolute which sets every mode of experience in opposition to reason and the rational, depends accordingly, upon an arbitrary preconception as to what experience and its limits *must* be" (p. 37, 38 op. cit.).

With this insistence Dewey makes it clear that he wants the term experience to refer indiscriminately to the reasoned and the non-reasoned.

In the light of his insistence on having the rational made indistinguishable from the non-rational and the conscious rendered indistinguishable from the unconscious, it can be readily understood, that he is eager to overrule any and all "distinction between, say, temporal and eternal objects, perception and conception, and, more generally, matter and form," (p. 38 op. cit.) within the framework in which he himself chooses to reason.

Were he to allow for any cognitive distinction between the temporal and eternal objects, perception and conception, and last, but not least, matter and form, Dewey is well aware, he could not sustain his presumption in favor of the unreflective.

By way of a post-scriptum, Dewey registers the existence of "a discrepancy between means that are employed and consequences that ensue" (p. 39 op. cit.).

How in the face of his insistence on the overriding factor of "continuum" he could permit himself to register a discrepancy between means and consequences in any specific form, Dewey does not disclose at this point.

He goes on to state that "sometimes this discrepancy is so serious that its result is what we call mistake and error" (p. 39 op. cit.).

He is not thinking, Dewey is quick to remark, in this connection of a mistake and error as something which can be definitely ascertained. He is but eager to point out the indeterminable source of any mistake and error, Dewey insists.

"The discrepancy exists," he solemnly declares, "because the means used, the organs and habits of biological behavior and the organs and conceptions employed in deliberate inquiry, must be present and actual, while consequences to be attained are future" (p. 39 op. cit.).

"Present actual means," he adds, "are the results of past conditions and past activities" (p. 39 op. cit.).

What he does not care to spell out in this instance, are the strictures which he had previously imposed upon the cognitive differentiation between the actual present, the actualized past, and the non-actual future.

Since Dewey denies "the organs and habits of biological behavior" a cognitive distinction between organism and environment, since he, moreover, does not permit "the organs and conceptions of deliberate inquiry" to serve as cognitive marks by which the reasoned can be distinguished from the unreasoned, he rules out the cognition of time sequences and makes it cognitively impossible to say, whether the actual is more or less indeterminable than the non-actual.

Chapter Two

THE DISASSEMBLING OF THE SUBJECT-MATTER OF SOCIAL SCIENCE

Dewey's dissolution of the subject-matter of natural science, which the opening chapter of this critical exposition has brought out, is followed by the dissolution of the subject-matter of social science on the part of the author of *"Logic, the Theory of Inquiry,"* which is to be disclosed in the present chapter.

Dewey introduces the social plane in a rather matter of course manner. "The environment," he states, "in which human beings live, act and inquire, is not simply physical. It is cultural as well." (*"Logic, the Theory of Inquiry,"* p. 42).

"Problems," he continues in a matter of course way, "which induce inquiry grow out of the relations of fellow beings to one another" (p. 42 op. cit.).

Some suspicion is raised by Dewey's subsequent declaration that "the organs for dealing with these relations" (i.e., relations of fellow beings to one another, P.C.) "are not only the eye and ear, but the meanings which have developed in the course of living" (p. 42 op. cit.).

Is Dewey, the question presses itself upon the reader of the just cited passage, getting ready to deal with what he calls meanings in the same way in which he treated the biological function of the human organs?

Is he not to make what he terms as meaning appear as indeterminable, as he had made the functioning of the eye and ear appear? Is he not aiming at correlating the indefiniteness to which he reduced the biological aspect of living with an indefiniteness of the social aspects of living?

The answer is not long in forthcoming.

"To a very large extent," Dewey touches upon the subject of the correlation of the biological and social aspects of life, "the ways in which human beings respond even to physical conditions are influenced by their cultural environment" (p. 42 op. cit.).

"Light and fire," Dewey recounts, "are physical facts" (p. 42 op. cit.).

"But," he warns, "the occasions in which a human being responds to things as merely physical in purely physical ways are comparatively rare" (p. 42 op. cit.).

"Such occasions," he implements his warning statement," are the act of jumping when a sudden noise is heard, withdrawing the hand when something hot is touched, blinking in the presence of a sudden increase of light, animal-like basking in sunshine, etc." (p. 42 op. cit.).

"Such reactions," Dewey emphasizes, "are on the biological plane." (p. 42 op. cit.).

Those reactions, Dewey should have pointed out in this instance, are the only ones on the biological plane the individual can become aware of under the provisions of the cognitive strictures imposed by the author of "Logic, the Theory of Inquiry."

When he goes on to assert that "the typical cases of human behavior are not represented by such examples" (p. 42 op. cit.), i.e., by examples in the range of physiological reflexes, he should have added that those typical cases present but one and the most primitive part of human behavior on a biological plane.

In not mentioning that the mere reflex reactions are not wholly representative of the biological range of human life activity, he leaves a vast sphere of the biological subject-matter, the one which extends beyond the range of instinctive reflexes, without any place in his treatment of the subject-matter of natural science.

By limiting himself to bringing up merely the instinctive biological functions, he provides himself with a methodological possibility of turning the vast area of biological functions which are not merely instinctive to a non-biological sphere of inquiry;

and that exactly appears to be the reason why Dewey refrains from extending the biological matrix of inquiry beyond the cognitive range of instinctive reflexes.

In his subsequent formulation which presents as "things representative of distinctly human (read social, P.C.) activity... the *use* of sound in speech and listening to speech, making and enjoying music; the kindling and tending of fire to cook and to keep warm; the production of light to carry on and regulate occupations and social enjoyments" (p. 42 op. cit.), Dewey most definitely cites factors of physical life the conceptual range of which cannot be placed within the narrow limits which are reserved for the comprehension of instinctive reflexes, along with manifestations of human living which undoubtedly belong to the social range of cognition.

The undifferentiation or, let us better say in this instance, the intermingling of biological and social factors in life activity, is being reemphasized by Dewey in his reference to the correlation of biological and cultural aspects.

"To indicate the full scope of cultural determination of the conduct of living," Dewey recites, "one would have to follow the behavior of an individual throughout at least a day; whether that of a day laborer, of a professional man, artist or scientist, and whether the individual be a growing child or a parent" (p. 43 op. cit.).

The listing of occupational or strictly social characteristics on the same level with physiological attributes of growth, can well be regarded as an exemplification of his indiscriminate treatment of biological and social manifestations of life.

His subsequent claims that the result of such indiscriminate treatment of physiological and social properties "would show how thoroughly saturated behavior is with conditions and factors that are of cultural origin and import" (p. 42, 43 op. cit.) can, in turn, be viewed as a demonstration of his determination to have the cultural or social area overextended at the expense of the biological or physiological areas of inquiry.

His insistence on having the social area of investigation include large areas of the physical or biological subject-matter is but reemphasized by Dewey's assertion that "of distinctively human behavior it may be said that the strictly physical environment is so incorporated in a cultural environment that our interactions with the former, the problems that arise with reference to it, and our ways of dealing with these problems, are profoundly affected by incorporation of the physical environment in the cultural" (p. 43 op. cit.).

Though he cites with approval Aristotle's postulation that "Man is a *social* animal" (p. 43 op. cit.) and admits that "this fact introduces him into situations and originates problems and ways of solving them that have no precedent upon the organic biological level" (p. 43 op. cit.), he has no intention of providing for a cognitive differentiation between the social and the non-social.

In the very next sentence Dewey is giving a hint that he is determined to hold on to the cognitive undifferentiation of the social and the non-social.

In the beginning of the following sentence he apparently reasons within a cognitive framework which provides for a qualitative distinction between the social and non-social when he states that "for man is social in another sense than the bee and ant, since his activities are encompassed in an environment that is culturally transmitted" (p. 43 op. cit.).

The second qualifying part of that sentence makes it clear, however, that he is bent on subverting that Aristotelian conception into its opposite, by having man's activities, as well as the activities of the animal placed into an identical cognitive fold.

In stating that "what man does and how he acts, is determined not by organic structure and physical heredity *alone* (italics by the author of this volume) " (p. 43 op. cit.), he gives a clear indication that he is determined to adhere to a comprehension which intermingles the actions of man and animals, without providing for the recognition of any principal marks of distinction.

The indication that he is determined to bring in the biological subject-matter once more, in order to blur the cultural subject-matter, becomes a certainty, when Dewey bluntly states that "even the neuro-muscular structures of individuals are modified through the influence of the cultural environment upon the activities performed" (p. 43 op. cit.).

The blunt statement makes it unmistakably clear that the comprehension of cultural activity is slated by Dewey for a submergence in the comprehension of a non-cultural activity.

He becomes even more outspoken in his determination not to allow for any essential cognitive difference between the cultural and non-cultural when he proclaims that "the acquisition and understanding of language with proficiency in the arts (that are foreign to other animals than men) represent an incorporation within the physical structure of human beings of the effects of cultural conditions, *an interpenetration so profound that resulting activities are as direct and seemingly "natural" as are the first reactions of an infant*" (underlining mine, P.C.) (p. 43 op. cit.).

With the latter half of the sentence in the just cited quotation Dewey devises a general procedure for the recommitment of cultural activity to the non-cultural fold.

He, moreover, paves the way with the just cited statement for having primitive or infantile human expression rendered cognitively undifferentiated from more advanced forms of human expression.

"To speak, to read, to exercise any art, industrial, fine or political, are instances of modification wrought *within*" (italics Dewey's, P.C.) "the biological organism by the cultural environment" (p. 43 op. cit.).

With this statement Dewey is actually disposing of the claim of the subject-matter of social science for an area of investigation of its own, by having its area assigned to the area of inquiry which had been reserved for natural science.

In the just quoted sentence Dewey is actually identifying speech, reading, any exercise in any art, industrial, fine or political as manifestations of the animal nature in man, thus fully disqualifying the Aristotelian proposition which made a provision for a qualitative distinction between the way in which animals and men express themselves.

Actually, Dewey wants to make sure with the just stated sentence, that, as far as cognition is concerned, no difference is to be made between the barking of a dog, the meowing of a cat, and the speech of a man.

In subsequently stating that the "modification of organic behavior in and by the cultural environment accounts for, or rather *is* (italics mine, P.C.) the transformation of purely organic behavior into behavior marked by intellectual properties" (p. 43 op. cit.), he is reinforcing his conception of the cognitive indistinctiveness of the cultural and non-cultural, by presenting it as a limitation of man's reasoning power.

With the reference to the "modification of organic behavior *in* and *by* the cultural environment" Dewey blurs the causative relation of organic behavior and cultural environment.

If one is not given cognitive means by which the *in* as the non-causative can be distinguished from the *by* as the causative, the causative range of comprehension in the relation of "modification of organic behavior" and "cultural environment" is rendered inoperative.

Since Dewey has insisted on having the cognition of cultural environment merged with the cognition of organic behavior, his reference to either *in* or *by* is, in effect, purely verbal.

To him the cultural activity, as he had explicitly stated before, is an activity *within* the biological range of activity.

The sequence in which he cites organic behavior and cultural behavior is therefore without any relevance; with any causal linkage absent, it does not make any difference whether he relates "modification of organic behavior in cultural environment" or "cultural environment in the modification of organic behavior."

Neither "cultural environment" nor "modification of organic behavior" is identifiable, as such, in Dewey's conception.

Environment, as has been demonstrated in the previous chapter is postulated as interchangeable with organism in Dewey's comprehension. A conceptual provision for a cognitive distinction between "modification of organic behavior" and "cultural environment" is, therefore, to be rated as being absent from the framework of Dewey's reasoning.

The indistinctiveness to which he reduces the factor of organic behavior and cultural environment is, in turn, bound to result in the indistinctiveness of what he calls "transformation of purely organic behavior into behavior marked by intellectual properties" (p 43 op. cit.).

Dewey bides his time before he makes an unquestionable admission that the intellectual properties he is talking about are as indeterminable as the organic behavior the transformation of which those properties are supposed to present.

He lowers the subject of intellectual properties into the realm of the indeterminable, step by step.

Though he concedes that intellectual operations are merely "foreshadowed in behavior of the biological kind" and that "to foreshadow is not to exemplify" (p 43 op. cit.), he does not care to admit that the realization of what is being foreshadowed presents something principally different from the foreshadowing factor.

He prefers to present intellectual operations as something unrealizable, as something which never moves beyond the stage of the foreshadowed.

Though he solemnly declares that "any theory that rests upon a naturalistic postulate must face the problem of the extraordinary differences that mark off the activities and achievements of human beings from those of other biological forms" (p. 43 op. cit.), he does not shrink from furnishing devices by which the cognition of the "mark-off" is to be made inconceivable.

With his assertion that "these differences (i.e. the differences in behavior of the biological kind and the intellectual operation, P. C.) that have led to the idea that man is *completely separated* (italics mine, P.C.) from other animals by properties that come from a *non-natural* source (italics mine, P.C.)" (p. 43, 44 op. cit.), he registers his unrelenting opposition against any "markoff" of the differences.

In his citing of the complete separation of man and other

animals and his referring to intellectual properties as coming from a non-natural source, Dewey, it should be noted, states the extreme position which is the opposite of his kind of extremity.

To head off a marked differentiation of intellectual and non-intellectual operations, which are respectively placed within contrary extreme ranges, he suggests something completely unmarked.

He undertakes to develop a conception of a representative intellectual pursuit which is not supposed to be comprehended as something in any way differing from organic behavior.

He assigns to the conception of "the development of language (in its widest sense) out of prior biological activities in its connection with wider cultural forces" (p 44 op. cit.) the role to demonstrate that the transformation of the biological kind of behavior into intellectual operation is something which is unascertainable.

The unascertainability of what constitutes a transformation of the biological into the intellectual is brought into full play by Dewey's assertion that "the problem . . . is not the problem of the transition of organic behavior into something wholly *discontinuous* with it" (p. 44 op. cit.) (italics mine, P.C.).

We are back in the realm ruled by Dewey's primary postulate. The preconception of continuum is being invoked to rule out any distinctive conception of the intellectual, as it had been made to rule out any distinctive conception of the non-intellectual.

Dewey does not mind reasserting his addiction to the continuum in quite unmistakable terms.

"It is a special form," he states, "of the general problem of continuity" (p. 44 op. cit.).

Though he hastens to add that "the general problem of continuity refers to a continuity of change and the emergence of new modes of activity—the problem of development at any level" (p. 44 op. cit.), he cannot be unaware that the very principle of continuum is supposed to make for an undifferentiation of new and old modes of activity and the indistinguishability of one level of development from another.

The postulate of continuity, Dewey as its postulator cannot fail to know, precludes even a cognitive distinction between emergence and non-emergence and development and non-development.

Under the overall rule of the principle of continuum a reference to emergence and development does not provide for more cognitive distinctiveness than a reference to continuum itself.

In the cognitive context in which he uses them, the words emergence and development do not mean anything which differs in any way from the meaning or, better said, meaninglessness of the word continuum.

To underscore the complete reign of the principle of continuum, Dewey moves for a disqualification of the aspect of the particular.

"The *special* constitution of an individual organism which plays a role in biological behavior is so irrelevant in controlled inquiry that it has to be discounted" (p. 44 op. cit.), Dewey insists.

He then moves to have his dictum of the continuum reinforced by a non-recognition of the subjective factor.

"To be intellectually 'objective,'" Dewey asserts, "is to discount and eliminate merely personal factors in the operations by which a conclusion is reached" (p. 44 op. cit.).

Dewey rules out the aspect of the particular as a basis for inference and the aspect of the subjective in the effecting of an inference, since his recognition of the two factors would interfere with the overall rule of the principle of continuum, which by its very definition excludes any cognitive distinction between the singular and the general, as well as between the subjective and the objective.

After having eliminated all cognitive obstacles for the unchallenged rule of the principle of continuum, Dewey proceeds to demonstrate its application in the sphere of language, as far as "transformation from organic behavior to intellectual behavior" (p. 45 op. cit.) is concerned.

To comply with the principle of continuum, he starts out

by referring to language "in its widest sense, a sense wider than oral and written speech" (p. 46 op. cit.).

"It includes the latter," Dewey amplifies, "but it includes also not only gestures but rites, ceremonies, monuments and the products of industrial and fine arts" (p. 46 op. cit.).

Thus language comes to include, without any qualification, every range of language development, from the most primitive sign language on, to the most advanced forms of wording.

No room is left in this all inclusiveness for the cognitive recognition of specific stages in linguistic development, even such a drastic change as the one which characterized the advance from the language of gestures and signs, which were conceived as means of holding off an evil eye, to the language of words, which were conceived as rational propositions, is denied specification.

The undifferentiation of linguistic means, which manifest superstitions, from linguistic means, which demonstrate reason, is being underscored by the inclusion of rites and ceremonies in Dewey's conception of language.

Rites and ceremonies range from the means of imploring evil spirits, to demonstrative means in praise of the highest level of human understanding, within the stated range of Dewey's comprehension.

Dewey does not care to make any provision for a cognitive distinction between the reasoned and unreasoned with respect to rites and ceremonies.

In further widening the scope of undifferentiation for his conception of language, Dewey includes material embodiments of human expression, along with the non-material form of human expression, in his range of language.

He thus overextends the application of his conception of language in a way, which makes it conceptually impossible to distinguish, what language is, and what it is not.

This overextension of the language concept presents, in turn, a demonstration of Dewey's disregard for the conceptual differences between object and subject, which he was proud to announce in his bid for the removal of any cognitive obstacles which stand in the way of an overall cognitive rule of the principle of continuum. (See chapter one of this exposition).

The indiscriminate inclusion of monuments and the products of industrial and fine arts in the overextended conception of language adds, in itself, a note of undifferentiation.

He makes no cognitive provision, it should be noted, for a distinction between the embodiments of esthetic or pleasurable expression, in the form of monuments and products of fine arts, and the embodiment of a utilitarian effort, in the form of products of industrial arts.

Dewey's subsequent insistence that "a tool or machine, for example, is not simply a simple or complex physical object having its own physical properties and effects, but is also a mode of language" (p. 46 op. cit.) can be only taken as a reiteration of his determination to keep the conception of language in an overextended form.

Dewey's contention that a tool or a machine *"says* something to those who understand it, about operations of use and their consequences" (p. 46 op. cit.) sounds but an added note of undifferentiation, it discounts the distinction between metaphorical and non-metaphorical use of linguistic expressions, with the consequence, that the cognitive distinctions between forms of human and non-human expression become erased.

The mode of operation which Dewey devises for his overextended conception of language fits in well with the undifferentiated view on linguistic expressions which he advances.

Though he makes a passing remark that language "institutes *communication*" (p. 46 op. cit.), he does not care to discuss the subject of language as communicative instrumentality.

Though he makes reference to linguistic communication as a means of "making of something common" (p. 46 op. cit.), he does not care to specify the something.

Though he insists that "language is made up of physical existences; sounds, or marks on paper, or a temple, statue, or loom" (p. 46 op. cit.), he shies away from an attempt to formulate a common denominator for his heterogenous listing.

Being conscious that he includes animate and inanimate

objects, humans and non-humans, in his conception of language, he prefers not to be confronted with the question of how those factors can communicate with each other.

He is wise to avoid the embarrassment of having to contend with the question, how, and by what means a written word can be communicated to a monument, and how, and by what means a statue can communicate with a loom.

He considers it the better part of wisdom, to maintain that sounds, or marks on paper, or a temple, statue, or loom . . . "do not *operate* or function as mere physical things, . . . they operate in virtue of their *representative* capacity or *meaning*" (p. 46 op. cit.).

With this assertion Dewey makes it clear that he intends to substitute the concept of the generator of communications, as well as the conception of generation of communication, by something which neither of the two represent.

In introducing the aspect of *representative* capacity and meaning Dewey provides himself with the opportunity to advance propositions in regard to linguistic expressions in which the factor that they are supposed to originate in a rather indiscriminate manner from sounds, or marks on paper, or a temple, statue or loom is left out of consideration.

In seeking to disqualify further the function of language with reference to its communicator, Dewey postulates that "the particular physical existence which has meaning is, in the case of speech . . . agreement in *action*" (p. 46 op. cit.).

The factor of understanding, which has a definite bearing on meaning, is thus being removed from the area of investigation of linguistic expressions, in favor of an activity concept, in which understanding and, hence, meaning, are not to be required to play any definite or, better said, definable part.

Dewey's insistence that "even when the meaning of certain legal words is determined by a court, it is not the agreement of the judges which is finally decisive" (p. 47 op. cit.) but emphasizes his defiance of the factor of understanding as related to meaning (agreement of the judges in the stated quotation can be read as understanding of the judges).

The decision occurs, Dewey insists, "for the sake of determining future agreements in associated *behavior*" (p. 47 op. cit.) — it is not therefore the understanding of the decision, or its meaning, but the acting, which is to count, regardless whether it is properly understood, or not.

Dewey is helpful in providing a clue that he is using the word meaning in an unaccepted form.

He states that his reference to the decision of the judges is among other things to prove that the "meaning, which a conventional symbol has, is not itself conventional" (p. 47 op. cit.).

Meaning, in the sense in which Dewey uses the term, is applied in a form in which no cognitive provision is made for the distinguishing of one meaning from another.

Since he removes the generator of meaning, as well as the factor of the generation of meaning, from his cognitive range, he deprives himself of the cognitive means to provide even for a differentiation of meaning and meaninglessness.

If more were needed to prove the undifferentiation of meaning, in the sense in which that term is used by Dewey, his insistence that "the meaning is established by agreements of different persons in existential activities having reference to existential consequences" (p. 47 op. cit.) provides ample testimony to the looseness with which he is determined to deal with meaning.

Existential, one is not to forget, means in Dewey's terminology something unspecifiable, something which can hardly be comprehended. (See chapter one of this exposition).

How a meaning can be attached to something unspecifiable, appears to be baffling.

Dewey, however, is helpful again, he does not mind stating that "the particular existential sound or mark that stands for *dog* or *justice* in different cultures is arbitrary or conventional in the sense that although it has *causes* there are no *reasons* for it" (p. 47 op. cit.).

He implies with this statement that the origination of a word is not a meaningful act and, therefore, of no interest to his, Dewey's, kind of linguistic inquiry.

When he goes on to assert that *"in so far* as it (a word P.C.) is a medium of communication, its meaning is common, because it is constituted by existential conditions" (p. 47 op. cit.), he but underwrites his paradoxical conception of the meaning of words as a function determined by "existential conditions" which, in themselves, are indeterminable.

With his subsequent postulation in which he states that "there is no such thing as a *mere* word or *mere* symbol" (p. 47 op. cit.), Dewey aims at rendering the question of what is meaningful, and what is meaningless insoluble.

He wants to advance with the stated assertion a stricture against the making of a cognitive distinction between a literal ("mere word") and a representative ("mere symbol") interpretation.

He is in particular set against language as a means of expressing or communicating "thoughts"—which he otherwise defines, as—"a means of conveying ideas or meanings that are complete in themselves apart from communal operational force" (p. 48 op. cit.).

He but repeats in the just quoted statement that he is unwilling to make any cognitive provision for a distinction between thoughtful and thoughtless expressions.

All that he is concerned with in the just quoted statement, is the relegation of any wording to a means for undertaking inexplicable actions which he, oddly enough, chooses to call "communal operational force."

He concedes that the connection of the reading of words with action which he demands is supposed to refer to *"possible* ways of operation rather than with those found to be *actually* and immediately required" (p. 49 op. cit.).

He admits in the just cited sentence, that he is referring to an activity which has but the remotest connection with the wording of what is being read.

The reader is to feel free to pay little, if any, attention, Dewey inferentially advises, to the question, of whether the writer of the written word wanted to advance a certain meaning, and what that meaning was supposed to be.

Reading is to be done, to comply with Dewey's conception, in order to receive a stimulation for action, regardless of the sounds which the words convey, and irrespective of their symbolic meaning.

Dewey derides "literature and literary habits" which "are a strong force in building up that conception of separation of ideas and theories from practical activity" (p. 49 footnote op. cit.), not with a view of advancing a balanced view of ideas and theories as they are expressed in literature and the action they effect, but with a view of discounting the presence of ideas and theories in literature, in order to free himself from the necessity to provide a distinct account of the way a meaningful wording effects a meaningful action, and a meaningless wording a meaningless action.

The indistinctiveness of what Dewey wants to be regarded as meaning is further emphasized by his insistence, that "any word or phrase has the meaning which it has only as a member of a constellation of related meanings" (p. 49 op. cit.).

"Words," he states, "as representatives are part of an inclusive code" (p. 49 op. cit.).

He then goes on to declare that "the code may be public or private" (p. 49 op. cit.).

He amplifies the latter statement, in turn, by declaring that "a public code is illustrated in any language that is current in a given cultural group" (p. 49 op. cit.).

He formulates in turn a private code as a code which is "agreed upon by members of special groups so as to be unintelligible to those who have not been initiated" (p. 49 op. cit.).

"Between these two," he observes, "come argots of special groups in a community, and the technical codes invented for a restricted special purpose, like the one used by ships at sea" (p. 49 op. cit.).

He concludes his classification of language groups with a formal observation that "in every case, a particular word has its meaning only in relation to the code of which it is one constituent" (p. 49 op. cit.).

As the more real distinction between the different classes of language, he proffers the one "drawn between meanings that are determined respectively in fairly direct connection with action in situations that are present or near at hand" (he refers in this instance to a language that is current in a given cultural group, P.C.) "and meanings that are determined for possible use in remote and contingent situations" (in this instance he refers to a private code agreed upon by members of special groups, P.C.) (p. 49 op. cit.).

In any language, the just stated division implies, it is not of real importance what is said and by whom it is said, though, oddly enough, Dewey does not discount the importance of the person to whom the language is being addressed.

Of real import, in any language and its use, is to Dewey the stimulation which it provides for action.

It is a kind of language activism which Dewey proposes, in which the content of the spoken and written word is bound to lose much, if not all, of its significance.

Language within the generally accepted scope becomes an array of sounds, the specific meaning of which Dewey is prepared to discount, as his subsequent treatment of the matter amply demonstrates.

"While all language or symbol-meanings are what they are as parts of a system, it does not follow that they have been determined on the basis of their fitness to be such members of a system," Dewey protests; "much less," he insists, "on the basis of their membership in a comprehensive system" (p. 49, 50 op. cit.).

As far as language and the respective symbol-meanings are concerned, Dewey wants to make sure with his protestation, a system is not to be regarded as a system and a part of a system is, therefore, to be rated as something which is not in any way systematic.

The system which is not supposed to be a system becomes in Dewey's formulation "simply the language in common use" (p. 50 op. cit.).

"Its meanings," he amplifies his disqualification of a systematic analysis, "hang together not in virtue of their examined relationship to one another, but because they are current in the same set of group habits and expectations" (p. 50 op. cit.).

Thus the examination of relationships of linguistic expressions in any rational form loses any relevance to Dewey.

And, reaching out for his climactic point in his discounting of a correlated analysis of what he calls meanings in language, Dewey bluntly asserts that "they" (the meanings of language, P.C.) "hang together because of group activities, group interests, customs and institutions" (p. 50 op. cit.).

He thus rules out any analysis of linguistic expressions in their relation to each other, by shifting the analytical scope to factors which lie outside the range of linguistics.

By contrast, he is willing to admit, "scientific language . . . is subject to a test over and above this criterion" (p. 50 op. cit.), i.e., the criterion of uncoordinated group activities.

Instead of having an interrelated analysis of linguistic expressions carried out, he suggests an investigation of uncoordinated group activities, group interests, customs and institutions.

"Each meaning that enters into the (scientific, P. C.) language," Dewey states, "is expressly determined in its relation to other members of the language system" (p. 50 op. cit.).

He thus reiterates the formalistic distinction, which he is willing to make, between the generally spoken and written language group and the specific languages devised by special groups and designed for special purposes.

The catch, however, in the distinction, which he is willing to provide, lies in the indistinctiveness of what he considers to be "meaning."

A systematic correlation of indistinct meanings of scientific language, Dewey can be sure, as no doubt he is, can well become as indistinct as an unsystematic correlation of the indistinct meanings of a generally used language.

Dewey, nonetheless, expounds the formalistic argument according to which "the resulting difference in the two types of language meanings" (the meanings of the generally spoken and written language and the scientific language, P.C.) "fundamentally fixes the difference between what is called common sense and what is called science" (p. 50 op. cit.).

He then goes on to state that "in the former cases" (the cases of the generally spoken and written language, P.C.), "the customs, the *ethos* and spirit of a group is the decisive factor in determining the system of meanings in use" (p. 50 op. cit.).

As if, the ethos, or, to use a plainer expression, a general predisposition can determine anything in any specific form.

As if, the ethos, or, to use the plainer expression, a general predisposition can come to mean anything specifiable.

As if, to sum up the case against Dewey in the stated connection, the ethos, which presents nothing more than an unspecifiable predisposition, can ever determine anything in any specifiable form.

Dewey is at least candid in this case, in stating that "the system" (of the generally used language, P.C.) "is one in a practical and institutional sense rather than in an intellectual sense" (p. 50 op. cit.).

He contrasts, in the stated context, the unreasoned—read practical and institutional—with the reasoned—read intellectual.

He owes an explanation in the stated connection, on what ground he is using the word system in referring to the unreasoned, unless he considers that the word system is not supposed to express any specifiable meaning.

He is, nonetheless, frank to admit that "meanings that are formed on this basis" (i.e., meanings which are referred to the unreasoned, P.C.) "are sure to contain much that is irrelevant and to exclude much that is required for intelligent control of activity" (p 50 op. cit.).

Meanings for which the unreasoned is used as frame of reference cannot ever provide a rational basis for judging what is irrelevant and what is relevant for an intelligent control of activity, Dewey could and should have added in the stated connection.

Dewey, to be sure, does testify that he considers meanings the frame of reference of which is the unreasoned to be "coarse and many of them ... inconsistent with each other from a logical point of view" (p. 50 op. cit.).

He thus admits that the meanings, the frame of reference of which is the unreasoned, are bound to be blurred and incoherent, as far as their relation to each other is concerned.

He could and should have stated in the stated connection, that it is hardly conceivable with reference to the unreasoned, to make a distinction between meaning and meaninglessness.

The disorderliness which results from an attempt to make sense out of a condition which does not provide for anything sensible, is, nonetheless, fairly accurately pictured by Dewey, when he relates that "one meaning is appropriate to action under certain institutional group conditions; another, in some other situation, and there is no attempt to relate the different situations to one another in a coherent scheme" (p. 50 op. cit.).

He concludes the statement on disorderliness by saying that the "multiplicity of language-meaning constellations is also a mark of our existing culture" (p. 50 op. cit.).

"This fact," he throws up his hands, "is the real Babel of communication" (p. 50 op. cit.).

He thus concludes his probing into the meaning of what he terms as common language, by an admission that language in his, Dewey's, time has ceased to be a medium of communication of thought.

Language as means of communication comes thus to serve in Dewey's comprehension as a vehicle for spreading disorientation.

The disorderliness and disorientation which he imputes to the commonly used language, Dewey wants to have inferred, will be overcome when "the ideal of scientific language" is realized, which is to constitute a "construction of a system in which meanings are related to one another in inference and discourse and where the symbols are such as to indicate the relation" (p. 51 op. cit.).

It is not the science language designed for limited use to which Dewey refers in this instance, it is an ideal scientific language which is designed for use by any group and devised

57

for general use which Dewey has in mind in the stated instance.

He is obviously tending to erase the distinction between a coded and an uncoded language, in pleading for an ideal scientific language.

The use to which Dewey puts the denotation of symbol clearly indicates that he is engaged in an effort to substitute artificialities for commonly used words.

The symbol language, which Dewey posits as an ideal scientific language for everybody's everyday use, is to be predicated upon the exclusion of material evidence, Dewey wants to make it sure.

He concedes in his exemplification "that the *word* 'smoke' stands in the English language for an object of certain qualities" (p. 51 op. cit.).

"In some other language," Dewey admits, "the same vocable and mark may stand for something different, and an entirely different sound stand for 'smoke'" (p. 51 op. cit.).

He wants such cases of representation referred to as representation by *"artificial signs"* (p. 51 op. cit.).

Artificial, in this sense, refers to the use of different combinations of sounds in different languages as identical evidence.

In subsequently stating that "when it is said that smoke as an actual existence, points to, is evidence of an existential fire, smoke is said to be a *natural* sign of fire" (p. 51 op. cit.) he makes the word smoke refer not to the evidence of smoke but to the evidence of something which is not smoke.

In making the word smoke appear as identifying some material factor which is not smoke, he makes the use of the word smoke appear doubly senseless.

First, the particular sound combination of smoke in a particular language group, as compared with the sound combination of another language group, which refers to the same evidence, is presented as making little, if any, sense.

On top of it, the specific sound combination of smoke is made to appear as senseless, since it refers to an evidence which, although related to the natural factor of smoke, does not by itself constitute an identification of that actual material factor.

Similarly, Dewey points out, "heavy clouds of given qualities are a natural sign of probable rain, and so on" (p. 51 op. cit.), but they are not natural signs, in his argument, of a material evidence of clouding.

The use of the specific sound combination of the word clouds in the English language makes as little sense as any sound combination which is used in any other language which refers to the identical evidence, to restate Dewey's line of argumentation; nor does the evidence to which the sound combination of the word clouds refers in its usage in the English language, so Dewey's argumentation runs, constitute a sensible evidence since it does not encompass a material beclouding factor for the comprehension of which it had been devised, but a material factor for the comprehension of which the word rain has been devised.

According to the path which Dewey charts, the word rain is, in turn, bound to refer to something which by its material evidence does not constitute rain, but to something which is not rain, aside from the factor that the sound combination of the word rain is by itself to be considered as something which has no basis in any material evidence.

His disqualification of natural signs referred to by words, Dewey argues, is based on the notion that "the representative capacity in question" (i.e. the representative word or better, words, as the representation of material evidence, P.C.) "is attributed to *things in their connection with one another*, not to marks whose meaning depends upon agreement in social use" (p. 51 op. cit.).

That his reference to things in their connection with each other requires a placing of the emphasis on connection at the exclusion of the specification of things, as his performance in the case of the words smoke and rain has shown, Dewey does not care to have recorded in this context.

Nor is he willing to have it explained how marks, i.e. words, can be commonly used without there being any agreement in regard to their social use.

His subsequent statement that "there is no doubt of the existence and the importance of the distinction designated by the words 'natural' and 'artificial' signs" (p. 51 op. cit.) can only become misleading, since he has made what he calls "natural" signs appear unnatural.

His subsequent reference to the effect that "the fundamentally important difference is not brought out by these words" (p. 51 op. cit.), (i.e. the words of natural and artificial) constitutes but a veiled admission that he has used the word natural in the sense of unnatural, and thus has made it methodologically, if not cognitively, unfeasible for himself to contrast what he calls natural signs, and what he names artificial signs.

He prefers to turn his back on words, in the sense of natural signs which he makes appear as artificial signs, in order to introduce artificial signs of his own through the employment of, what he calls, symbols.

The rationalization behind that move involves the inference that the substitution of one kind of artificiality for another kind cannot be attacked on logical and methodological grounds within his frame of reference.

"Smoke, as a thing having certain observed qualities," Dewey expands his line of argumentation, "is a sign of fire only when the thing exists and is observed" (p. 52 op. cit.).

The common word can, in other words, be applied, according to the just quoted statement, to identify a material factor for the comprehension of which it was devised, only when the basis for the observation of that factor is granted reality in the spacial-temporal context.

Such spacial-temporal reality, Dewey admits, "is highly restricted, for it exists only under limited conditions" (p. 52 op. cit.).

Spacial-temporal reality, and the words which are formed to represent it have to submit to certain cognitive requirements and cannot be applied at will—Dewey is willing to concede in this instance.

In testifying to the methodological prerequisites for the employing of common words Dewey is again trying to present the rules which apply to the use of common words as a kind of artificial imposition.

Though he characterizes the common word as a natural sign, he once more tries to taint the natural sign with unnaturalness.

"The situation is very different," he exclaims, "when the *meaning* 'smoke' is embodied in an existence, like a sound or a mark on paper" (p. 52 op. cit.).

A real meaning is to be ascribed to the word smoke only under the condition that the question of a respective material evidence is not supposed to be asked; a real meaning is, in other words, to be imputed to the word smoke only under a condition that it amount to a purely verbal reference.

Real existence and real meaning is not being granted to anything in the stated connection which might conceivably lie beyond the cognitive range of the sound and paper mark of "smoke."

A purely verbal meaning of the word smoke, a meaning which is not burdened with non-verbal factors, Dewey is well pleased to announce, can be used without any regard to anything which might occur within the non-verbal range of cognition.

"It"—(the sound or paper mark of "smoke," P.C.)—"can be related to other meanings in the language-system"; (p. 52 op. cit.), i.e., to meanings in a language system which constitutes but a correlation of sound effects and paper meanings, Dewey is highly pleased to notice.

"Ideas as ideas, hypotheses as hypotheses," in Dewey's assertion, "would not exist were it not for symbols and meanings as distinct from signs and significances" (p. 53 op. cit.).

It is to be noted in the stated connection, that signs do not constitute the whole of observable realities, they are but guides to the observing of reality, or as Dewey puts it, "this something being at the time *inferred* rather than observed" (p. 52 op. cit.).

Dewey is, in turn, bent on blocking any cognition which probes beyond the readily apparent.

Though he admits that to him words or symbols do not provide *"evidence* of any existence," he expresses preference for their use in that cognitive form in stating that "what they" (words and symbols, P.C.) "lack in this capacity" (i.e. capacity for providing evidence of any existence, P.C.) "they make up for in creation of another dimension. They make possible ordered discourse or reasoning" (p. 52 op. cit.), i.e. reasoning which is purely formal in character.

Dewey's utter disregard for any objective factors of validation cannot be expressed in a more blatant form than is the case in his subsequent exclamation in which he states that "this" (ordered discourse or reasoning, P.C.) "may be carried on without any of the existences to which symbols apply being actually present: without, indeed, assurance that objects to which they apply anywhere actually exist, and, as in the case of mathematical discourse, without direct reference to existence at all" (p. 52, 53 op. cit.).

The word symbol thus does come to stand for something which is not a symbol.

Symbolic expressions thus come to express nothing but themselves.

Symbol thus does not constitute a representative sign to Dewey, since it does not represent anything.

The word symbol becomes but an array of sounds which does not refer to anything but its own sound combination.

The sterilization of the word symbol by Dewey is accompanied by his ruling, according to which a sign in his discourse is under no circumstances to be rated as a symbolic sign.

The denotation of sign is being postulated by Dewey as an antidote to the denotation of symbol.

Since to him symbol does not constitute a representative denotation, but a denotation which encompasses what he calls the whole of the situation, he is logically entitled to postulate the word symbol as a denotation which refers to something which is not a sign.

The discarding of the word symbol for the identification of representative expressions has made symbol express nothing in Dewey's formulation.

A symbol which expresses nothing in a symbolic sense is very close to a meaning which does not bring out anything which is particularly meaningful.

The word meaning, in the sense of lack of meaning, expresses as little, if anything, as the word symbol, in the sense of non-symbol.

In that context, Dewey is perfectly justified to ally his use of the word symbol with his application of the word meaning.

As compared to a meaningless meaning and a non-symbolic symbol, even a non-typical sign can be made to appear significant.

In that sense, Dewey is once more logically correct in positing sign and significance, as against symbols and meanings.

Dewey's assertion, which has been cited here before, that "ideas as ideas, hypotheses as hypotheses, would not exist were it not for symbols and meanings as distinct from signs and significances" (p. 53 op. cit.) has to be placed within the cognitive framework in which he applies the words meaning and symbol.

With reference to a meaning and a symbol which is not supposed to refer to any non-verbal evidence, ideas can only rate as cobwebs and hypotheses cannot come to amount to more than fictions.

Dewey's reference in the stated connection to "ideas as ideas" and "hypotheses as hypotheses" but underscores his insistence on having an idea regarded as being expressive of nothing but that idea in a sense of a sound-combination and having a hypothesis refer to nothing but that hypothesis in the sense of a sound-combination.

It is, in a sense, a tautological proposition which Dewey expounds in this instance. His admission that "the greater capacity of symbols for manipulation is of practical importance" (p. 53 op. cit.) but underscores that he is not willing to marshal more than a subjective notion to support his insistence that "ideas as ideas" and "hypotheses as hypotheses" would not exist, were it not for symbols and meanings, as distinct from signs and significance.

His subsequent proclamation that the manipulative subjectivistic angle in using symbol in a non-symbolic manner is paled "in comparison with the fact that symbols introduce into inquiry a dimension different from that of existence" (p. 53 op. cit.) constitutes but an underscoring of his disqualification of objective factors.

"Clouds of certain shapes, size and color may signify to us the probability of rain; they portend rain" (p. 53 op. cit.), Dewey tries to exemplify.

"But the *word* cloud when it is brought into connection with other words of a symbol-constellation enable us," Dewey goes on, "to relate the meaning of being a cloud with such different matters as differences of temperature and pressures, the rotation of the earth, the laws of motion and so on" (p. 53 op. cit.).

What he actually states in the just quoted sentences is that the word clouds when referred to something which can be expected to take place outside the person has little, if any, meaning.

When, however, the word cloud is used in a manner in which it relates nothing but an array of sounds which an individual pronounces, or marks on paper made by an individual, it conveys as much meaning as to allow for its correlation with any number of other sounds.

Dewey certainly does not expect the words "differences of temperature and pressures" and the words "rotation of the earth," or the words "the laws of motion," to express anything which exists in nature, since such expectation on his part would logically force him to take those words out of the framework of the symbol-constellation, within the range of which he is apparently determined to keep them, and to have them placed into the fold of sign significance, from which he is apparently likewise determined to keep those words out.

The integration of scientific and non-scientific language to which his kind of symbol meaning designation is supposed to lead, turns out to be a means of greater obfuscation of scientific terminology along with the obfuscation of non-scientific wording.

The scientific terminology which had come to be agreed upon to express specific factors for specific purposes of observation, as Dewey himself had come to recognize it before he moved in his symbol-constellation proposition, is now being supplanted by a wording which has no reference to any observation of nature.

Scientific terms along with common wording come to be linked to each other by nothing but sound effects or paper marks, which are not supposed to explain anything about man, or nature, or man in nature.

The order into which Dewey promises to put scientific terms along with common words constitutes, as far as any objective fgactors are concerned, but a patent case of disorderliness.

It is in the sense of disorderliness that a meaningless meaning and a non-symbolic symbol lead to the same results, as Dewey expects them to.

His unremitting committment to the promotion of a "Babel of communication" is once more demonstrated by Dewey by his recounting of an incident which Ogden and Richards report in their widely heralded volume on the "The Meaning of Meaning," (reference is made to Page 174 of "The Meaning of Meaning" in Dewey's "Logic, the Theory of Inquiry," Page 53, footnote).

"A visitor in a savage tribe wanted on one occasion "the word for table," Dewey recounts the incident to which Ogden and Richards refer.

"There were five or six boys standing around, and tapping the table with my forefinger I asked "What is this?" (p. 53 op. cit.)," Dewey restates the incident to which Ogden and Richards refer.

"One boy said it was *dodela,* another that it was an *etanda,* a third stated that it was *bokali,* a fourth that it was *elamba,* and the fifth said it was *meza*" (p. 53, op. cit.), according to the account given by Ogden and Richards.

"After congratulating himself on the richness of the vocabulary of the language," Dewey restates Ogden and Richards, "the visitor found later "that one boy had thought he wanted the word for tapping; another understood we were seeking the word for the material of which the table was made; another had the idea that we required the word for hardness; another

65

thought we wished the name for that which covered the table; and the last . . . gave us the word *meza,* table." (p. 53 op. cit.).

This incident but underscores the distinction between a supposed meaning and a verified meaning, and between a presumed symbol and an ascertained symbol.

The incident further testifies to the distinction between the imaginary, in the sense of the evidentially unconfirmed, and the non-imaginary, in the sense of the evidentially confirmed.

Dewey, on his part, looks to the incident for a support for his proposition which, as far as meanings are concerned, relies on supposed meanings and, as far as symbols are involved, takes recourse to presumed symbols.

Verified meaning and ascertained symbol, it should be noted, are not known in Dewey's vocabulary by that name, they are replaced by the denotation of sign significance.

The symbol-constellation within which Dewey's scientific language is supposed to operate is to leave room only for the imaginary, the confirmed he is intent on leaving to the non-scientific, the common language.

In regard to the specific incident the word table, which was the word in the understanding of the questioner, does not fall within the purview of Dewey's symbol-constellation, all the other words, however, which were based on a misunderstanding of the questioner, do fall within Dewey's range of symbol-constellation.

If any other proof were needed that Dewey's conception of symbol-constellation is being designed by him as a means of obfuscating a communication from person to person, the tribal incident, to which he approvingly refers, can well furnish the test.

Dewey himself does not undertake to deny that his symbol-constellation technique can be most appropriately used to create misunderstanding.

"This story" (i.e., the incident referred to by Ogden and Richards), Dewey is proud to announce, "might have been quoted earlier as an illustration of the fact that there is not possible any such thing as a direct one-to-one correspondence of names with existential objects" (p. 53 op. cit.).

The very seeking of any correspondence between words and objects is disavowed by Dewey when he subsequently states "that words mean what they mean in connection with conjoint activities that effect a common, or mutually participated in, consequence" (p. 53 op. cit.).

A word is to be sought not for expression of anything but the consequence of a conjoint activity which a searching of a word constitutes.

The reaching of the word comes thus to be rated as an activity which has no other meaning than the searching of the word.

The searching of the word is thus elevated to an end by itself, since the word to be found is supposed to conform only to the conjoint activities, regardless of what had prompted that activity.

The action which effects the conjoint activity comes to be wholly lost in Dewey's symbol-constellation conception.

The answers which fall within Dewey's range of symbol-constellation are so unrelated to any specific action which they were intended to elicit, that it would have hardly made any difference whether the questioner in the stated case related by Dewey had made any other gesture than the one he actually did.

The misunderstanding created among the questioned tribesmen could hardly have been greater, had the questioner just raised a finger in the direction of the table, or swung his leg towards the table instead of tapping the table, as he actually did, according to the report.

What exactly the gesture of the tapping of the table had to do with the statements which the individual tribesmen made, remains, as Dewey wants them to remain, anybody's guess.

The very fact that it is a gesture, not a word, which is made to elicit the answers, is in itself not to be overlooked; the "symbol-constellation" proffered by Dewey is so unprecise a factor, as to make it rather difficult, if not cognitively impossible, to fit words within it.

Primitive gestures which by their very nature are unprecise, fit much better into the kind of "symbol-constellation" which Dewey propounds.

The instance that the tribesmen answered with words to a gesture makes the whole incident sound rather improbable.

It would have been much more in keeping with Dewey's conception of "symbol-constellation," if he had reported the incident in a form in which the tribesmen had been made to react to a gesture with gestures.

Yet, even an expression with gestures, it can be said, is a more accurate expression of life than a "symbol" which is being deliberately conceived without reference to any manifestation of nature.

A live gesture is more expressive than a dead symbol, there should be little doubt about that.

Dewey refers to a most abortive form of expression in this instance.

His reference to a symbolic-constellation constitutes a misnomer, he actually refers to non-symbolic-constellations.

Nonchalantly he proceeds to reinforce his proposition of symbolic meaning, which is neither symbolic nor has a meaning, by insisting that in their respective relation to each other they refer to "implications."

He obviously implies, in this instance, that a symbol which is not supposed to be representative of anything, and a meaning which is not supposed to have any particular sense, can be said, as having no other implication, than the one, that they are related to each other.

He complains about the ambiguity in which the word relation is being applied, "not merely in ordinary speech but in logical texts" (p. 54, 55 op. cit.) as well. "The word "relation," " he argues, "is used to cover three very different matters which in the interest of a coherent logical doctrine must be discriminated" (p. 55 op. cit.).

He then goes on to state the three different matters as follows:

"(1) Symbols are "related" directly to one another.

(2) They are "related" to existence by the mediating intervention of existential operations.

(3) Existences are "related" to one another in the evidential sign-signified function" (p. 55 op. cit.).

He then wants it accepted without challenge that the three modes of "relation" are so different from one another that they do not warrant the use of the word relation in all three instances.

He insists that the use of the word relation in all the three cited matters tends to create a confusion in regard to what those matters really are.

He then proffers this declaration that in order "to avoid negatively, the disastrous doctrinal confusion that arises from the ambiguity of the word *relation,* and in order to possess positively, linguistic means of making clear the logical nature of the different subject-matters under discussion, I shall reserve the word *relation* to designate the kind of "relation" which symbol-meanings bear to one another *as* symbol-meanings" (p. 55 op. cit.).

He thus reserves the use of the word relation for the indication of a relation which has no relation to either existential operations or existences, to cite his own classification.

He wants the word relation applied in a sense of non-relation as far as existential operations and existences are concerned.

Dewey does not consider it opportune to admit that the use of the word relation with reference to either "symbols," or "existential operations," or "existences" makes it cognitively feasible to refer to any of the three cited factors as but differences in degree.

He does, furthermore, not consider it proper to concede that, contrary to his allegation, the use of the word relation with reference to either "symbols," "existential operations" and "existences," made it cognitively feasible for him to relate similarities as well as differences of the three factors with one another.

As regards the empty symbols which Dewey propounds, it

makes, in turn, very little difference, if any, as far as the advancement of their respective understanding is concerned, whether those symbols are being related to each other or not.

Nor is there, in regard to the arbitrary designation of symbols by Dewey, much difference, as regards the conveying of their meaning is concerned, which of those arbitrary symbols is being related to another arbitrary symbol and in what order, or, for that matter, whether the relation is one of complete disorder.

Dewey could rightly bring logic to his side when he wants it inferred that it might be advisable to keep the word related —which he is bent on bringing into ill repute by way of reference to empty and arbitrary symbols—out of a sphere in which he is willing to concede that a real and significant relation continues to exist.

In the latter sense, Dewey can feel logically justified to "reserve the word *relation* to designate the kind of 'relation' which symbol-meanings bear to one another *as* symbol-meanings" (p. 55 op. cit.).

In the same sense, he can consider himself logically justified to proclaim that he will "use the term *reference* to designate the kind of relation they sustain to existence; and the words *connection* (*and involvement*) to designate that kind of relation sustained by *things* to one another in virtue of which *inference* is possible" (p. 55 op. cit.).

The distancing of the spheres in which the word relation is granted and the spheres in which the word relation is denied application, it should be noted, however, is not limited to a contrasting of the spheres in which the word relation is to have and is not to have currency.

Dewey goes further in his dictum of keeping the spheres of "symbol-meaning" apart from "existential operation" and "existences" with reference to the use of the word relation which he is determined to discredit.

He is providing for a widening of the cognitive gap between the spheres of "existential operation" and "existences," by ordering the substitution of two different words for the word relation, which he wants to have excluded from any usage in regard to the stated two spheres.

He wants the word reference substituted for the word relation in regard to "existential operations."

The word connection or involvement is in turn suggested as a substitute for the word relation in regard to "existences."

The suggestion that the word reference be used instead of the word relation to "designate the kind of relation symbol-meanings sustain to existence," (p. 55 op. cit.) as Dewey phrases it, indicates that, as far as "existential operations" are concerned, he, Dewey, is determined not to go beyond a nominal identification.

The words reference and relation both refer to but an outer manifestation, and the substitution of one by another does not provide for much change, as far as the range of cognition is concerned.

The substitution of the word relation by the word reference suggests a merely verbal performance on the part of Dewey.

Only in regard to the factor of things and the inference which they invite, Dewey appears to be prepared to acknowledge more than an outer manifestation.

The substitution of the word relation by the word connection or the word involvement, does suggest a change in the cognitive range of the sphere to which those two substitute words are made to apply.

Should one, however, be inclined to interpret Dewey's demand for the use of the words connection and involvement in regard to things and the inference they invite, as indication that he is granting the comprehension of things and the way they hang together a cogency which he has denied "symbol-meanings" and their "existential operation," one is taught the better.

Dewey insists that "no inference could be made that was not blind and blundering" (p. 56 op. cit.).

"Moreover," he asserts, "since *what* is inferred . . . is not present in observation, any anticipation that could be formed of it would be vague and indefinite, even supposing an anticipation could occur at all" (p. 56 op. cit.).

The connection and involvement in regard to things, it turns out, does not really refer to "things in virtue of which *inference* is possible" (p. 55 op. cit.), as he had at first contended but to the connection and involvement of inferences in regard to which the matter of existence and non-existence of things becomes but a wholly irrelevant factor.

With this contradiction of his own previous statement, Dewey places the factor of existence in the fold of the imaginary.

The imaginary, the non-real, he thus invites the conclusion, is less real than any verbosity which is treated as such.

In this context he is logically justified to argue, that the relation of "symbol-meanings" which refer to the vaguest of "existential-operation," exercise a comparatively greater cogency than the connection of inferences which have no existential basis whatsoever.

It is the just stated sense, which is to be read into Dewey's contention, that "it is language, originating as a medium of communication in order to bring about deliberate cooperation and competition in conjoint activities, that has conferred upon existential things their signifying or evidential power" (p. 56 op. cit.).

A language which, according to Dewey, constitutes an array of meaningless symbols, as well as the activity which those meaningless symbols engender, are ostensibly granted by the author of "Logic, the Theory of Inquiry" the cognitive power to signify and thus legitimize any evidence which could be conceivably derived from "existential things."

It is implied in this instance, that meaningless symbols and the kind of activity they engender can be best used to slur over any cognitive distinction which could conceivably be made between the imaginary and the really existing, in any attempt to marshal significant evidence for a relevant inference.

Chapter Three

THE DEGRADATION OF KNOWLEDGE

The devolution of the subject-matter of social science by Dewey, it should be noted, ends upon the same note as the dissolution of the subject-matter of natural science. The dissolution of the subject-matter of natural science is sounded off by Dewey, as has been demonstrated in the first chapter of this exposition, with an argumentation, which is to prove that no cognitive distinction can be made between the actual and non-actual within his cognitive frame. The disassembling of the subject-matter of social science by Dewey ends, in turn, as has been shown in the second chapter of this exposition, with the reassertion that any attempt to distinguish between the imaginary and non-imaginary is to have no relevance within the range of his comprehension.

The end result at which Dewey arrives in both cases is essentially the same, it amounts to a denial of the feasibility to draw a cognitive distinction between fictitious and non-fictitious propositions.

The cognitive position at which Dewey has arrived is of such destructive magnitude that anything he has to offer by way of a follow up, strikes one as an anti-climax.

Although he had originally set himself the limited task to disqualify the contents of natural and social science, he went much further than that in the course of his argumentation. He did not only make the content of both natural and social science meaningless, he made a division between natural and social science appear senseless. More than that, he proceeded to erase the cognitive marks by which a scientific comprehension can be distinguished from a non-scientific.

His subsequent argumentation presents but a rationalization of the extreme position at which he has arrived.

In his follow up he first offers a summary of his position. "Upon the biological level," he states, "organisms have to respond to conditions about them in ways that modify those conditions and the relations of organisms to them, so as to restore the reciprocal adaptation that is required for the maintenance of life-functions" (*"Logic, the Theory of Inquiry"* p. 60).

The emphasis in the just quoted sentence has to be placed on what Dewey calls "reciprocal adaptation" which, in the cognitive range proffered by the author of "Logic, the Theory of Inquiry," does not mean more than adaptation to adaptation, to adaptation and so on, and so forth, since the question of adaptation of what to what has remained unanswered, in view of Dewey's prohibition against having either the organism or the environment comprehended in any distinctive form.

Dewey's subsequent statement which relates that "human organisms are involved in the same kind of predicament" (p. 60 op. cit.) can be taken at its face value, as far as the cognitive bearing of that statement is concerned.

Since the cultural factor in environment has been rendered as meaningless as the natural factor, the specification of a particular adaptation of the human organism becomes a cognitively unsoluble problem.

With the question of adaptation to what left unanswered again in any specifiable form, the factor of adaptation is once more reduced to the level on which nothing more can be said about adaptation that it is an adaptation to something about which nothing specific is known.

Since, moreover, the human organism is postulated as unspecifiable as the non-human organism, the cognition of adaptation is being further impeded by the cognitive impossibility of answering in any specific form the question of what is being adapted; adaptation in the social sphere remains as empty a proposition with Dewey as in the non-social sphere.

In view of the stated dismal cognitive situation, it appears strange at first sight, that Dewey finds it necessary to designate "the environment in which human beings are *directly* involved the common sense environment or "world" and inquiries that take place in making the required adjustments in behavior, common sense inquiries" (p. 60 op. cit.).

In his placing of emphasis on the factor "directly involved" Dewey but restates the position he had previously taken, which did not allow for a distinction between environmental and non-environmental factors. In placing the word world in quotation marks he but once more stresses that he considers any cognitive distinction between the outer and the inner world in the form of objective and subjective factors a preposterous proposition.

What is new in the just stated connection, what has not been stated before by Dewey in regard to his cognitive position, is the designation of the cognitive indistinctiveness to which he subscribes as a *common sense* comprehension.

New also is his designation of "inquiries in making the required adjustments in behavior" as *common sense* inquiry.

The renaming of "inquiries in making the required adjustments in behavior" as *common sense* inquiries provides, however, but a new name for an entirely unsettled condition.

What sense can an inquiry into "required adjustments in behavior" make, in the face of a resolution to have any specific adjustment regarded as inconceivable.

How an adjustment which is comprehended as a series of unspecifiable correlations is to be effected in any meaningful manner in any "common sense inquiry," one is prone to inquire.

What sense is the entering of the factor of behavior into a "common sense inquiry" to make, in the face of a cognitive prohibition of having behavior conceived in any determinable form?

"As is brought out later," Dewey declares, "the problems

that arise in such situations of interaction may be reduced to problems of the use and enjoyment of the objects, activities and products, material and ideological (or "ideal") of the world in which individuals live" (p. 60 op. cit.).

In the stated listings Dewey throws together everything and anything—the subjective and objective, the rational and the non-rational, the material and the non-material, the real and the ideal.

Those listings can in no way provide any specific explanation of what constitutes what Dewey calls "situations of interactions." But that is not intended by the author of "Logic, the Theory of Inquiry." The very incongruity of the listing is but to demonstrate once more that "situations of interactions" are inexplicable in any specific form. On that point Dewey is quite specific, he has no hesitancy to proclaim that "such inquiries (i.e. common sense inquiries P.C.) are accordingly different from those which have knowledge as their goal" (p. 60 op. cit.).

Though he asserts that "the attainment of knowledge of some things is necessarily involved in common sense inquiries," he finds it necessary to warn that "it occurs for the sake of settlement of some issue of use and enjoyment, and not, as in scientific inquiry, for its own sake" (p. 60, 61 op. cit.).

According to the stated assurance, the search for knowledge remains an extraneous factor to common sense inquiry; if any knowledge is gained in a common sense inquiry, it is to be regarded as purely incidental and how could it be otherwise, Dewey is helpful, since "in the latter (i.e. common sense inquiry) there is no *direct* involvement of human beings in the *immediate* environment—a fact which carries with it the ground for distinguishing the theoretical from the practical." (p. 61 op. cit.).

Dewey's reference to *direct* involvement underlies that the common sense inquiry is based upon the cognitive prohibition to set the subject apart from the object.

His reference to *immediate* involvement underscores, in turn, that the common sense inquiry is predicated by the cognitive undifferentiation of environmental and non-environmental factors.

Lest it be inferred that he uses the term common sense in any accepted sense, Dewey takes pains to point out that he does not intend to conform to any available formulation of common sense.

To Dewey "the use of the term *common sense* is somewhat arbitrary from a linguistic point" (p. 61 op. cit.).

He means by that statement that the known delineations of common sense are arbitrary.

By throwing the onus of arbitrariness on the known formulations of common sense, he provides himself with an ostensible reason to declare that, by contradistinction, "the kinds of situations referred to and the kind of inquiries that deal with the difficulties and predicaments they present cannot be doubted" (p. 61 op. cit.) i.e., the common sense situations, as long as they remain undefined, are not arbitrary.

Dewey tries his best to make what to him are common sense situations undefinable.

"They are (the common sense situations, P.C.) those which continuously arise in the conduct of life and the ordering of day by day behavior" (p. 61 op. cit.).

The common sense situations are presented in the just stated sentence as the most crude and primitive sense reactions.

Dewey makes sure that any attempt of discrimination, any attempt which is to be made to be selective in the grasping of what is involved in a common sense situation, is to be doomed to futility.

"They are" (common sense situations, P.C.), he declares, "such as constantly arise in the development of the young as they learn to make their way in the physical and social environments in which they live; they occur and recur in the life activity of every adult, whether farmer, artisan, professional man, law-maker or administrator; citizen of a state, husband, wife, or parent." (p. 61 op. cit.).

As far as the common sense situation is concerned, Dewey thus disallows any distinction between a situation in which a child and an adult finds himself. Since he denies the conceivability of any differentiation between a situation in which a child and an adult is involved, he is logically bound to consider that the detecting of differences in various adult situations is a cognitively impossible proposition. A cognitive apparatus which is so crude that it does not provide for a discrimination of problems of children and adults, is certainly not subtle enough to record a distinction between the life-activity of a farmer, artisan, professional man, law-maker or administrator or, for that matter, citizen of a state, husband, wife or parent.

In the stated context, Dewey's subsequent proclamation that "on their very face they (the common sense situations, P.C.) need to be discriminated from inquiries that are distinctly scientific" (p. 61 op. cit.) presents but an anti-climax.

Nor does his follow-up statement in which he disclaims that the common sense situations "aim at attaining confirmed facts, 'laws' and theories" (p. 61 op. cit.) add anything to what he had just stated before, except for his volunteering of the admission that facts are not confirmable within a common sense situation.

The kind of common sense situation which Dewey describes is so broad and all inclusive, as to defy almost any delineation. For the kind of common sense situation which he has in mind, Dewey has reason to surmise, there are hardly any terms available which could adequately express it.

In scanning the Oxford Dictionary he finds the following definition of common sense: "Good sound practical sense; combined tact and readiness in dealing with the ordinary affairs of life" (p. 61 op. cit.).

In trying to make sense of that definition, Dewey observes that "common sense in this signification applies to behavior in its connection with the *significance* of things" (p. 61).

He implements his observation by stating that *"good sense* is, in ordinary language, good *judgment"* (p. 61 op. cit.).

The stated signification, Dewey realizes, is too intellectual, as he himself admits, too discriminating to fit his indiscriminatory view of the common sense situation which he propounds.

He therefore hastens to provide an implementation of what

he considers the Oxford Dictionary definition of common sense means. He further qualifies the Oxford Dictionary definition as "sagacity . . . power to discriminate the factors that are relevant and important in significance in given situations; it is power of discernment" (p. 61 op. cit.) —and then follows the descent— the discrimination and discernment is not supposed to go beyond the range of the 'ability to tell a hawk from a hernshaw, chalk from cheese, and to bring the disciminations made to bear upon what is done and what is to be abstained from, in the 'ordinary affairs of life' " (p. 61 op. cit.).

At this point Dewey has brought the Oxford Dictionary definition down to the level on which it means no more than the most immediate sense reaction.

He is aware, however, that there exists another dictionary definition, he finds that the dictionary formulates common sense in still another manner. That other definition refers to common sense, Dewey finds, as "the general sense, feeling, judgment of mankind or a community" (p. 62 op. cit.).

In musing upon this definition, Dewey observes that it speaks of "the *deliverances* of common sense as if they were a body of settled truths" (p. 62).

"It applies," he continues his observation, "not to things in their significance but to *meanings* accepted" (p. 62 op. cit.).

With those observations Dewey states that the second dictionary definition which he had discovered refers to outer appearances, as if they constitute all the characteristics of a given situation. That Dewey himself is instrumental in propounding that kind of conception, the author of "Logic the Theory of Inquiry" does not care to discuss at this point.

He probably does not want to be reminded that his whole cognitive effort is directed towards parading outer appearances and nothing but outer appearances.

Although he casually refers to "the Scottish school of Reid and Stewart" which "erected 'common sense' into an ultimate authority and arbiter of philosophic questions" and remarks that "they (Reid and Stewart P.C.) were carrying this signification to its limit" (p. 62 op. cit.), he wants to avoid any linking of his cognitive stand with the position taken by the obscurantist Scottish school. He quickly changes the subject in an obvious effort to preclude the disclosure that he himself is a much more radical expounder of appearances than Reid and Stewart ever were.

Dewey is in a hurry at this turn; without any further explanation, he shifts the range of discussion. He quickly turns to a more literal discussion of the second definition of common sense.

He advances a formal linguistic interpretation of that definition, by insisting that common sense in the said definition does not mean more than "general" (p. 62 op. cit.).

On the basis of that formalistic interpretation he goes on to contend that the second definition "designates the conceptions and beliefs that are currently accepted without question by a given group of mankind in general" (p. 62 op. cit.).

"They are *common*," he amplifies, "in the sense of being widely, if not universally, accepted" (p. 62 op. cit.).

That is as far as he is willing to go in exploring the formalistic aspect of the second common sense definition. Without any further explanation, he suddenly shifts to the content of what he considers the second common sense definition involves.

The wide acceptance, he unequivocably states, refers to "something of the same ultimacy and immediacy for a group that 'sensation' and 'feeling' have for an individual in his contact with surrounding objects" (p. 62 op. cit.).

He has once more descended to the level of comprehension which is compatible with a common sense situation of his own making.

Both definitions of common sense, which are cited by Dewey, have now been adapted by him to serve as indicators of a situation which, as far as the dictionary shows, are not identified as common sense situations.

None of the two dictionary definitions would, for instance, list taboos as expressions of common sense.

Dewey is, however, quick to claim, and rightly so, that, within the low level of comprehension to which he makes the two cited common sense definitions refer, taboos can well rate as common sense expressions.

Within the low level of comprehension to which he makes the two available definitions refer, Dewey is well justified in claiming, there is no way to detect preconceived opinions and prejudiced judgments.

He has made the two available definitions of common sense refer to such a low level of comprehension, Dewey is again justified in claiming, that there remains hardly a difference between the two definitions.

Within the low level of comprehension to which he has reduced the cognitive range of his kind of common sense inquiry reasoning can hardly become more than a tautological proposition. Dewey is again helpful in stating that, as he puts it, "I do not suppose that a generalization of the inquiries and conclusions of this type (i.e. the type of his, Dewey's, common sense inquiry, P.C.) under the caption of 'use and enjoyment' needs much exposition for its support" (p. 63 op. cit.).

The statement indicates that Dewey considers it self-evident that his designation of use and enjoyment as subject-matters of common sense inquiry is so inclusive, as to require no further elaboration.

He, nonetheless, proceeds with an implementation of what he considers a self-explanatory statement, in an effort to make sure that a due lack of discrimination and discernment be exercised in the determination of the range of subjects which a common sense inquiry is to cover.

"Use and enjoyment," he relates, "are the ways in which human beings are directly connected with the world about them" (p. 63 op. cit.).

Directly, should one have forgotten, refers in Dewey's vocabulary to the cognitive impossibility to distinguish human beings and the world about them in any specifiable form.

He subsequently states that "questions of food, shelter, protection, defense, etc., are questions of the use to be made of materials of the environment and of the attitudes to be taken practically towards members of the same group and to other groups taken as wholes" (p. 63 op. cit.).

In this sentence he makes sure that no cognitive distinction is made between subjective and objective factors, as far as their common sense use is concerned.

Fully in line with his cognitive lack of discernment in relating objective and subjective factors, is his assertion that "use, in turn, is for the sake of some consummation or enjoyment" (p. 63 op. cit.).

With this sentence he makes clear that use and enjoyment are but interchangeable terms for him; since he makes both use and enjoyment refer to undifferentiated subjective and objective factors, he deprives himself of any cognitive criterion by which he could uphold a meaningful distinction between the respective two words.

His cognitive disability in the stated connection is well illustrated by his relating that "some things that are far beyond the scope of direct use, like stars and dead ancestors, are objects of magical use, and of enjoyment in rites and legends" (p. 63 op. cit.).

The just quoted statement reveals that he has no cognitive criterion left by which he could distinguish between usefulness and uselessness and between enjoyable and non-enjoyable, in any rational terms.

His follow-up statement is not more than declaratory.

Although he declares with much aplomb that "if we include the correlative negative ideas of disuse, of abstinence from use, and toleration and suffering, problems of use and enjoyment may be safely said to exhaust the domain of common sense inquiry" (p. 63 op. cit.)—he fails to notice that he is not in a cognitive position to account for the factors which distinguish use from disuse and enjoyment from toleration or suffering.

To provide himself with a cognitive absolution for placing everything and anything within the range of his kind of common sense inquiry, Dewey introduces the aspect of the qualitative.

"There is direct connection," he proclaims, "between this fact (i.e. the all inclusiveness of his type of common sense inquiry, P.C.) and the concern of common sense with the *qualitative*" (p. 63 op. cit.).

Qualitative, in the stated connection, becomes something which is not readily discernible.

Though Dewey insists that "it is by discernment of qualities that the fitness and capacity of things and events for use is decided" (p. 63 op. cit.), he is cognitively unable to provide for the comprehension of a quality, in the sense in which quality means a lasting attribute.

Since he does not allow for any cognitive recognition of objects as objects, he is left without a cognitive frame of reference to which qualities could be attributed.

Within his cognitive frame he can attest to no more than passing impressions.

When he subsequently relates "that proper food stuffs, for example, are told or discriminated from those that are unfit, poisonous or tabued" (p. 63, 64 op. cit.), he but offers a listing which has no cognitive impact as far as his way of reasoning is concerned.

He is likewise engaged in a mere verbalistic venture when he states that "tanning skins is a process qualitatively different from that of weaving baskets or shaping clay into jars; the rites that are responsive to death are qualitatively different from those appropriate to birth and weddings" (p. 64 op. cit.).

All those items are without any cognitive relevance in Dewey's mode of cognition.

To make sure that no human or non-human factor escapes the range of common sense inquiry, Dewey provides for a system of cognitive devolution by which each succeeding stage of technological and social development is successively cast into the range of common sense comprehension.

"Every invention of a new tool and utensil, every improvement in technique" (p. 64 op. cit.) any "changes in the regulative scheme of relations within a group, family, clan or nation" (p. 64 op. cit.) are to be respectively degraded in the cognitive sense, Dewey wants to see to it, by being placed within the range of the common sense inquiry.

Regardless of whether "the business of one age becomes the sport and amusement of another age" (p. 65 op. cit.), regardless of whether "scientific theories and interpretations continue to be affected by conceptions that have ceased to be determinative in the actual practice of inquiry" (p. 65 op. cit), they cannot, Dewey insists, be permitted to escape a successive cognitive devolution, in the sense that their cognitive range is to become reduced to the level of common sense comprehension.

The scheme for the degrading of comprehension, Dewey is eager to stress, is a progressive one.

He spreads his common sense comprehension device out as a net in which he intends to catch any conceivable human and non-human development, step by step, at the very point it comes to show its respective effectiveness.

He thus provides himself with a device by which he can stand ready to resist an attempt to overturn the cognitive barriers of common sense comprehension at every conceivable turn of human and non-human evolution.

His pattern of progressive cognitive devolution constitutes no less than a bid on the part of Dewey to arrest an advance of the rule of reason, and Dewey is proud to call attention to it.

In his sly manner he remarks that "the very fitness of the Aristotelian logical organon in respect to the culture and common sense of a certain group in the period in which it was formulated unfits it to be a logical formulation of not only the science but even of the common sense of the present cultural epoch" (p. 65 op. cit.).

Dewey is willing to abstain from opposing Aristotle's proposition, as long as he can make Aristotle's form of cognition appear as a kind of early upsurge of human thought which is rather primitive in its expression.

Aristotle's form of cognition has been left far behind by Dewey's kind of common sense comprehension, the author of the "Logic the Theory of Inquiry" wants to have implied.

The real contradistinction Dewey does not care to have mentioned.

Dewey could hardly relish the prospect of having it dawn on

anybody, that the real contradistinction between Aristotle's logical organon and his, Dewey's, approach to logic, lies in the factor that Aristotle had dedicated himself to the task of elevating with his propositions the level of human comprehension in his time as well as for all time to come, while he, Dewey, had devoted his labors to an attempt to degrade human comprehension in his time and for all time to come.

Aristotle was animated by the vision of the Logos, the world as embodiment of reason, while Dewey was guided by an outlook in which unreason was allowed to play a preponderant part.

Should there yet remain the slightest doubt, that Dewey is bent on having the range of common sense inquiry prevail over any other mode of inquiry, his subsequent treatment of the relation of scientific and non-scientific inquiry removes any such doubts.

"Both the history of science and the present state of science prove," he relates, "that the goal of the systematic relationship of facts and conceptions to one another is dependent upon *eliminatoin* of the qualitative as such and upon reduction to non-qualitative formulations" (p. 65 op. cit.).

The *elimination of the qualitative as such* in the just quoted statement refers to the elimination of any qualitative specifiability, and thus to the elimination of any meaningful interpretation, in the sense of the relation of outer forms to a material content.

Science in this context is being reduced to a kind of system of hieroglyphics, the deciphering of which is prohibited.

That the history of science and the present state of science abounds with examples of a reduction of science to the level on which it presents no more than a manipulation of meaningless signs, can be granted.

It can also be admitted, that those scientists who disguise their manipulations of meaningless signs, by engaging in a quantification of something which is not supposed to be known, consider such a scheme as the goal of any future science.

It is not admissible, however, if science is to be viewed as a means for the advancement of knowledge about human and non-human nature, to regard all science of the past, of the present and of the future, as signifying nothing more than the parading of empty symbols.

Dewey's subsequent statement in which he asserts that "the problem of the relation of the domain of common sense to that of science has notoriously taken the form of opposition of the qualitative to the non-qualitative; largely but not exclusively the quantitative" (p. 65 op. cit.) constitutes but a half-truth, since it neglects to take into account the division between those scientists who are content with evolving meaningless formulas and those who strive for a meaningful interpretation of data.

Dewey's counterposition of the common sense inquiry as "an application in *qualitative* use and enjoyment of the environment" (p. 65 op. cit.) is, in the sense in which Dewey refers to the qualitative, no counterposition at all.

Since qualitative, in the sense in which Dewey applies the term with reference to his range of common sense inquiry, does not allow for any cognitive distinctiveness of the factor of quality, his reference to qualitative use and enjoyment of the environment is not more than verbal.

Between the verbalistic form of scientific inquiry and the verbalistic mode of common sense inquiry there is no real distinction, and Dewey admits it inferentially.

He does not deny that the relativistic frame which he postulates as the "systematic relations of coherence and consistency" (p. 65 op. cit.) is wide enough to take in all meaningless propositions, regardless of whether they originate in the sphere originally assigned to science, or in the sphere reserved by him for common sense inquiry.

Nor is Dewey willing to dispute that the cognitive problems which continue to trouble scientific inquirers, the questions which pertain to "the difference . . . between perceptual material and a system of conceptual constructions" (p. 65 op. cit.) has any relevance on a level of comprehension for which the cognitive range of common sense inquiry can be made to serve as a common denominator.

In a statement which follows, Dewey tries to make sure that the range of common sense inquiry is to be treated as the ultima ratio of all inquiry.

When he complains that "the separation and opposition of scientific subject-matter to that of common sense, when it is taken to be final, generates those controversial problems of epistemology and metaphysics that still dog the course of philosophy" (p. 66 op. cit.), he is actually issuing a warning against any detachment of the common sense subject-matter from the science subject-matter in any cognitive form.

His insistence that the "scientific subject-matter is intermediate" (p. 66 op. cit.) but indicates that he wants the cognitive range of science to remain subordinated to the cognitive range of common sense inquiry.

In what follows, Dewey but elaborates on the theme of the cognitive congruity of common sense and scientific inquiry.

"I begin the discussion," Dewey starts off his follow-up proposition, "by introducing and explaining the denotative force of the word *situation*" (p. 66 op. cit.).

"What is designated by the word "situation"—Dewey formulates in the negative—"is *not* a single object or event or set of objects and events" (p. 66 op. cit.).

The stated formulation indicates that Dewey is introducing the term situation in order to obstruct a cognitive identification of either a single object or event, or set of objects and events.

Dewey's subsequent assertion makes it even more certain that he is bent on obstructing any cognition of a single object or event, or set of objects and events.

His assertion that "we never experience nor form judgments about objects and events in isolation, but only in connection with a contextual whole" (p. 66 op. cit.) constitutes a firm invitation to obstruct the forming of analytical judgments about objects and events.

Dewey is, nonetheless, not content with the effectuation of an obstruction of an analytical discernment of specific factors, he wants to prevent analytical discernment as such.

"Psychology," he relates, "has paid much attention to the

question of the process of perception, and has for its purpose described the perceived object in terms of the results of analysis of the process" (p. 66 op. cit.).

As indistinct as the object emerges from the stated psychological analytical approach, for Dewey that degree of indistinctiveness is insufficient.

He calls attention to the factor that "by the very nature of the case the psychological treatment takes a *singular* object or event for the subject-matter of its analysis" (p. 67 op. cit.) with the implied intention to deny the very conceivability of an object as such.

The very next sentence makes the just stated implication explicit.

"In actual experience," he asserts, "there is never any such isolated singular object or event; *an* object or event is always a special part, phase, or aspect, of an environing experienced world—a situation" (p. 67 op. cit.).

An object is i.e. not identifiable as an object; an object is only identifiable as a part, a phase or aspect of an environing world—a situation, which is, by itself, not identifiable in any cognitive form.

In an obvious effort to soothe the impact of his sweeping disqualification of the cognition of an object Dewey introduces an intermediary term.

"There is always," he states, "a *field* in which observation of *this* or *that* object or event occurs" (p. 61 op. cit.).

He has no intention, however, to make the so called "field" any more distinctive than the "situation," as his subsequent sentence discloses.

"Observation of the latter" (i.e. this or that object or event, P.C.), he insists, "is made for the sake of finding out what that *field* is with reference to some active adaptive response to be made in carrying forward a *course* of behavior" (p. 67 op. cit.).

Since within Dewey's cognitive range "adaptive response to be made in carrying forward a *course* of behavior" does not signify more than a mere animal reflex—as has been demonstrated in chapter one of this critical exposition—the observation of "this or that object, for the sake of finding out what that *field is*" can hardly lead to anything distinct.

The introduction of the intermediary term field which is to take the place of the term situation, results but in a compounding of cognitive indistinctiveness.

Dewey is helpful in making it clear that the cognitive range, within which he is trying to operate in his demonstration of what he considers to be a situation or a field, is not one which encompasses more than the crudest of animal sense reactions.

"One has only to recur to animal perception, occurring by means of sense organs," Dewey observes, "to note that isolation of what is perceived from the course of life behavior would be not only futile, but obstructive, in many cases fatally so" (p. 67 op. cit.).

This statement discloses that he has a non-reflective factor in mind when he refers to the lack of isolation in his discussion of 'field' and 'situation.'

The inference which Dewey wants to be drawn from the cognitive indistinctiveness in which the "field" and the "situation" are made to linger by him is, as has been indicated, far reaching.

"When the act and object of perception are isolated from their place and function in promoting and directing a successful course of activities in behalf of use-enjoyment," Dewey insists, "they are taken to be exclusively *cognitive*" (p. 67 op. cit.).

With this assertion Dewey provides that an *act* or *object* of perception cannot be made subject of cognition as *act* or *object* of perception, but as something which is neither an act nor an object of perception.

"The perceived object, orange, rock, piece of gold, or whatever, is taken to be an object of *knowledge per se*" (p. 67 op. cit.), Dewey complains.

An object, the complaint implies, cannot become known as an object.

"In the sense of being discriminatingly noticed, it *is* an object of knowledge, but," he insists, "not of knowledge as ultimate and self-sufficient" (p. 67 op. cit.).

The object is, in other words, an object of such knowledge which does not properly constitute knowledge of the object.

"It" (the object, P.C.) "is noted or 'known' only so far," Dewey insists, "as guidance is thereby given to direction of behavior; so that the situation in which it is found can be appropriately enjoyed or some of its conditions be so used that enjoyment will result or suffering be obviated" (p. 67 op. cit.).

An object can, in other words, be known only as something which is not knowable as an object.

The object is made to disappear from the analytical sphere to make place for a "situation" which, in its turn, is being denied analytical treatment in either a perceptual or conceptual range.

The elimination of the object as an object, in the sense of an analytical factor, makes, in turn, for a compounded indistinctiveness, as far as Dewey's treatment of the factor of situation is concerned.

"Recurring to the main topic" (the topic concerning the situation, P.C.), Dewey relates, "it is to be remarked that a situation is a whole in virtue of its immediately pervasive quality" (p. 68 op. cit.).

This sentence is open to an interpretation that the totality in the situation is linkable to an immediate sense reaction.

Dewey, however, wants no part in that kind of interpretation, and he is eager to state it.

"When," he relates, "we describe" (the immediately pervasive quality, P.C.) "from the psychological side, we have to say that the situation as a qualitative whole is sensed or *felt*" (p. 68 op. cit.).

"Such an expression is, however, valuable only as it is taken negatively to indicate that it is *not,* as such, an object in *discourse*" (p. 68 op. cit.), Dewey continues.

What he is driving at in the stated context, is made clear in the very next sentence.

"Stating that it is *felt,*" he insists, "is wholly misleading if it gives the impression that the situation *is* a feeling or an emotion or anything mentalistic" (p. 68 op. cit.).

He denies with the stated sentence that, what he calls situation, is explicable in terms of a sense reaction.

"On the contrary," he asserts, "feeling, sensation and emotion have themselves to be identified and described in terms of the immediate presence of a total qualitative situation" (p. 68 op. cit.).

With this statement Dewey places himself on record in linking the totality of the situation with the totally inexplicable factor of the "presence of a total qualitative situation."

In this sentence Dewey links one inexplicable proposition to another inexplicable proposition and thus renders both propositions meaningless.

The meaninglessness of the proposition of "presence of a total qualitative situation" deprives, in turn, the factor of sense reaction of any meaningful form of reference and leaves the factors of "feeling, sensation and emotion" dangling in the air, analytically speaking.

The analytically anarchical stand, which Dewey takes in the stated connection, is being further emphasized by him.

"The pervasively qualitative is not only that which binds all constituents into a whole but it is also unique"; he stresses, "it constitutes in each situation an *individual* situation, indivisible and unduplicable" (p. 68 op. cit.).

Analytically, there is no way of either denying or confirming Dewey's stated assertion.

Since he denies the identifiability of what he terms "pervasively qualitative," he has no way of either proving or disproving that the "pervasively qualitative" does or does not duplicate itself.

It is inconceivable by any cognitive standards to establish whether something unidentifiable does or does not reoccur.

The reference to the uniqueness of "the pervasively qualitative" would by itself not mean anything in Dewey's stated presentation, were he not to use that reference in relation to something else.

It is only when he states that the "distinctions and relations are instituted *within* a situation" (p. 68 op. cit.) and when he relates that *"they"* (the distinctions and relations *within* a situation, P.C.) "are recurrent and repeatable in different situations" (p. 68 op. cit.), that he indicates that he is bent on using the unidentifiability of "the pervasively qualitative within a situation" as a means to deprive identifiable factors of any specifiable frame of reference.

In placing the "distinctions and relations *within* a situation" which is bound to remain unidentifiable, Dewey makes the distinctions and relations to which he refers also unidentifiable.

His insistence that the "distinctions and relations *within* a situation . . . are recurrent and repeatable in different situations" is thus rendered meaningless, since it refers to distinctions and relations which, since they are placed within the "situation," are not identifiable as distinctions and relations in any specifiable form.

Dewey's reference to duplication and reoccurrence thus comes to be as meaningless as his reference to non-duplication and uniqueness.

By having made the unidentifiability of "the pervasively qualitative" become so pervasive as to engulf any conceivable identifiable factors, he has lost any cognitive means for either proving or disproving either uniqueness or reoccurrence in the stated context.

Dewey seals his anarchistic cognitive position in regard to what he terms a situation by insisting that "discourse that is not controlled by reference to a situation is not discourse" (p. 68 op. cit.), by which he means that reasoning cannot be regarded as valid if the unspecifiability and unidentifiability of what he calls a situation are not posted as guides to reasoning.

His insistence that a refusal to recognize the unspecifiability and unidentifiability of a situation as a guiding principle in reasoning is likely to result in "a meaningless jumble" (p. 68 op. cit.) constitutes a most patent example of what can be readily recognized as a perversion of truth by any common sense definition but that of Dewey's.

After he had made it abundantly clear that he had introduced what he calls "the pervasive qualitative of a situation" in order to reduce anything which he places within its range to the level of unspecifiable and unidentifiable factors, Dewey does not consider it at all perplexing to refer inferentially, in the just-cited quotation, to the cognitive proposition which is predicated upon the recognition of identifiable and specifiable factors, as a road to a meaningless jumble.

He does, to be sure, recognize the cognitive incongruity of his proposition when he states that "the universe of experience surrounds and regulates a universe of discourse but never appears as such within the latter" (p. 68 op. cit.).

The stated recognition but reemphasizes his determination to make reasoning ineffective.

Dewey, it becomes evident, has reached a point at which he has no cognitive means left by which he could conceivably distinguish the alogical from the logical.

He has reached the destination at which he was aiming all along, to having the common sense inquiry established as an alogical form of inquiry, in contradistinction to the logical form of scientific inquiry.

Having reached the great divide, Dewey considers himself entitled to proclaim the reversion of the logical form of scientific inquiry to the alogical form of common sense inquiry, as the most pressing cognitive problem of any time in the history of human thought.

In his call for a cognitive counter-revolution, he does not hesitate to claim that the reversion to the amorphic form of human knowledge, from which the systematic ordering of science has emerged, constitutes a pre-conditioning factor for any social advance.

B — IN LIEU OF ART

Chapters Four and Five

THE REMOVAL OF THE ART OBJECT FOLLOWED BY A DISPOSAL OF THE ARTIST

The alogical cognitive position at which Dewey arrives in his dealing with the subject-matter of science is carried over by him into the sphere of art.

The cognitive counter-revolution by which he is enabled to reduce scientific to non-scientific propositions makes it, in turn, feasible for him to reduce esthetic to non-esthetic factors.

He starts off his attack against the cognition of beauty as such, by a disqualification of art objects as such.

"By one of the ironic perversities," Dewey declares, "that often attend the course of affairs, the existence of the works of art upon which formation of an esthetic theory depends has become an obstruction to theory about them" (*"Art as Experience"* p. 3).

He thus registers his opposition to having art objects identified as art objects.

"For one reason," he admits, "these works are products that exist externally and physically" (p. 3 op. cit.).

He thus becomes more specific in his objection.

"In common conception," he complains, "the work of art is often identified with the building, book, painting, or statue in its existence apart from human experience" (p. 3 op. cit.).

He thus makes it clear that he is determined not to recognize that art objects can be identified as such within the cognitive framework of a specified and specifiable sphere of esthetic inquiry.

He is unequivocably stating in the sentence which follows

that "the actual work of art is what the product does with and in experience" (p. 3 op. cit.).

The work of art comes thus to be cognitively placed within the realm of indeterminableness, for which the term experience is made to stand by Dewey.

The product of art is not only denied cognition as an art product, it is even denied cognition as a product in Dewey's subsequent deliberations.

The cognitive stricture of an indeterminable experience does not merely preclude the identification of a building, a book, a painting or a statue as art objects; it precludes the cognition of a building as a building, a book as a book, a painting as a painting, and a statue as a statue.

The cognitive stricture of indeterminable experience has been devised by Dewey, it should be recalled, in order to make it cognitively unfeasible to set an object apart from something which is not an object.

When he subsequently complains that "the very perfection of some of these products (i.e. art products, P.C.) the prestige they possess because of a long history of unquestioned admiration, creates conventions that get in the way of fresh insight" (p. 3 op. cit.), he but underscores his objection to having art objects placed within an artistic frame of reference.

Although he refers in the just quoted sentence to prestige and unquestioned admiration which creates conventions, he is attacking the very cognitive basis by which an artless evaluation can be distinguished from an artful evaluation, as the very next sentence indicates.

"When the art product once attains classic status" Dewey insists, "it somehow becomes *isolated* (italics mine, P..C.) from the human conditions under which it was brought into being and from the human consequences it engenders in actual life experience" (p. 3 op. cit.).

Isolation in the sense in which Dewey uses the term stands for negation of analytical separation of spheres of inquiry.

In the context in which the term isolation is being used in the just stated instance, it merely reemphasizes Dewey's opposition to having the status of an art product determined on the basis of specific conditions; it but reaffirms his determination to have an art product treated as an unspecifiable factor.

He is definitely opposed, as he unabashedly states, to having "art . . . remitted to a separate realm, where it is cut off from that association with the materials and aims of every other form of human effort, undergoing, and achievement" (p. 3 op. cit.).

He is fully committed as he unequivocably declares "to restore *continuity* (italics mine, P.C.) between the refined and intensified forms of experience that are works of art and the every-day events, doings, and sufferings that are universally recognized to constitute experience" (p. 3 op. cit.).

He thus records it as his very special task in regard to the philosophy of art, to have the art factor engulfed by an interminable chain reaction.

His use of the word continuity in the stated connection makes it clear that he is determined not to permit a range of art analysis which would refer to more than a correlation of one indeterminable factor with another.

Dewey reexemplifies the application of the term continuity, in the sense in which he defines it, by stating that the "mountain peaks do not float unsupported; they do not even just rest upon the earth. They *are* the earth," he insists, "in one of its manifest operations" (p. 3 op. cit.).

Mountains, the stated quotation brings out, cannot be regarded as something which has a definite shape and a specified substance.

A mountain, the stated quotation is supposed to convey, is not something which is in any way distinct from the general conception of earth.

The stated reexemplification is used by Dewey to reassert his demand for having scientific inquiry submerged in indistinctiveness and indefiniteness.

"It is the business of those," he declares, "who are concerned with the theory of the earth, geographers and geologists, to make this fact evident in its various implications" (p. 3, 4 op. cit.), by which he means the fact that the subject-matter of a respective scientific inquiry is indistinct and as such is to be made indistinguishable from the subject-matter of any inquiry in a related sphere.

When he subsequently declares that "the theorist who would deal philosophically with fine art has a like task to accomplish" (p. 4 op. cit.), he means by like the task of having esthetic inquiry rendered indistinct and indistinguishable from any non-esthetic inquiry.

In the elaboration which follows, Dewey aims at a demonstration of what he does not consider to be the sphere of esthetic inquiry.

He takes recourse to the paradoxical device of discounting objects of art, as art objects, in an effort to devise an art theory.

"In order to understand the meaning of artistic products, we have to forget them for a time" (p. 4 op. cit.), he suggests.

Then follows an even more perplexing proposal. He urges that the turning aside from the artistic products be followed up by taking "recourse to the ordinary forces and conditions of experience that we do not usually regard as esthetic" (p. 4 op. cit.).

He thus pleads for an abandonment of the entire range of esthetic inquiry as a means of arriving at an esthetic theory.

"We must arrive at the theory" (read esthetic theory, P.C.), he declares, "by means of a detour" (p. 4 op. cit.).

"For theory," he amplifies, "is concerned with understanding, insight, not without exclamations of admiration, and stimulation of that emotional outburst often called appreciation" (p. 4 op. cit.).

He thus sets the stage for having esthetic and non-esthetic factors treated as an inseparable mixture.

"It is quite possible to enjoy flowers," he states, "in their colored form and delicate fragrance without knowing anything about plants theoretically" (p. 4 op. cit.).

He thus makes a direct reference to artistic enjoyment as a non-reflective factor.

"But if one sets out to *understand* the flowering of plants, he is committed to finding out something about the interactions of soil, air, water and sunlight that condition the growth of plants" (p. 4 op. cit.).

Understanding in this sentence is being referred to as the preponderably reflective and non-esthetic.

"By common consent," Dewey elaborates, "the Parthenon is a great work of art" (p. 4 op. cit.).

"Yet," he asserts, "it has esthetic standing only as the work becomes an experience for a human being" (p. 4 op. cit.), an experience, to spell it out, in which the work of art is not permitted to rate as a work of art.

"If one is to go beyond personal enjoyment into the formation of a theory about that large republic of art of which the building is one member," Dewey maintains, "one has to be willing at some point in his reflections to turn from the bustling, arguing acutely sensitive Athenian citizens, with civic sense identified with a civic religion, of whose experience the temple was an expression, and who built it not as work of art but as civic commemoration" (p. 4 op. cit.).

The work of art thus comes to rate as work of art only to a point subject to the non-reflective "personal enjoyment."

The work of art ceases to rate as work of art, according to the just quoted citation, at a point at which it is made subject to reflection.

The reflection by virtue of which the object of art is being replaced by any number of non-artistic factors is made to count as an art theory.

Dewey amplifies his approach to an art theory in which objects of art are not recognized as such by stating that "the turning to them (as Athenian citizens, P.C.) is as human beings who had needs that were a demand for the building and that were carried to fulfillment in it" (p. 4 op. cit.).

It is not a demand of humans for an artistic object, nor is it a matter of artistic fulfillment of humans which is involved in the formulation of Dewey's esthetic theory, as the just quoted statement discloses.

"The one who sets out to theorize about esthetic experience

embodied in the Parthenon must realize in thought," Dewey cautions, "what the people into whose lives it entered had in common, as creators and as those who were satisfied with it, with people in our own houses and on our own streets" (p. 4 op. cit.).

Dewey thus warns that his theory of esthetic experience, as exemplified by him in the case of the Parthenon, does not provide for any distinction between the factors which account for the generation of the object of art and the factors which are involved in art appreciation.

In the statement which follows Dewey attempts to establish inexplicable enjoyment as an all embracing art factor.

"In order to *understand* the esthetic in its ultimate and approved forms," Dewey lectures, "one must begin it in the raw; in the events and scenes that hold the attentive eye and ear of man, arousing his interest and affording him enjoyment as he looks and listens: the sights that hold the crowd—the fire-engine rushing by; the machines excavating enormous holes in the earth; the human-fly climbing the steeple-side; the men perched high in air on girders, throwing and catching red-hot bolts" p. 4, 5 op. cit.).

The numerous and varied instances which Dewey cites in the stated connection, provide a clear indication of his intention to bury the theory of the esthetic in a medley of everything and anything which could possibly elicit some undefinable pleasure.

Inexplicable enjoyment and undefinable pleasure are not only posted by Dewey as the key factor of art appreciation but as key factors in the origination of art as well.

"The sources of art in human experience," Dewey instructs, "will be learned by him who sees how the tense grace of the ball-player infects the onlooking crowd; who notes the delight of the housewife in tending her plants, and the intent interest of her goodman in tending the patch of green in front of the house" (p. 4 op. cit.).

After having refused to rate an art object as an art object, Dewey has made it feasible for himself, as the just quoted sentence shows, to rate any object as an art object.

He inferentially admits that the objects he had referred to in the just quoted citation are not regarded as art objects by those who deal with them.

"These people," he states, "if questioned as to the reason for their actions, would doubtless return reasonable answers. The man who poked the sticks of burning wood would say he did it to make the fire burn better" (p. 6 op. cit.).

"But," Dewey insists on his own accord, "he (the man who poked the sticks of burning wood, P.C.) is nonetheless fascinated by the colorful drama of change enacted before his eyes and imaginatively partakes in it" (p. 5 op. cit.).

With the stated assertion Dewey identifies the esthetic with an interminable and indeterminable sense reaction and leaves it there.

In his subsequent elaboration Dewey attempts to square the esthetic factor with what is generally called job satisfaction.

"The intelligent mechanic engaged in his job, interested in doing well and finding satisfaction in his handiwork," Dewey insists, "is artistically engaged" (p. 5 op. cit.).

The irony of this proposition of Dewey's, aside from the specific aspects of job satisfaction which he intends to convey, lies in the factor that his disqualification of the art object as art object on the ground that art objects have tended to become ossified in the mind of art appreciators, is followed here by an implicit granting of an artistic quality to the most stagnant form of an object—the work product of an artificer.

The removal of objects of art as objects of art from the range of his analysis leaves Dewey without a criterion, not only in regard to his judging whether objects are art objects or not, it leaves him also without any cognitive basis for the evolving of standards by which he could determine what is and what is not an artistic appreciation.

Since he finds himself free to rate anything and everything in human experience as esthetic within the distorted scope of his analysis, he could not possibly detect any perversion of esthetic appreciation in his plea for the discounting of any distinctions in the quality of artistic expressions.

"So extensive and subtly pervasive are the ideas that set Art upon a remote pedestal," Dewey complains, "that many a person would be repelled rather than pleased if told that he enjoyed his casual recreations, in part at least, because of their esthetic quality" (p. 5 op. cit.).

Were standards for an esthetic quality to be set so low, as to allow for an inclusion of any kind of artistic expression, no matter how degrading the performance, it will not happen, Dewey infers, that "the arts which today have most vitality for the average person are things he does not take to be arts" (p. 5 op. cit.).

Since he has deprived himself of any objective artistic standards, Dewey feels at liberty to instruct the average person not to be so discriminating as to deny "the movie, jazzed music, the comic strip, . . . newspaper accounts of love-nests, murders, and exploits of bandits" (p. 5, 6 op. cit.) an esthetic value.

He tries to twist his argument by referring to the keeping of art objects in a museum as a factor which works against the elevation of popular taste.

"For, when what he (the average person, P.C.) knows as art is relegated to the museum and gallery," he complains, "the unconquerable impulse towards experiences enjoyable in themselves finds such outlet as the daily environment provides" (p. 6 op. cit.).

The just quoted citation gives expression to a compounded distortion.

The placing of art objects in a museum or a gallery, which is usually being done in order to maintain standards of art creation and art appreciation through the exhibition of those objects in a museum or a gallery, is represented in the just cited quotation as a major factor which contributes to the lowering, if not dissipation, of art standards.

Coupled with his disqualification of museum pieces as art standards is Dewey's inferential demand that his kind of art analysis, which is predicated upon the degrading of the conception of art objects to a level on which it becomes conceptually unfeasible to discriminate between the artistic and the non-artistic in an object, be recognized as a proper means for the dissemination of esthetic evaluation.

In line with his indirect attack on the art object as the objective standard of art lies Dewey's assault on the conception of evolution of art standards.

"We do not have to travel to the ends of the earth nor return many millennia in time," he insists, "to find peoples for whom everything that intensifies the sense of immediate living is an object of intense admiration. Bodily scarification, waving feathers, gaudy robes, shining ornaments of gold and silver, of emerald and jade," he asserts, "formed the contents of esthetic arts and, presumably, without the vulgarity of class exhibitionism that attends their analogues today" (p. 6 op. cit.).

Dewey refuses to make any distinction between the artistic bearing of the most primitive and the most refined objects, as the cited quotation shows.

He, moreover, infers that instead of an evolution of artistic standards, there has taken place a devolution of artistic criteria.

The primitives are credited with a more developed and refined sense of art appreciation than the civilized in Dewey's just stated proposition.

He does not shrink from decrying the entire course which art development has taken.

To him the removal of mysticism from the adoration of inanimate objects and the division between art proper and religious art constitutes a step backward, as far as art creation and art appreciation is concerned.

"Dancing and pantomime, the sources of the art of the theater, flourished as part of religious rites and celebrations" (p. 7 op. cit.), Dewey states with regret for its passing.

"Musical art abounded in the fingering of the stretched string, the beating of the taut skin, the blowing with reeds" (p. 7 op. cit.), Dewey notices with remorse.

"Even in the caves, human habitations were adorned with colored pictures that kept alive to the senses experiences with the animals that were so closely bound with the lives of humans" (p. 7 op. cit.), Dewey recalls with nostalgia.

Art as an expression of tribal customs is considered by Dewey as the apex of art development.

He expresses his preference for art as an integral part of religion in citing with a sense of loss, as far as its passing is concerned, that the "structures that housed their gods and the instrumentalities that facilitated commerce with the higher powers were wrought with especial fitness" (p. 7 op. cit.).

The separation of art from religious cults is inferentially regarded by Dewey as a primary factor which is responsible for the disintegration of art.

The time when art ceased to be the handmaiden of religion is being inferentially identified by Dewey as the period of the downfall of the arts.

The evolvement of art as an intellectual discipline in its own right, the establishment of art as a specific range of inquiry is considered by Dewey as merely a manifestation of the degeneration of art.

When he subsequently recalls that "the arts of the drama, music, painting, and architecture thus exemplified (i.e. in their primitive tribal manifestations, P.C.) had no peculiar connection with theaters, galleries, museums" (p. 7 op. cit.), he forgets to add that neither drama, nor music, nor painting, nor architecture were regarded as art in those times and could therefore not rate a place in a theatre, or museum, or gallery, the very designation of which is preconditioned by the recognition of the existence of art as a phenomenon sui generis.

The non-recognition of art as art in the distant past is being inferentially acknowledged by Dewey in his pointing out in a subsequent statement that "the collective life that was manifested in war, worship, the forum, knew no division between what was characteristic of these places and operations, and the arts that brought color, grace, and dignity, into them" (p. 7 op. cit.).

In its more direct import, the just stated quotation is supposed to convey the thought that, at a time when art did not exist as such, and was not recognized as such, it served as means of social elevation, and to bring out, by contradistinction, that the time in which art came to exist as such, and became recognized as such, is characteristic of a period in which art has become a concomitant of social degradation.

The role of the arts at the time when they were given recognition as a factor of social elevation is restressed by Dewey when he states that "painting and sculpture were organically one with architecture, as that was one with the social purpose that buildings served" (p. 7 op. cit.).

He continues to refer to art as an instrumentality of social elevation when he cites that "music and song were intimate parts of the rites and ceremonies in which the meaning of group life was consummated" (p. 7 op. cit.), and when he relates that "drama was a vital reenactment of the legends and history of group life" (p. 7 op. cit.).

As preoccupied as he is with his effort to picture the evolution of art as a phenomenon sui generis as a factor in social degradation, he fails to realize that the actual beginning of art in the cognitive sense is presented by a break with the conception which held that art *is* life and the rise of the conception that art *is a reflection upon life.*

It is his preoccupation with the presumed devolution of art which makes him close his eyes, or pretend to have his eyes closed, to the real significance of the phase in the development of art which had taken place in ancient Greece.

When he singles out the Greeks for a commendation because, as he states it, "not even in Athens can such arts be torn loose from this setting in direct experience and yet retain their significant character" (p. 7 op. cit.), he fails to note that the actual significance of the art development in Athens does not lie in the factor that it *does not* fully emerge from the stage at which art was not distinguished from a general manifestation of life, but, on the contrary, in the factor that artistic expressions *of* social life had come to be differentiated at that time from artistic expressions *in* social life.

Dewey presents but a superficial observation as far as the

esthetic factor is concerned when he states with regard to ancient Athens that "athletic sports, as well as drama, celebrated and enforced traditions of race and group, instructing the people, commemorating glories, and strengthening their civic pride" (p. 7 op. cit.).

What is really significant, as far as the esthetic development in Athens is concerned, Dewey does not seem to realize, is not the mere factor that the Athenians celebrated and enforced traditions by way of athletic sports and drama, but the perfection they had reached in the institution of the differentiation of artistic means which were to be used in those celebrations.

It is a patent misrepresentation of the development of art as a specific factor, to ascribe, as Dewey does, the postulation of art as "an act of reproduction, or imitation" by the Athenian Greeks (Dewey must have Aristotle in mind in this case, P.C.) "to the close connection with daily life" (p. 7 op. cit.).

The very conception of an art theory as a discipline of its own, with a range of inquiry of its own, is, as Dewey could not have failed to note, predicated upon the cognitive differentiation of an artistic form of expression and a non-artistic manifestation of ordinary life.

It constitutes, moreover, a complete reversal of the respective cognitive position in regard to art which had been taken at the time of the flowering of the ancient Greek philosophy when Dewey characterizes Plato's conception of art as one which "reflected the emotions and ideas that are associated with the chief institutions of social life" (p. 7 op. cit.).

Plato, Dewey should be reminded, was the one Greek thinker who in his conception of art took the exceptional position that art in the ideal sense *is* life in the ideal sense and that therefore there is no place for art as *reflection* upon life.

Dewey's unrelated insistence that "the idea of 'art for art's sake' would not have been understood" (p. 8 op. cit.), has to be placed in a proper historical perspective, if one is to make sense of it.

The period of the flourishing of the arts in Ancient Greece was a period of the emergence of art as discipline in its own right, with a range of inquiry of its own, as has been stated here before.

The severance of the conceptual bonds of art creation and art appreciation from non-artistic conceptions had been but recently performed, an attempt to discount all content in art through evolvement of the formalistic conception of art for art's sake was yet far off.

In what follows, Dewey deplores what he calls the "compartmental" conception of fine art (p. 8 op. cit.) which had taken place in more recent history.

Compartmental in this connection means intellectual, it means art as a distinct intellectual discipline, it signifies art with an intellectual radius of operation of its own.

Dewey would like to deintellectualize the arts, he would like to have the conception of art revert to a level at which art and artless become hopelessly intermingled again.

When he cites "our present museums and galleries to which works of fine art are removed and stored" as "some of the causes that have operated to segregate art instead of finding it attendant of temple, forum, and other forms of associated life" (p. 8 op. cit.), he is actually pleading for the resubmergence of art into the misty sphere of mysticism.

He restresses his longing for a reconfinement of art to the realm of unreason in giving some highlights concerning the "history of modern art . . . in terms of the formation of the distinctively modern institutions of museum and exhibition gallery" (p. 8 op. cit.).

"Most European museums," he relates with dissatisfaction, "are among other things, memorials to the rise of nationalism and imperialism" (p. 8 op. cit.).

"Every capital," Dewey deplores, "must have its own museum of painting, sculpture, etc., devoted in part to exhibiting the greatness of its artistic past, and, in other part, to exhibiting the loot gathered by its monarchs in conquest of other nations; for instance, the accumulations of the spoils of Napoleon that are in the Louvre" (p. 8 op. cit.).

"They testify," he cites with disapproval, "to the connection between the modern segregation of art and nationalism and militarism" (p. 8 op. cit.).

While plundering and nationalistic exhibitionism as means of filling museums and galleries with art pieces can be considered deplorable, that is not the underlying reason which prompts Dewey's resentment in the stated instance.

At the bottom of the stated tirade lies his objection to militarism, nationalism and imperialism as secular movements.

What he really resents, is the creation of art objects which have been dedicated to secular purposes.

He somehow does not seem to realize that the establishment of the arts as a discipline of its own with its own range of inquiry has been predicated upon the emancipation of the arts from ecclesiastical tutelage in all of its forms.

He is unwilling to recognize that without a secularization of the general flow of social life, art, as such, governed by its own rules, would not have been permitted to exist.

This lack of discernment in his drawing of a historical perspective of art finds a patent illustration in his placing of the case of Japan which "saved much of her art treasures by nationalizing *the temples* (italics mine, P.C.) that contained them" (p. 8 op. cit.) into the same category with the accumulation of secular art treasures in Western museums and galleries.

The philosopher Dewey should not mind being reminded here, that it makes quite a difference as to what is being stored away.

The placing of objects which have not been created as art objects and were not supposed to be rated as art objects into a museum, can hardly be considered as having the same significance as an art factor as the placing of objects which have been created as art objects and are supposed to be rated as art objects into a museum or gallery.

Temples placed in museums do not become art pieces per se, on account of having a place in a museum; the place of those temples in the history of the development of art is unaffected, it remains the same, regardless of whether those temples can be found in a museum or not.

The architecture and the paintings of temples and churches of the period at which art as art was not as yet recognized as such, is, as far as its respective content and form is concerned, bound by religious tenets.

It should be admitted that, within the bounds of religious tenets, there was room for artistic creativeness.

In the selection of religious images and the use of the form of molding those images, the producers of temple and church architecture and paintings were allowed some discretion.

Nonetheless, the flight of the imagination of the artist remained restricted by the social and economic necessity imposed upon him by the all powerful ecclesiastical authorities to design church symbols.

The meaning and the purpose of those symbols had been largely predetermined.

It can be admitted, in turn, that, within the restricted artistic area in which he was bound to operate, the producer of temple and church architecture and paintings did manage to effect what can be called changes in style.

Changes in form became marked in the later stages of the production of church architecture and paintings in Western countries.

Those changes which broke with the traditional primitivism in the creation of religious objects constituted a precursor of the break with the ecclesiastical restrictions which had been placed on the selection of subject-matter.

It is only in the latter sense that the temple and church paintings and architecture can be placed in the category of art objects.

Only in the sense in which the temple and church architecture and paintings, and, we may add here, temple and church music as well, represented an early stage in the emergence of art as art, can they be granted a place in art development, regardless of whether those objects are found in museums or not.

Dewey's lack of discernment in drawing a historical perspective is further revealed by his treatment of the economic aspect of the development of art.

He finds that "the growth of capitalism has been a powerful influence in the development of the museum as the proper home for works of art, and in the promotion of the idea that they are apart from the common life." (p. 8 op. cit.).

"The *nouveaux riches*," he observes, "who are an important by-product of the capitalist system, have felt especially bound to surround themselves with works of fine art which, being rare, are also costly" (p. 8 op. cit.).

"Generally speaking," Dewey remarks, "the typical collector is the typical capitalist" (p. 8 op. cit.).

While he has a point there, that art has become a product which is more accessible to the rich than the poor in capitalist society, the placing of art products in a museum or a gallery can, however, hardly be cited as a means by which capitalists promoted "the idea that they (the works of art) are apart from common life," as Dewey charges.

While the influence of capitalist society on the development of art was not a positive one in all its aspects, what is all important, and what Dewey forgets to mention, is the factor that capitalism had created a market for art products which before the rise of capitalism did not exist.

Dewey, in the distorted view on the history of art development which he expounds, expresses opposition to the drawing of art products into the marketing stream.

"Modern industry and commerce have an international scope" (p. 9 op. cit.), he cites.

"The contents of galleries and museums testify to the growth of economic cosmopolitanism" (p. 9 op. cit.), he relates.

And then follows the specific objection: "the mobility of trade and of populations, due to the economic system, has weakened or destroyed the connection between works of art and the *genius loci* of which they were once the natural expression. As works of art have lost their indigenous status they have acquired a new one—that of being specimens of fine art and nothing else" (p. 9 op. cit.).

He recognizes in the just quoted statement that the growth

of the market for art products went hand in hand with the growth of art as a phenomenon sui generis.

To him, however, such a development signifies a backward step; he sees in the factor that art products came to be related to a wider social horizon than the one which was circumscribed by the range of local folk-lore in the course of the creation and enlargement of a market for art products an indication of the downfall of the arts.

His scornful remark that "works of art are now produced, like other articles, for sale in the market" (p. 9 op. cit.) is meant to be a castigation of the entire marketing nexus, as far as it expresses itself in the dealing in art objects.

His principal opposition to the marketing of art products is well in line with his critical views on the place of the artist in capitalist society.

"Because of changes in industrial conditions," he relates, "the artist has been pushed to one side from the main streams of active interest" (p. 9 op. cit.).

"Industry," he observes, "has been mechanized and an artist cannot work mechanically for mass production" (p. 9 op. cit.).

"He" (the artist P.C.) "is less integrated," Dewey expresses resentment, "than formerly in the normal flow of social services" (p. 9 op. cit.).

The thought behind the thought refers, in the stated connection, to Dewey's proposition according to which art as a profession is not supposed to be recognized as a legitimate social and economic phenomenon.

The pre-capitalist society which is postulated as the ideal period by Dewey, as far as the conditions of the arts and the position of the artist is concerned, did not know art products as art products, and artists as artists.

In the ideal conception of art and the artist which Dewey is trying to revive, art was a by-product in the production of a utilitarian product and the artist was a producer of a utilitarian product who excelled in his skill in the production of the stated product.

That is the sense in which Dewey's reference to integration "in the normal flow of social services" is to be understood in the stated context.

In his subsequent bemoaning of "a peculiar esthetic individualism" as well as in his subsequent complaint that "artists find it incumbent upon them to betake themselves to their work as an isolated means of self-expression" (p. 9 op. cit.) Dewey is not content to dwell on the difficulties which the artist has in asserting himself as a professional artist in modern industrial society.

What Dewey has in mind in the stated connection, is to interpret the obstacles to the self-assertion of the artist as an artist in contemporary capitalist society as a sign which indicates the necessity of the abandonment of the whole conception of artistic work as a profession and a return to the conception which does not recognize any distinction between an artist and an artisan.

He bolsters his case for a return of the artist to the fold of the artisan by citing extremities in the artist's position which grow out of his struggle for the survival of the artist as an artist, in the face of the vicissitudes of the capitalist economy and society.

"In order not to cater to the trend of economic forces, they (the artists, P.C.)," he observes, "feel obliged to exaggerate their separateness to the point of eccentricity" (p. 9 op. cit.).

"Consequently artistic products," Dewey relates, "take on to a still greater degree the air of something independent and esoteric" (p. 8, 9 op. cit.).

The problem-complex which he touches upon here is the one which is involved in the proposition of art for art's sake.

Dewey had casually mentioned the proposition of art for art's sake when he discussed the condition of the arts in Athenian Greece.

At that time, as had been pointed out by this writer, the stated proposition could not have become acute.

In the context in which Dewey mentioned the art for art's sake proposition, it constituted but an added note of historical misprojection.

When he reaches the historical period to which the art for art's sake proposition properly belongs, he does not even care to have the subject-matter mentioned by that name.

He contents himself with a less specific objection to "exaggerated separateness to the point of eccentricity" on the part of the artist and the "still greater degree of the air of something esoteric" in art products, which he wants to have regarded as an added evidence that it has become high time to discount the conception of the artist as an artist, along with the conception of artistic products as artistic products.

Dewey, to be sure, is not at once disclosing as to what his indictment of the self-isolation of the artist is supposed to lead.

He divests himself of quite a few exclamations before he divulges the course he is taking.

He decries the "chasm between ordinary and esthetic experience" (p. 10 op. cit.).

He derides "the philosophies of art that locate it in a region inhabited by no other creature, and that emphasize beyond all reason the merely contemplative character of the esthetic" (p. 10 op. cit.).

He attacks the "confusion of values" which "enters in to accentuate the separation" (p. 10 op. cit.).

He assails as "adventitious matters, . . . the pleasure of collecting, of exhibiting, of ownership and display" which "simulate esthetic values" (p. 10 op. cit.).

"Criticism is affected" (p. 10 op. cit.), Dewey notices with dissatisfaction.

"There is much applause for the wonders of appreciation and the glories of the transcendent beauty of art indulged in without much regard to capacity for esthetic perception in the concrete" (p. 10 op. cit.), he observes with disapproval.

None of those critical statements are followed up, however.

All those critical remarks are left to be just remarks and nothing more.

A respective explanation is not even attempted by Dewey.

At this point he shifts the area of his deliberations.

He shows signs of being determined to leave the social and economic factors, as far as they have a bearing on the arts, unattended.

By way of overstating the respective problem involved, he bans the economic aspect from the subsequent range of his deliberation.

"My purpose," he declares, "is not to engage in an economic interpretation of the history of the arts, much less to argue that economic conditions are either invariably or directly relevant to perception and enjoyment, or even to interpretation of individual works of art" (p. 10 op. cit.).

In disclaiming crude economic determinism for the kind of art philosophy he is trying to advance, Dewey does not seem to realize that he does not remove (by his disclaiming of crude economic determinism) the economic factor, as such, as a legitimate aspect of an inquiry into the arts.

His discounting of all economic questions as factors affecting the arts under the pretense that those questions can be dealt with only within the cognitive framework of a crude economic determinism, is bound to result in an incompleteness of his inquiry, in the narrowing of its range, it is of necessity to thwart a rounded approach to a philosophy of the arts.

Dewey's very next statement constitutes an indictment of his own position which he is taking with regard to the economic aspects within the range of a philosophy of the arts.

His banning of any and all economic questions which include not only problems which pertain to the economic factor involved in the relation of the producer and the buyer of art products, but, in addition, the whole social and economic matrix within which the producer and the acquirer of art operate, is hardly compatible with what he subsequently states about what he regards as a proper approach to a philosophy of the arts.

"It is to indicate," Dewey states it as his deliberate aim, "that *theories* which isolate art and its appreciation by placing them in a realm of their own, disconnected from other modes of experiencing, are not inherent in the subject-matter but arise because of specifiable extraneous conditions" (p. 10 op. cit.).

"Embedded as they (theories which isolate art, P.C.) are in institutions and in habits of life," Dewey continues his declaratory statement, "these conditions operate effectively because they work so unconsciously" (p. 10 op. cit.).

"Then," he asserts, "the theorist assumes they are embedded in the nature of things" (p. 10 op. cit.).

One would think that the cognitive recovery of the social and economic institutions and social and economic habits of life from the conceptual wreckage, which Dewey calls the unconscious, would be a preconditioning factor in the realization of the program which Dewey is ostensibly setting for himself.

What could prompt Dewey, one is bound to ask, to persist in discounting social and economic institutions and social and economic habits of life, should he be determined to evolve a realistic art theory.

Well, the answer is not long in forthcoming.

Dewey, it turns out, is not committed to the maintaining of a strict theoretical position.

"The influence of these conditions (i.e. institutions and habits of life, P.C.), is not confined to theory" (p. 10 op. cit.), he declares.

The theoretical, the equivocable statement implies, cannot be set apart from the non-theoretical.

In order to confound the "theories which isolate art," he sets out to disqualify the cognitive basis for any conceivable art theory.

His subsequent lamentation that the non-recognition of institutions and habits of life as a specific factor in the evolvement of an art theory "deeply affects the practice of living, driving away esthetic perceptions that are necessary ingredients of happiness, or reducing them to the level of compensating transient pleasurable excitations" (p. 10 op. cit.) is followed by a less equivocal statement on what he suggests as a remedial proposition.

"Even to readers who are adversely inclined to what has been said," he declares, "the implications of the statements which have been made may be useful in defining the nature of the problem" (p. 10 op. cit.).

As the crux of the stated declaration, he proffers the proposition "of recovering the *continuity* (italics mine, P.C.) of esthetic experience with normal processes of living" (p. 10 op. cit.).

The reintroduction of the conception of continuity constitutes a clear enough indication that Dewey is committed to the dissolution of all art theories, and that he is, in turn, resolved to keep the art theories in a state of dissolution on the basis of a claim that nothing else is knowable about art factors than that one factor is related to another, and still to another, and so on, and so forth, ad infinitum.

The specification of factors, their cognitive distinctiveness, is ruled out within the range of Dewey's conception of continuity.

The factors involved in the respective correlation are reduced to such insignificance in Dewey's relativistic approach which revolves around his conception of continuity, that it makes little, if any difference, whether the stated proposition is referred to as a relation of one factor to another, and still to another, and so on, and so forth, or, whether the proposition is stated in the form of relation of a relation, of a relation and so on, and so forth, without the word factor even being mentioned.

Dewey himself does not mind providing some leads at this turn as to what "recovering the *continuity* of esthetic experience with normal processes of living" involves within his frame of reasoning.

"The understanding of art and of its role in civilization, is not furthered by setting out with eulogies of it," he observes, "nor by occupying ourselves exclusively at the outset with great works of art recognized as such" (p. 10 op. cit.).

The just quoted statement carries Dewey's contradictory position with regard to what he calls "theories that isolate art" to its logical conclusion.

The condemnation of eulogies to art, which is supposed to constitute a condemnation of a kind of art appreciation which does not grant specific recognition to social and economic factors which are embedded, to use Dewey's expression, in art creations, is followed by a refusal to recognize the existence of great works of art, as works of art, as a preconditioning factor for approaching the kind of inquiry into the arts which he is about to outline.

His remark that the removal of the great works of art as art objects from the sphere of his kind of inquiry into the arts is to constitute but a temporary device—it is to be effected, as he states, "at the outset"—can hardly be taken as a legitimate excuse.

A cognition and perception of the arts which starts out with the supposition that the art object is non-existent, can hardly be viewed as constituting an inquiry into the arts.

By removing the art object as art object as an analytical factor from the kind of art theory he is about to evolve, no matter what the time limit for that removal is to be, does cognitive violence to the subject-matter which he is supposed to discuss.

The cognitive violence which the removal of art objects as art objects as an analytical factor from the kind of art theory he is about to evolve is of such serious nature that the return of the art object into the fold of inquiry, after it had been left out of consideration in the evolvement of the basic principles of that inquiry, cannot restore to that kind of inquiry the character of an inquiry into the arts.

A return of the art object into the fold of inquiry the basic principles of which are stated with disregard of the existence of the art object can but lead to a disqualification of the art object as art object, since the cognitive propositions of an inquiry which are laid down in disregard of the factors of the art object are lacking of cognitive means to recognize art objects as art objects.

It should be noted in the stated connection, that Dewey finds it opportune to advocate a discounting of *great* works of art as a preconditioning factor of his devising of an art theory.

A great work of art, generally recognized as such, Dewey is not unaware, can be well classed as a representative work of art for a certain period and a certain form of art; the exclusion of great works of art as great works of art as a preconditioning factor of his art theory, Dewey could not have been unaware of it, leaves him without any art standard, it leaves the approach to the art theory which he is about to devise at the mercy of passing impressions about art objects.

Were he to leave only non-representative art objects within the range of his inquiry from the very outset of his devising of the framework of that inquiry, Dewey can then be led to reason, these art objects cannot really count as art objects in any significant form in the absence of comparative standards of the evaluation of art objects as art objects.

Fleeting impressions about art objects, Dewey can thus cogitate, can hardly have any effect on the evolvement of basic principles.

He thus can see himself cognitively unable to discern either the representative or the non-representative in art objects.

The just stated consideration is no doubt guiding Dewey when he subsequently proclaims that "the comprehension which theory essays will be arrived at by a detour; by going back to experience or the common or mill run of things to discover the esthetic quality such experience possesses" (p. 11 op. cit.).

"Theory," Dewey subsequently insists, "can start with and from acknowledged works of art only when the esthetic is already compartmentalized, or only when works of art are set in a niche apart instead of being celebrations, recognized as such, of the things of ordinary experience" (p. 11 op. cit.).

"Even a crude experience," he asserts, "if authentically an experience, is more fit to give a clue to the intrinsic nature of esthetic experience than is an object already set apart from any other mode of experience" (p. 11 op. cit.).

The just stated quotations make it clear that Dewey is set to discount in his kind of art theory any cognitive framework in which the art factor is allowed to play any definable role.

When he adds that "the trouble with existing theories is that they start from a ready-made compartmentalization, or from a conception of art that "spiritualizes" it out of connection with the objects of concrete experience" (p. 11 op. cit.) he is but reasserting his intention not to tolerate any conceptualization in which the art object is made to rate as art object.

Compartmentalization, as had been stated by this writer in the preceding part of this chapter, can be well interpreted as intellectualization, in the sense in which Dewey uses the term.

Dewey's disapproval of compartmentalization can be well taken to mean disapproval of art as either a proper subject for cognition or perception.

Any theory of art which makes cognitive provisions for the recognition of art as an art factor is, for that very reason, rejected by Dewey.

Dewey's rejection of the conception of art that "spiritualizes" can, in the context in which it is placed by him, be taken as a rejection of any conception of art on the grounds that art is a factor which does not merit a conception of its own.

When he subsequently states that "a conception of fine art that sets out from its connection with discovered qualities of ordinary experience will be able to indicate the factors and forces that favor normal development of common human activities into matters of artistic value" (p. 11 op. cit.) he manifests his determination to have the art factor engulfed in a welter of extraneous propositions.

Qualities of ordinary experience and normal development of common human activities, no matter what they are, are by any reasonable definition non-artistic in character.

A conception of fine art which sets out from a connection with non-artistic factors, which in other words, sets out with the proposition that there is no principal distinction between the artistic and non-artistic, can hardly lead to an understanding of what is involved in art.

Though Dewey tries to acquit himself by insisting that the alternative to what he calls spiritualization does not constitute a degrading and crude materialization of works of fine art, his conception of fine art which sets out from its connection with ordinary experience, i.e. non-artistic experience, can lead but to a disqualification of the art factors within the range of his comprehension.

Connection, in Dewey's vocabulary, it should be restressed in this instance, means inseparable connection; it signifies a cognitive tieup which does not allow for any distinctiveness.

Connection, in the way the word is being used by Dewey, becomes but another expression for continuity.

A conception of fine arts which sets out from its connection with ordinary experience, becomes thus a conception which is characterized by an undifferentiation of the factors which are supposed to be connected.

The word connection, in the way in which Dewey uses it, over-shadows the factors which are supposed to be connected.

The conception of fine arts that sets out from its connection with ordinary experience, in the way Dewey formulates it, means nothing more than a connection of two undifferentiated factors.

It should be added, that the reference to discovered qualities, in the sense in which Dewey uses the word qualities, does not introduce any note of differentiation.

It is, therefore, difficult to see how a conception of fine arts that sets out from its connection with discovered qualities of ordinary experience, in the sense in which Dewey formulates it, can ever be effectively applied for the indication of the factors and forces that favor the normal development of human activities with reference to matters of artistic value.

The undifferentiation with which he starts out his formulation of fine arts can serve as but an indicator of undifferentiation.

The undifferentiation to which his conception of fine arts is bound to lead his inquiry into the arts can most certainly not be of any assistance "to point out those conditions that arrest its (the factors and forces that favor the normal development of common human activities into matters of artistic value P.C.) normal growth" (p. 11 op. cit.), Dewey's assertion to the contrary.

Dewey's undifferentiated conception of fine arts can form merely an obstacle to the normal development of common human activities into matters of artistic value, since it does not provide for cognitive means by which the factors and the forces that favor the normal development of common human activities into matters of artistic value can be determined.

Dewey's conception of the fine arts can thus merely contribute to the abnormal development of common human activities into abnormal factors of artistic range.

Dewey's conception of fine arts can thus lead merely to a widening of the chasm between artistic values and the currents of social and economic life, a chasm, the castigation of which was supposed to provide the raison d'être for his, Dewey's, kind of inquiry into the arts.

What follows in the stated connection can hardly be expected to provide a lead to any understanding of the art factor and its place in social and economic life.

A misprojection in the premise can hardly fail to result in a misprojected conclusion.

A reasoning based on a misconception can hardly fail to lead to another misconception.

Dewey, on his part, is proceeding as if there is nothing misleading in his basic formulation.

Dewey, on his part, continues to argue as if his conception of fine arts is designed to clarify and not to confound the respective issues involved.

"Writers on esthetic theory," he nonchalantly remarks, "often raise the question of whether philosophy can aid in cultivation of esthetic appreciation" (p. 11 op. cit.).

"The question," he observes, "is a branch of the general theory of criticism, which, it seems to me, fails to accomplish its full office if it does not indicate what to look for and what to find in concrete esthetic objects" (p. 11, 12 op. cit.).

How the stated observation is to be squared with Dewey's insistence on having concrete art objects discounted as art objects in the conception of fine arts which he is evolving, Dewey does not care to explain.

As a matter of fact, he is in a great hurry to drop the stated subject.

He is quite quick to relate that "in any case, it is safe to say that a philosophy of art is sterilized unless it makes us aware of the function of art in relation to other modes of experience, and unless it indicates why this function is so inadequately realized, and unless it suggests the conditions under which the office would be successfully performed" (p. 12 op. cit.).

What is new in the just quoted statement, is the relation of the function of art to other modes of experience.

What is significant in the just cited quotation, is Dewey's effort to establish a link between the function of art and the mode of experience which is distinctly not of an art character.

A link within the framework of Dewey's reasoning is an inseparable link, it should not be forgotten in this connection.

The function of art philosophy in the setting of standards of the artistic perception of the creative artist and the artistic taste of the art appreciator is thus presented as being explainable in terms of an experience which is not one of art.

The function of the art philosophy, which Dewey is trying to establish, is thus rendered inexplicable by him in terms of art.

In suggesting a probe into the factors of why art philosophy has not so far been adequately expressed in terms of experience other than the one of art, to provide a clue for the conditions under which such a function of the art philosophy can be adequately performed, Dewey evolves a scheme for a progressive deterioration of art as a specific and specifiable factor in the current of life.

A cumulative deterioration of the arts as a factor in the current of life, Dewey is well aware, is conditioned, if not preconditioned, by the deterioration of artistic production.

Should the artist be able to maintain artistic production standards, should he be able to adhere to artistic conceptions in the selection of subject-matter, the deterioration of the arts as a distinctive and distinguishable factor in life could not be complete and lasting, Dewey is fully conscious.

He therefore undertakes a major attack which can have but

the effect of undermining the conceptual and perceptual prerequisites of art creation.

"The comparison of the emergence of works of art out of ordinary experiences to the refining of raw materials into valuable products," Dewey is apologetic, "may seem to some unworthy, if not an actual attempt to reduce works of art to the status of articles manufactured for commercial purposes" (p. 12 op. cit.).

"The point, however," he elaborates on his excuse, "is that no amount of esthetic eulogy of finished works can of itself assist the understanding or the generation of such works" (p. 12 op. cit.).

With the two stated sentences Dewey tries to present the issue of comprehension of art creation as one which can be approached either as a factor of mere material production or as a purely emotional factor.

As between the two, he chooses the factor of material production for his approach to the comprehension of art creation in this instance.

A third possibility, a possibility according to which esthetic concepts are permitted to rate as constituent elements of art creation along with material elements and emotional factors, Dewey does not care to grant.

"Flowers," he asserts, "can be enjoyed without knowing about the interactions of soil, air, moisture, and seeds of which they are the result" (p. 12 op. cit.).

With this assertion he, by contrast, emphasizes the purely emotional aspect in esthetic comprehension.

"But they cannot be *understood*," he insists, "without taking just these interactions into account—and theory is a matter of understanding" (p. 12 op. cit.).

With the stated quotation he draws away, in turn, from the emotional approach, and at the same time discounts the material approach to esthetic comprehension.

In posting interactions as a decisive factor in understanding art, he is paving the way for an utter formalistic form of esthetic comprehension.

"It is a commonplace," he argues, "that we cannot direct, save accidentally, the growth and flowering of plants, however lovely and enjoyed, without understanding their causal conditions" (p. 12 op. cit.).

The word causal, which Dewey uses in the stated quotation, has to be brought into relation with his conception of interaction.

In devising interaction as a clue to understanding, he clearly indicates that he is determined to concentrate on surface manifestations.

Within the cognitive range of interaction to which Dewey is committed, causation can come to mean no more than an interrelation.

Within the cognitive range of interaction, causative elements as such, in the sense of specific material factors of causation, cannot be made to count.

It is with an eye to the causative indistinctiveness at which he is aiming that the subsequent passages of Dewey's "Art as Experience" are to be read.

"It should be just a commonplace," he declares, "that esthetic understanding—as distinct from sheer personal enjoyment—must start with the soil, air, and light out of which things esthetically admirable arise" (p. 12 op. cit.).

Though he lists the physical factors of soil, air and light, his cognitive proposition of interaction makes it unfeasible for him to recognize these elements as specific causative factors.

His subsequent declaration which states, that "the more we recognize this fact, the more we shall find ourselves faced with a problem rather than with a final solution" (p. 12 op. cit.) constitutes a candid admission that the kind of understanding he is setting out to promote in regard to the bearing of external factors on art creation and art appreciation, is to render the cognitive and perceptual problems which are involved in art comprehension insoluble.

In the light of what has just been stated, the question which he subsequently asks is merely rhetorical.

His question "*if* artistic and esthetic quality is implicit in every normal experience, how shall we explain how and why it so generally fails to become explicit?" (p. 12, 13 op. cit.) can be readily answered by saying, that by postulating the esthetic as *merely* implicit in normal experience Dewey himself sets up a cognitive roadblock which prevents the artistic and esthetic quality from becoming explicit and discernible within the range of his comprehension.

Dewey, however, is not content with leaving it to the reader to enforce the cognitive strictures, which he, Dewey, wants to have imposed.

Dewey himself is eager in this instance to implement his general proposition.

He undertakes to resolve the puzzlement, which the just quoted question is supposed to create, by stating that the question cannot be answered "any more than we can trace the development of art out of everyday experience, unless we have a clear and coherent idea of what is meant when we say 'normal experience'" (p. 13 op. cit.).

"Fortunately," he claims, "the road to arriving at such an idea is open and well marked" (p. 13 op. cit.).

"The nature of experience," he lectures, "is determined by the essential conditions of life" (p. 13 op. cit.).

He then goes on to recommit the essential conditions of human life to the fold of the essential conditions of non-human life.

"While man," he intones, "is other than bird and beast, he shares basic vital functions with them and has to make the same basal adjustments if he is to continue the process of living" (p. 13 op. cit.).

"Having the same vital needs, man derives the means by which he breathes, moves, looks and listens," Dewey reintones, "the very brain with which he coordinates his senses and his movements from his animal forebears" (p. 13 op. cit.).

This tune of reincorporation of the social into the biological is being sounded off by Dewey with his by now usual refrain that "the organs with which he (the human being, P.C.) maintains himself in being are not of himself alone, but by the grace of struggles and achievements of a long line of animal ancestry" (p. 13 op. cit.).

"Fortunately," he then proclaims, "a theory of the place of the esthetic in experience does not have to lose itself in minute details when it starts with experience in its elemental form" (p. 13 op. cit.).

"Broad outlines suffice" (p. 13 op. cit.), he promises.

After that his statements become once more redundant.

"No creature lives merely under its skin," he recites; "its subcutaneous organs are means of connection with what lies beyond its bodily frame, and of which, in order to live, it must adjust itself, by accommodation and defense but also by conquest" (p. 13 op. cit.).

The aspect of redundancy is not relieved by his recitation that "at every moment, the living creature is exposed to danger from its surroundings, and at every moment, it must draw upon something in its surroundings to satisfy its needs" (p. 13 op. cit.).

The aspect of redundancy becomes even more evident when he states that "the career and destiny of a living being are bound up with its interchanges with its environment, not externally but in the most intimate way" (p. 13 op. cit.).

If one reminds oneself of the pains Dewey took to undifferentiate environment, if one recalls that within Dewey's range of cognition environment cannot be set apart from factors which do not constitute environment, his reference to "interchanges with environment not externally but in the most intimate way" assumes a purely verbal character, since the factor of environment is not recognizable as such within his, Dewey's, cognitive framework.

In what follows Dewey provides illustrations for his conception of the identity of human and non-human factors of living.

"The growl of a dog crouching over his food," he relates, "his howl in time of loss and loneliness, the wagging of his tail at the return of his human friend are expressions of the implication of a living in a natural medium which includes man along with the animal he has domesticated" (p. 13 op. cit.).

The theme that man's living conditions as well as his manner of living is identical with the living conditions and the manner of living of the animal is further exploited by Dewey.

"Every need, say hunger for fresh air or food," he observes, "is a lack that denotes at least a temporary absence of adequate adjustment with surroundings" (p. 13, 14 op. cit.).

In subsequent statements he reverts to the factor of undifferentiation which, by and large, make those pronouncements meaningless.

When he states that "it" (the denotation of the temporary absence of adequate adjustment with surroundings) "is also a demand, a reaching out into the environment to make good the lack and to restore adjustment by building at least a temporary equilibrium" (p. 13 op. cit.), he forgets to mention that environment is something unfathomable within his range of cognition and that an adjustment to something which cannot be discerned and differentiated from something else, is hardly conceivable.

His statement that "life itself consists of phases in which the organism falls out of step with the march of surrounding things and then recovers unison with it—either through effort or by some happy chance" (p. 14 op. cit.) can be considered as fitting only in part into his cognitive framework.

Since a conscious effort to recover the unison of the organism and environment is inconceivable under the stricture which provides for a cognitive undifferentiation of organism and environment, the recovery of a unison of the organism and environment has, within Dewey's range of comprehension, to be invariably ascribed to a happy chance.

With regard to his subsequent statement that "in a growing life, the recovery is never mere return to a prior state, for it is enriched by the state of disparity and resistance through which it has successfully passed" (p. 14 op. cit.) Dewey should not mind being reminded that his prior insistence on undifferentiation as supreme cognitive factor makes a distinction between a prior and a succeeding state well nigh inconceivable within his cognitive range; if a disparity and resistance to the growing of life does actually take place, its effects have to be rated as haphazard as its causes within the scope of his, Dewey's, comprehension.

When he observes that "if the gap between organism and environment is too wide, the creature dies" (p. 14 op. cit.), he should not mind having it recalled that the degree of the gap between organism and environment cannot be determined if, as he insists, the organism is to remain cognitively undifferentiated from environment.

Whether the live creature dies or survives has to be left to an unhappy or happy chance, if Dewey's conception that an organism cannot be differentiated from environment and environment cannot be differentiated from an organism is to be made to stand.

His argumentation that "if its activity (the organism's activity, P.C.) is not enhanced by the temporary alienation, it merely subsists" (p. 14 op. cit.) cannot be granted any specific meaning since cognitive provisions for the differentiation of what is enhancement and what is not enhancement are thoroughly lacking within Dewey's range of comprehension.

His observation that "life grows when a temporary falling out is a transition to a more extensive balance of the energies of the organism with those of the conditions under which it lives" (p. 14 op. cit.) cannot be considered as signifying more than an exclamation, if the cognitive stricture of undifferentiation is to be made to prevail.

"These biological commonplaces," i.e. the commonplace of cognitive undifferentiation of the human and non-human factors in life as well as the commonplace of the undifferentiation of organism and environment, to fill in for Dewey, "are something more than that; they reach to the roots of the esthetic in experience" (p. 14 op. cit.), Dewey subsequently proclaims.

With this proclamation he goes on record in favor of having the sphere of art creation and art appreciation confined to the same cognitive range to which he has committed human life along with animal life.

Art creation and art appreciation come to be cast by the said programmatic statement into that sphere of the cognitive twilight which is characterized by the undifferentiation of human and non-human life.

The subsequent statements, in which the correlation of organism with environment are offered as the root of esthetic experience, are all based on the premise of cognitive undifferentiation.

The subsequent observation that "the world is full of things that are indifferent and even hostile to life; the very processes by which life is maintained, tend to throw it out of gear with its surroundings" (p. 14 op. cit.) pictures life as a contradictory process.

The statement can be accorded meaning, however, only under the condition that the ban on the cognition in any specific form of the things that are indifferent and even hostile to life be lifted by Dewey, which, it should be observed, is not the case.

The following assertion in which Dewey contends that "nevertheless, if life continues and if continuing it expands, there is an overcoming of factors of opposition and conflict; there is a transformation of them into differentiated aspects of higher powered and more significant life" (p. 14 op. cit.) can be only regarded as paradoxical within his cognitive framework.

How "differentiated aspects" can come to be recognized as such within the scope of his comprehension, in the face of his systematic effort at an all pervading cognitive undifferentiation, Dewey does not care to mention in the said connection.

Nor would he care to be reminded in the stated connection that his reference to "a higher powered and more significant life" can make little sense within his framework of reasoning, in the face of his persistent attempt to have the cognition of life reduced to a level at which a distinction between differing manifestations of life is not supposed to register.

Dewey's subsequent exaltation about "the marvel of organic, of vital, adaptation through expansion (instead of by contraction and passive accommodation)" (p. 14 op. cit.) uses the word marvel in the literal sense.

Within Dewey's range of comprehension vital adaptation

through expansion, if it is to be granted any recognition, can be rated as but a miracle.

The comprehension of organic, vital adaptation, in the sense of a specific cause and a specific effect which would allow for a rational explanation, remains inconceivable within Dewey's cognitive frame of reference.

His subsequent insistence that "here (in the organic, vital adaptation, P.C.) in germ are balance and harmony attained through rhythm" (p. 14 op. cit.), can, in view of the meaninglessness of the preceding statements, not be rated as more than an exclamation.

Dewey himself but underscores the meaninglessness of his reference to "balance and harmony attained through rhythm" when he proffers as a corollary to the said contention the statement that "equilibrium comes about not mechanically and inertly but out of, and because of, tension" (p. 14 op. cit.).

None of the terms used in the just quoted sentence can be made to mean anything specifiable, if Dewey's general stricture of undifferentiation is to be maintained.

Equilibrium is rendered indistinguishable from tension within the stated range of Dewey's comprehension.

Were a creative artist, a composer, to try to follow Dewey's advice and attempt to look for the roots of an esthetic experience within what Dewey calls a sphere of organic, vital adaptation, he would be unable to distinguish between harmony and disharmony, between the rhythmical and the non-rhythmical, were he to respect Dewey's unrelenting opposition against having the factor of organic, vital adaptation conceived in any specifiable form.

Compliance with the general stricture of undifferentiation is bound to make it even inconceivable for the prospective composer to suspect that harmony is something different from disharmony and the rhythmical something distinguishable from the arhythmical.

The general cognitive framework of undifferentiation is based on the proposition that cognition and perception cannot reach a level at which an imbalance can be distinguished from a balance—the two conceptions which lie at the root of the factors of harmony and disharmony, as well as at the root of the factors of the rhythmical and the non-rhythmical.

As if the cognitive level to which he is trying to link the esthetic experience were not low enough, Dewey is apparently proceeding to descend into still lower regions of comprehension.

"There is in nature," he declares, "even below the level of life, something more than mere flux and change" (p. 14 op. cit.).

"Form is arrived at," he contends, "whenever a stable, even though moving, equilibrium is reached" (p. 14 op. cit.).

Since within his cognitive range of indefiniteness, a non-moving equilibrium is to appear formless, a moving equilibrium can hardly assume any form within his cognitive framework, Dewey has to be reminded at this instance.

Since he is cognitively unable to specify what exactly is an equilibrium, his denotation of a moving equilibrium can be considered as but another move to avoid specification.

Should a prospective painter attempt to follow Dewey's advice in trying to locate the root of an esthetic experience, by attempting to learn something about form through an effort to comprehend a moving equilibrium, he would be in for a bitter disappointment.

In view of Dewey's cognitive incapacity to distinguish an equilibrium from a disequilibrium within his frame of reference, the prospective painter who remains within Dewey's cognitive framework would be unable to determine what makes for form and what for formlessness.

In view of the just stated considerations, the statements which follow can be considered as being bare of any import as far as the advancement of a reasoned understanding of what Dewey calls the roots of the esthetic in experience is concerned.

His subsequent exclamation that "wherever there is coherence there is endurance" (p. 14 op. cit.) means little if anything since he has deprived himself of cognitive means for the distinguishing of coherence from non-coherence and endurance from non-endurance.

His subsequent attempt to evolve a conception of order is bound for a cognitive shipwreck since his all prevailing cognitive stricture of undifferentiation renders him cognitively incapable of distinguishing order from disorder.

As far as the conception of order is concerned, Dewey does not mind demonstrating the cognitive aspect of undifferentiation.

His assertion that "order is not imposed from without but is made out of the relations of harmonious interactions that energies bear to one another" (p. 14 op. cit.) is meant to convey the thought that order is something which is not caused by anything which is not qualified as order.

Order thus comes to be presented as a self-generating factor, as something which possesses the quality of emanation.

The undifferentiation of the conception of order is carried a point further by Dewey's subsequent contention that "it" (order, P.C.) "comes to include within its balanced movement a greater variety of changes" (p. 14 op. cit.).

The indefiniteness of the conception of order is being advanced by the just stated contention to a degree, at which it does not make any difference whether the conception of disorder is or is not included in the stated conception of order, order becomes a meaningless word with the stated contention.

A prospective artist, be he a prospective composer, or a prospective painter, or for that matter a prospective novelist, who, in taking Dewey's advice, would try to discover the roots of esthetic experience by attempting to discern the order "of harmonious interactions that energies bear to one another," is bound to fail in the most miserable fashion.

In view of the cognitive undifferentiation of order and disorder, the prospective creative artist, were he to remain within Dewey's cognitive frame, would not be able to discriminate between the chaotic and the non-chaotic.

After having failed to provide a reasoned criterion for the distinguishing of order from disorder, Dewey proceeds to cast the whole controversy about the cognition of order and disorder into the mold of the unreasoned.

"Order," he exclaims, "cannot but be admirable in a world

constantly threatened with disorder—in a world where living creatures can go on living only by taking advantage of whatever order exists about them, incorporating it into themselves" (p. 14, 15 op. cit.).

He contents himself in the just quoted statement with referring to order as an emotional factor, as a factor which is admirable, as he expresses himself.

While he indicates that the admiration of order is based on a reasoned expectation of survival through a kind of incorporating of order by living creatures, the factor of reasoned expectation constitutes no more than a feeling of reasoned expectation in the context into which he places it.

Dewey himself emphasizes that at this stage of his deliberations he is operating within a purely sensuous range, by subsequently stating that "in a world like ours, every living creature that attains *sensibility* (italics mine, P.C.) welcomes order with a response of harmonious *feeling* (italics mine, P.C.) whenever it finds a congruous order about it" (p. 15 op. cit.).

The finding of a congruous order by the living creature thus becomes a groping in the dark since reasoning as a means not only of finding, but even of comprehending what constitutes a congruous order, is ruled out by Dewey's respective stand on cognition.

The finding of a congruous order remains a matter of chance within the range of comprehension which Dewey is willing to permit the live creature to retain.

In the passage which follows, Dewey undertakes to remove the factor of the esthetic from the mold of the reasoned.

In the subsequent statements Dewey moves for a presentation of the whole complexity of the problems which surround the issue of the esthetic as a non-reasoned proposition.

"For only when an organism shares in the ordered relations of its environment does it secure the stability essential to living" (p. 15 op. cit.), Dewey remarks in a rather apodictic mood.

He then goes on to contend that "when the participation comes after a phase of disruption and conflict, it bears within itself the germs of a consummation akin to the esthetic" (p. 15 op. cit.).

Since he had just stated that the live creature lives in a world constantly threatened with disorder, disruption and conflict come to be the normal procedure within the range of his comprehension.

Participation in the ordered relations of its environment after a phase of disruption and conflict expresses, within Dewey's range of comprehension, the struggle of the live creature for survival.

In linking the consummation of the participation in the ordered relations of its environment after a phase of disruption and conflict with the esthetic, Dewey makes the esthetic rate as a feeling of animal satisfaction of the animal over his being an animal.

In his subsequent deliberation Dewey devotes himself to the specific task of deintellectualizing the operation of the esthetic.

"The rhythm of loss of integration with environment and recovery of union," Dewey relates, "not only persists in man but becomes conscious with him" (p. 15 op. cit.).

Relevant in the stated connection is the question to what degree does man become conscious.

On that point Dewey first asserts that "its" (i.e. the rhythm of loss of integration with environment and recovery of union) "conditions are material out of which he (man, P.C.) forms purposes" (p. 14 op. cit.).

He then declares however that, "emotion is the conscious sign of a break, actual or impending" (p. 14 op. cit.).

Dewey's rating of emotion as a conscious sign constitutes an inadvertent admission on his part that consciousness, within the range of comprehension which he is willing to permit in the stated contention, is a strictly sensuous consciousness.

Within the range of a merely sensuous consciousness, purposes cannot rate more than sensual premonitions which also can be termed as anticipated feelings.

While he states that "the discord is the occasion that induces reflection" (p. 15 op. cit.), reflection in the context of the stated deliberation cannot mean more than a sensuous reflex.

The subsequent statement which relates the "desire for restoration of the union converts mere emotion into interest in objects as conditions of realization of harmony" (p. 15 op. cit.) means what it says, in the sense that it does not refer to an interest in objects as objects, but objects as conditions of realization of harmony.

Objects do not rate as objects within Dewey's range of comprehension, it has to be recalled at this turn.

Interest in objects as conditions of realization of harmony thus signifies no more than a sensuous inclination towards an expected feeling.

The subsequent statement which relates that "with the realization," (i.e. realization of harmony, P.C.) "material of reflection is incorporated into objects as their meaning" (p. 15 op. cit.) has little, if any, meaning.

Objects are not granted a distinctive comprehension as objects within Dewey's range of comprehension.

His treatment of the subject-matter of organism and environment as well as his dealing with the factor of the art object bear ample testimony to that effect.

The expression "material of reflection" does not rate as more than an array of vague feelings within the stated range of Dewey's argumentation.

Hence there is little, if anything, available and little, if anything, present into which an incorporation can take place.

Thus Dewey's reference to the incorporation of meaning into objects becomes rather meaningless in the stated connection.

Dewey goes on to insist that "since the artist cares in a peculiar way for the phase of experience in which union is achieved, he does not shun moments of resistance and tension" (p. 15 op. cit.).

This statement, taken by itself, could be taken as an indication that the artist is in possession of some cognitive means by which he could relieve the resistance and tension.

Dewey is quick however to dampen the possibility of such an interpretation, he hastens to deny that the artist is imbued with any intellectual power.

"He" (the artist, P.C.), Dewey hastens to add, "rather cultivates them" (the resistance and tension, P.C.) "not for their own sake but because of their potentialities, bringing to living consciousness an experience that is unified and total" (p. 15 op. cit.).

The cultivation by the artist of resistance and tension thus comes to rate as a mere subconscious act, as a kind of subconscious cultivation of an anticipated consciousness.

By relegating the creative activity of the artist to the sphere of the unconscious, Dewey, it should be noted, places it on a level which fits his comprehension of roots of the esthetic in experience within which a conscious distinction between what is formless and chaotic, and what is not formless and not chaotic, is unrealizable.

As illustration of the absence of reason in the creative activity of the artist Dewey proffers a contradistinction between his conception of artistic and scientific activity.

"In contrast with the person whose purpose is esthetic," he insists, "the scientific man is interested in problems, in situations wherein tension between the matter of observation and of thought is marked" (p. 15 op. cit.).

This contrasting implies that the scientific man has cognitive means at his disposal through the use of which he can first recognize the existence of problems as problems in a reasoned manner, and then proceed to resolve those problems in a reasoned fashion, while the artist is neither imbued with a cognitive endowment to recognize the existence of problems in a reasoned way nor does he have the cognitive ability to resolve those problems by way of reasoning.

"Of course," Dewey asserts, "he (the scientist, P.C.) cares for their (the problems, P.C.) resolution" (p. 15 op. cit.).

"But," he counters, "he (the scientist, P.C.) does not rest in it; he passes on to another problem using an attained solution only as a stepping stone from which to set on foot further inquiries" (p. 15 op. cit.).

The two stated sentences are supposed to restress the factor that the scientist is concerned with bringing his intellect to bear on an unadjusted life situation in a conscious effort to resolve it, while the artist is bound to remain within the realm of the subconscious which comes to express itself in a feeling of a vague anticipation that the unadjusted life situation will somehow resolve itself.

In what follows, Dewey tries to bring his conception of artistic activity in line with the kind of conception of scientific activity to which he is committed.

"The difference between the esthetic and the intellectual," he starts backtracking, "is thus one of the place where emphasis falls in the constant rhythm that marks the interaction of the live creature with his surroundings" (p. 15 op. cit.).

"The ultimate matter of both emphases in experience is the same," he declares, "as is also their general form" (p. 15 op. cit.).

With this declaration he recommits scientific propositions to the same level of meaninglessness, as the one to which he has committed esthetic factors.

Experience, it should be note din the stated connection constitutes with Dewey a generic term, on the indefiniteness of which he makes his whole deconceptualization effort hinge.

In embedding scientific attainments in his conception of experience, he erases any distinction in the comprehension of scientific and esthetic attainments within his cognitive framework.

His subsequent remark that "the odd notion that an artist does not think and a scientific inquirer does nothing else is the result of converting a difference of tempo and emphasis into a difference in kind" (p. 15 op. cit.) means two things.

The distinction between the artist as a non-thinker and the scientific inquirer as nothing but a thinker refers to the distinction which Dewey himself maintained, when he contrasted his conception of esthetic activity as a non-intellectual pursuit with the conception of scientific activity as an intellectual pursuit.

The indistinctiveness between artistic activity and scientific inquiry, which is introduced in the stated citation under the guise of a difference in tempo, refers to the common ground on which the artistic activity as non-intellectual pursuit and the scientific activity as a deintellectualized pursuit are placed by Dewey, at this point of his deliberations.

In the latter sense, Dewey is justified to state that "the thinker has his esthetic moment when his ideas cease to be mere ideas and become the corporate meanings of objects" (p. 15, 16 op. cit.).

One has only to remind oneself of the meaninglessness to which Dewey had reduced the term meaning in the form in which he has applied it in dealing with the subject-matter of language, in order to realize that what he is actually trying to perform here, as far as the significance of the attainments of scientists is concerned, constitutes but an attempt to have scientific achievements rendered as lacking any specific significance as artistic achievements within the range of his comprehension.

In what follows, Dewey grants the artist the capacity for a kind of subdued thinking, a thinking which does not come to express itself in any definable manner.

"The artist," he asserts, "has his problems and thinks as he works" (p. 16 op. cit.).

"But," he insists, "his thought is more immediately embodied in the object" (p. 16 op. cit.).

The artist is here credited with a kind of thinking which is not traceable as such.

It is a kind of thinking to which Dewey refers in the stated connection, of which an outsider cannot be sure, whether it constitutes or does not constitute thinking.

As far as scientific activity is concerned, Dewey relates in the stated connection that "because of the comparative remoteness of his end, the scientific worker operates with symbols, words and mathematical signs" (p. 16 op. cit.).

Though the scientific worker is credited in this statement with the capacity to think openly and to be able to formulate his thoughts, the treatment which symbols, words and mathematical signs receive at the hands of Dewey, as has been demonstrated in the second chapter of this exposition, does not augur well for a use of symbols, words and mathematical signs as thought propositions.

Scientific symbols, words and mathematical signs emerge from Dewey's treatment in such a mutilated form, in the sense of their fitness to serve as meaningful propositions, that the question for what they are to be used and what the effect of that use is to be becomes rather irrelevant.

Dewey's concluding remark in the passage which is quoted here, that "the artist does his thinking in the very qualitative media he works in, and the terms lie so close to the object that he is producing that they merge directly into it" (p. 16 op. cit.), constitutes but a restressing that the artist is unable to express himself in reasoned terms.

In a subsequent passage Dewey revives his favored theme of an objectless esthetic experience.

"The live animal," he contends, "does not have to project emotion into the objects experienced" (p. 16 op. cit.).

"Nature is kind and hateful, bland and morose, irritating and comforting, long before she is mathematically qualified or even a congeries of 'secondary' qualities like colors and their shapes" (p. 16 op. cit.), he asserts.

"Even such words as long and short, solid and hollow, still carry to all, but those who are intellectually specialized, a moral and emotional connotation" (p. 14 op. cit.), he insists.

"The dictionary will inform any one who consults it that the early use of words like sweet and bitter was not to denote qualities of sense as such but to discriminate things as favorable and hostile" (p. 16 op. cit.), he wants it to be noted.

With the stated quotations Dewey wants to bring out that the attributes of things are actually not qualities of objects but mere subjective impressions.

His subsequent exclamation, "how could it be otherwise?" (p. 16 op. cit.), which is followed by the observation that "direct experience comes from nature and man *interacting* (italics mine, P.C.) with each other" (p. 16 op. cit.) constitutes but a restressing of his non-recognition of man and nature as specifiable factors.

Within the range of Dewey's conception of interaction, man is not permitted to gain a degree of consciousness which would enable him to project himself versus nature in any definite form.

Man apart from nature, man as a specimen sui generis, cannot function as such within Dewey's cognitive range of interaction.

His subsequent statement which relates that "in this *interaction* (of man and nature, italics mine, P.C.), human energy gathers, is released, dammed up, frustrated and victorious" (p. 16 op. cit.), forgets to mention that within the cognitive range of interaction, to which he, Dewey, subscribes, the factors of gathering up of human energy, its release and frustrations are indistinguishable as such.

The same is to be said in regard to the statement which follows in which he observes that "there are rhythmic beats of want and fulfillment, pulses of doing and being withheld from doing" (p. 16 op. cit.).

Want is indistinguishable from fulfillment within the cognitive range of interaction, and neither are rhythmic beats distinguishable from non-rhythmic beats within the stated cognitive range.

Within Dewey's cognitive range of interaction nothing else can become apparent than the factor that an interaction constitutes an interaction.

In a roundabout way, Dewey admits that his conception of the rhythmic is so devised, as to make it indistinguishable from a conception of the non-rhythmic.

The sequence of the argument in that connection runs as follows.

First, he asserts that "all interactions that effect stability and order in the whirling flux of change are rhythms. There is ebb and flow, systole and diastole: ordered change" (p. 16 op. cit.).

Then he goes on to state, and here follows the crux of the

argument: "The latter (ordered change, P.C.) moves within bounds. To overpass the limits that are set is destruction and death, out of which, however, new rhythms are built up" (p. 16 op. cit.).

Death, the height of disorder as far as the orderly functioning of the life process is concerned, is given the same credit as the life process in regard to the effectuation of the rhythmical.

Logically, Dewey is on sound ground here, since he has deprived the organism of cognitive means by which it can distinguish factors which favor its survival from factors which threaten its survival; Dewey is logically bound to make organic life indistinguishable from organic death.

With death and survival of organism ruled out as factors which have any distinct effect on the roots of the esthetic in experience, Dewey is free to argue that the esthetic in experience is not limited to animate nature; esthetic, he is logically free to assert, is a factor which operates in inanimate nature with the same effectiveness as in animate nature.

Dewey's subsequent assertion which states that "the proportionate interception of changes establishes an order that is spatially, not merely temporarily patterned: like the waves of the sea, the ripples of sand where waves have flowed back and forth, the fleecy and the black-bottomed cloud" (p. 16 op. cit.) is intended to establish an inferential claim that the esthetic is as much a form of expression of inanimate as of animate nature.

The just stated contention is, moreover, intended to place the factor of space as a factor which forms the basis for the evolvement of the conception of a perspective within the cognitive framework of interaction, within which form is bound to become indistinguishable from formlessness.

A subsequent statement which relates that "inner harmony is attained only when, by some means, terms are made with the environment" (p. 17 op. cit.) is but intended to further the undifferentiation of what Dewey calls the roots of the esthetic in experience.

His subsequent recitation that "when it (inner harmony, P.C.)

occurs on any other than an 'objective' basis, it is illusory—in extreme cases to the point of insanity" (p. 17 op. cit.) contains the germs of a self-contradictory statement.

In placing objective in quotation marks in the just stated quotation, he indicates that he does not intend to honor the factor of objective in any manner in which it could serve as an effective barrier against the illusory and, in extreme cases, the insane.

The very next sentence in which he states that "fortunately for variety in experience, terms are made in many ways—ways ultimately decided by selective interest" (p. 17 op. cit.) makes it quite clear that he is well on his way to having the objective basis on which inner harmony is attained dissolved.

"Pleasures," he relates, "may come about through chance contact and stimulation; such pleasures are not to be despised in a world full of pain" (p. 17 op. cit.).

Those pleasures which come through chance and stimulation, which are sensuous pleasures, are not considered, however, by Dewey as constituting a decisive factor in forming the objective means on the basis of which inner harmony is being established.

"Happiness and delight," he emphasizes, "are a different sort of thing. They come to be through a fulfillment that reaches to the depth of our being—one that is an adjustment of our whole being with the conditions of existence" (p. 17 op. cit.).

Happiness and delight, factors which are supposed to count as a decisive element in forming the objective means on the basis of which inner harmony is established, are treated here as something which cannot be specified.

An "adjustment of our whole being with the conditions of existence" is something which cannot readily be comprehended, even within a cognitive frame which is not Dewey's.

The subsequent statement which relates that "in the process of living, attainment of a period of equilibrium is at the same time the initiation of a new relation to the environment, one that brings with it potency of new adjustments to be made through struggle" (p. 17 op. cit.), does not mean much, if anything, within Dewey's range of comprehension.

Dewey's undifferentiation of organism and environment leaves him without any cognitive means to distinguish an equilibrium from a disequilibrium.

Within the cognitive range of the undifferentiation of organism and environment, the question of adjustment to what remains unanswerable.

Adjustment thus comes to rate within Dewey's cognitive range as what he terms a series which means that the answer to the question what constitutes adjustment is being sidetracked.

Adjustment comes to rate as a series of maladjustments, the resolution of which is being indefinitely delayed.

The just stated considerations have to be firmly kept in mind in reading Dewey's subsequent statements.

His assertion that "the time of consummation is also one of beginning anew" (p. 17 op. cit.) has a distinct ring of unreality, in the light of what has just been said in regard to Dewey's conception of adjustment.

His subsequent warning that "any attempt to perpetuate beyond its term the enjoyment attending the time of fulfillment and harmony constitutes withdrawal from the world. Hence it marks the lowering and loss of vitality" (p. 17 op. cit.) can carry little weight, in the face of Dewey's cognitive stricture, which intercedes with the realization of what constitutes fulfillment and harmony and interferes with the cognition and perception of fulfillment and harmony in regard to their specific bearing on enjoyment.

The concluding statement which Dewey makes in the stated connection has an undertone of resignation and, as such, has a ring of truth in it.

"But," he states, "through the phases of perturbation and conflict, there abides the deep-seated memory of an underlying harmony, the sense of which haunts life like the sense of being founded on a rock" (p. 17 op. cit.).

The reference to an *underlying* harmony, a harmony in other words which is not realizable as well as the reference to the memory of an underlying harmony in the sense which "haunts life like the sense of being founded on a rock" gives sufficient indication that Dewey had become resigned to see the factor of the esthetic in life committed to the realm of the fictitious, in which no objective basis is required for the ascertainment of the means for an attainment of an inner harmony.

In what follows, Dewey vies for no less than having all records of artistic creation and artistic perception removed from the range of experience which he tries to establish as the root of all esthetic comprehension.

He approaches his challenging task by launching an underhanded attack on the time factor as an element of cognition and perception.

"Most mortals," he declares, "are conscious that a split often occurs between their present living and their past and future" (p. 18 op. cit.).

When Dewey talks of a split in the cognition and perception of the past, the present and the future, he actually pleads for the application of his conception of "continuum" to the comprehension of time.

Dewey's complaint about the split in the cognition and perception of the past, the present and the future, is thus to be taken as an endorsement of a comprehension of time which is to make it cognitively and perceptually unfeasible for the mortal to have the past set apart from the present and to have the present set apart from the future.

In that connection a conscious realization of a contradistinction between the past, present and future, presents itself to Dewey as a disability, as his very next statement indicates.

"Then" (in consequence of the mortal's ability to tell the past from the present and the present from the future, P.C.), he laments, "the past hangs upon them (the mortals, P.C.) as a burden; it invades the present with a sense of regret, of opportunities not used, and of consequences we wish undone. It rests upon the present as an oppression, instead of being a storehouse of resources by which to move confidently forward" (p. 18 op. cit.).

Nothing is mentioned in the two just quoted statements about the conceptual and perceptual ability of the mortal to distinguish the past from the present and the future, as a preconditioning cognitive and perceptual factor of the mortal becoming conscious of his past errors.

Nothing is said in the two just quoted sentences about the necessity to grant the mortal the cognitive and perceptual ability to distinguish the past from the present and the future, as a requisite factor for the conscious realization by the mortal of his past attainment.

Dewey's subsequent statement, which he places within the framework of the cognitive and perceptual indistinguishability of the past as past, the present as present, and the future as future, does not provide any cognitive and conceptual basis for a comprehension in which errors made in the past and attainments effected in the past can come to be recorded as such in the mind of the mortal.

A mortal who is denied the capacity to set the past apart from the present and the future is unable to conceive of the past as a specifiable conceptual and perceptual frame.

A mortal who is denied the capacity to set the past apart from the present and the future, is conceptually and perceptually unable to array his experience in terms of time sequence.

In the light of what has just been stated, Dewey's subsequent statement in regard to past errors and attainment can be rated as no more than a reference to an extremely dim realization of those occurrences.

His apologetic statement in which he says, "but the live creature adopts its past; it can make friends with even its stupidities, using them as warnings that increase present wariness" (p. 18 op. cit.), can be rated as no more than a reference to a vague premonition, as far as the future is concerned, born out of a half-conscious realization of what had taken place in the past.

Dewey's subsequent assertion that "instead of trying to live upon whatever may have been achieved in the past, it uses past successes to inform the present" (p. 18 op. cit.) constitutes but a thinly veiled disclaimer of the past experience in terms of a reasoned experience as a basis for judging present and future experience, it postulates past experience as undigested information.

Dewey's subsequent observation which relates that "every living experience owes its richness to what Santayana well calls 'hushed reverberations'" but restresses Dewey's determination not to permit his kind of mortal to arrive at a conscious realization of time sequence and the bearing time sequence has on the distinguishing of a chaotic from an ordered experience.

With his follow-up remark in which he states that "art celebrates with peculiar intensity the moments in which the past reinforces the present and in which the future is a quickening of what now is" (p. 18 op. cit.) but reattaches the art factor to his disordered comprehension of experience to which he has committed himself by virtue of his determined opposition to the conscious realization of time sequence.

Dewey appears to be keenly aware that the inability to place the source of esthetic experience within the cognitive and perceptual range of time sequence is more likely to be creditable to a non-human than a human.

He shows that awareness by insisting that "to grasp the sources of esthetic experience, it is, therefore, necessary to have recourse to animal life below the human scale" (p. 18 op. cit.). "The activities of the fox, the dog, and the thrush," he continues, "may at least stand as reminders and symbols of that unity of experience which we so fractionize when work is labor, and thought withdraws us from the world" (p. 19 op. cit.).

This statement constitutes more than a disclaimer of the cognitive and perceptual capacity to comprehend time sequence as a means of locating the source of esthetic experience, it disavows all cognition and perception above the range of instinctive comprehension as a means for the identification of the source of esthetic experience.

In Dewey's subsequent statement which relates with regard to the animal that "all senses are equally on the *qui vive*" (p. 19

op. cit.), the qui vive can be well interpreted as meaning instinctive in this case.

The following statement has all the earmarks of a mockery of the human being.

"As you watch," Dewey states, "you see motion merging into sense and sense into motion—constituting that animal grace so hard for man to rival" (p. 19 op. cit.).

Dewey implicitly objects in this case, as far as the factor of the source of esthetic experience is concerned, to the human ability to use reflection as a means of controlling his senses and directing his movements.

The following statement is leading up to a stunt.

"What the live creature retains from the past and what it expects from the future operate as directions in the present" (p. 19 op. cit.), Dewey first restates what he has said before.

He then ventures to proclaim that "the dog is never pedantic nor academic; for these things arise only when the past is severed in consciousness from the present and is set up as a model to copy or a storehouse upon which to draw" (p. 19 op. cit.), in an obvious effort to create a shock which will make the reader forget the dead end into which he, Dewey, has maneuvered himself by his rooting for having the cognition and perception of time sequence eliminated from the comprehension of the sources of esthetic experience.

In a kind of follow-up statement, Dewey tries to soften the impression that he is making the human who is trying to discover the source of esthetic experience to regret that he is not a dog.

After all, Dewey is well able to contend that he was careful to remark that the comparison of the human with a dog, as far as the discovering of the source of esthetic experience is concerned, has but symbolic significance which was meant to assure the reader of *"Art as Experience"* that he, Dewey, did not intend to insist that animals, by virtue of being animals, can be expected to become concerned with discovering the sources of esthetic experience.

As a real exponent of the tracer of sources of esthetic experience to whom conceptual and perceptual ability to comprehend time sequence is denied, Dewey introduces a human monster.

"There is much in the life of the savage," he states, "that is sodden" (p. 19 op. cit.).

"But," he observes, "when the savage is most alive, he is most observant of the world about him and most taut with energy" (p. 19 op. cit.).

This statement is supposed to present the savage as the model exponent of mental power and physical prowess among humans. "As he (the savage, P.C.) watches what stirs about him," Dewey continues, "he too is stirred" (p. 19 op. cit.).

The impulsive, the instinctive is here favorably commented.

"His" (the savage's, P.C.) observation," Dewey relates, "is both action in preparation and foresight of the future" (p. 19 op. cit.).

Lack of discernment of the past in preparation for action is here selected for laudable mention.

"He" (the savage, P.C.), Dewey states, "is as active through his whole being when he looks and listens as when he stalks his quarry or stealthily retreats from a foe" (p. 19 op. cit.).

Lack of discrimination in the taking of action is here chosen for special commendation.

"His senses," Dewey concludes his extollment of the savage, "are sentinels of immediate thought and outposts of action, and not, as they so often are with us, mere pathways along which material is gathered to be stored away for a delayed and remote possibility" (p. 19 op. cit.).

He thus signs off his deliberations on the evolvement of a theoretical approach to the sources of the esthetic in experience, by holding up the case of the savage as a means of demonstration of supposedly adverse effects of all reflection.

He thus avails himself of an opportunity to complete his ambitious undertaking to devise an approach to an esthetic theory which was to rectify alleged misconceptions about artistic creation and artistic perception and cognition, by an illustration of the unavailability of any theoretical proposition for the marshalling of the sources of esthetic experience.

Chapter Six

THE DISSIPATION OF THE SENSE OF BEAUTY

The demonstration of the unavailability of any theoretical proposition to marshal the sources of esthetic experience, which was carried out by Dewey as a means of disqualifying the art object as art object and the artist as artist, is followed by a kind of rationalization which is supposed to demonstrate that a specific and specifiable esthetic factor in experience is unavailable.

Dewey starts out his deliberations which are intended to deprecate the sensing of beauty by man by insisting that "experience occurs continuously, because the interaction of live creature and environing conditions is involved in the very process of living. Under conditions of resistance and conflict, aspects and elements of the self and the world that are implicated in this interaction qualify experience with emotions and ideas so that conscious intent emerges" (*"Art as Experience"* p. 35).

The cognitive aspect of interaction looms large over this opening statement, thus Dewey's reference to conscious intent in the stated connection is placed under a cloud.

In view of the cognitive undifferentiation which embellishes Dewey's opening statement, the subsequent statement does not come off as much of a contrast, as Dewey intended it to be.

"Oftentimes, however," Dewey observes, "the experience had is inchoate. Things are experienced but not in such a way that they are composed into *an* experience. There is distraction and dispersion; what we observe and what we think, what we desire and what we get, are at odds with each other. We put our hands to the plow and turn back; we start and then we stop, not because the experience has reached the end for the sake of which it was initiated but because of *extraneous* (italics mine, P.C.) interruptions or of inner lethargy" (p. 35 op. cit.).

The mingling of subjective indecision and an objective lack of finality to which Dewey refers in this statement does not provide a marked contrast with undifferentiation of activity to which the preceding statement refers, in view of the cognitive factor of interaction.

Dewey, on his part, does not care to make much of an issue of the alleged contradistinction between the two just cited statements which follow each other, he is much more concerned with the pointing to the contrast between the factors involved in the kind of experience referred to in the just cited statements and the factor involved in another kind of experience.

"In contrast with such experience" (the experience referred to in the quotations cited above, P.C.), he states, "we have *an* experience when the material experienced runs its course to fulfillment" (p. 35 op. cit.).

"Then and then only," he solemnly declares, "is it integrated within and demarcated in the general stream of experience from other experiences" (p. 35 op. cit.).

The contrast between the just cited two statements and the two statements which preceded them does contain, it should be acknowledged, some contrasting elements.

In the preceding two statements he did not outwardly deny the presence of a causal factor, the first of the preceding statements contains a reference to "environing conditions," the second of those statements refers to "extraneous interruptions."

No matter how dubious those references are, as far as their real meaning is concerned in view of the all prevailing cognitive factor of interaction, the very fact that Dewey expressedly refers to those factors is to be taken as clear indication that he is not bent on having causation as such disqualified in the stated connection.

The second two statements, and in particular the introduction of the word "fulfillment" in the first sentence and the term "integrated" in the second sentence, can be taken as a clear sign that Dewey is determined to have no commerce with the factor of causation in the stated connection.

The demonstrations which follow make Dewey's unwillingness to have any track with causation in the just stated connection amply clear.

"A piece of work is finished," he observes, "in a way that is satisfactory; a problem receives its solution; a game is played through; a situation, whether that of eating a meal, playing a game of chess, carrying on a conversation, writing a book, or taking part in a political campaign, is so rounded out that its close is a consummation and not a cessation" (p. 35 op. cit.).

Consummation versus cessation in the just quoted statement refers to more of a contrast than meets the eye, it refers to a consummation within the range of which the factor of cessation is not acknowledged as such, since cessation refers to a cause and effect correlation.

Consummation in this instance refers to a consummation without any apparent or real cause.

The factor of causelessness is being brought into focus by Dewey when he relates that "such an experience is a whole and carries with it its own individualizing quality and self-sufficiency" (p. 35 op. cit.).

The words "a whole," "individualizing" and "self-sufficiency," all three of them, constitute but a veiled expression of causelessness.

In his subsequent reference, "it is *an* experience" (p. 35 op. cit.), the *an* can be readily interpreted as a stand-in for *a causeless*.

The deprecation of the causative continues to be the theme of Dewey's subsequent statements.

"Philosophers," Dewey observes, "even empirical philosophers, have spoken for the most part of experience at large" (p. 35 op. cit.).

In the context in which the just quoted phrase is placed, the expression "experience at large" is to be read as causative experience, as Dewey's immediately following statements reveal.

"Idiomatic speech, however," he cites as the respective contrasting proposition, "refers to experiences each of which is singular, having its own beginning and end" (p. 35 op. cit.).

Idiomatic, in the stated context, refers to a kind of speech which cannot be placed within a causative frame of reference.

Reference to its own beginning and end in the stated connection does not provide for a causal correlation of the beginning and the end, it is supposed to emphasize the singularity of the idiomatic, its irregularity, which makes the tracing of the end to the beginning an unrealizable proposition—a factor which is once more stressed in the very next sentence.

"For life," Dewey declares, "is no uniform uninterrupted march or flow" (p. 35 op. cit.), and thus places added stress on the futility of any attempt to relate one life manifestation to another in any specifiable causal form.

It should be noted in passing that Dewey's use of the word uninterrupted is misleading in the stated connection since he gives the impression that he is using the word uninterrupted with reference to ceaseless.

Dewey had just before used the word ceased as contrasted by the word consummation, in order to indicate the respective contradistinction between a non-causative and a causative experience.

In this instance, by implication, he refers to the "interrupted" and thus "ceasing" as a non-causal proposition.

"It," (life, P.C.), he continues his dilatory review, "is a thing of histories, each with its own plot, its own inception and movement toward its close, each having its own particular rhythmic movement; each with its own unrepeated quality pervading it throughout" (p. 35, 36 op. cit.).

"Unrepeated quality pervading it" means in this instance a quality which does not allow for any causal qualification, in the sense of having "its own plot, its own inception and movement towards its close" explained in causal terms.

In the stated context the factor of "its own plot, its own inception and movement towards its close" is not explainable in any other terms than by a reference that it constitutes a "particular rhythmic movement" which, in turn, refers to something inexplicable.

"Experience in this vital sense," Dewey amplifies, "is defined by those situations and episodes that we spontaneously refer to as being "real experiences" (p. 36 op. cit.).

In putting real experiences in quotation marks Dewey stresses the factor of spontaneity, in the sense that the stated kind of experience constitutes an experience which cannot be causally accounted for.

In following up the just quoted statement by amplifying it with a phrase, "those things of which we say in recalling them, "that *was* an experience" (p. 36 op. cit.), Dewey but restresses the factor that he is referring to an experience the coming and passing of which cannot be causally accounted for in any specifiable form.

The undifferentiation, as far as the causal factor is concerned, is illustrated by Dewey in his subsequent statement.

"It may have been something of tremendous importance—" he relates, "a quarrel with one who was once an intimate, a catastrophe finally averted by a hair's breadth" (p. 36 op. cit.).

"Or," Dewey continues, "it may have been something that in comparison was slight—and which perhaps because of its very slightness illustrates all the better what is to be an experience" (p. 36 op. cit.).

"There is that meal in a Paris restaurant," Dewey goes on, "of which one says 'that *was* an experience'" (p. 36 op. cit.).

"Then," he goes on and on, "there is that storm one went through in crossing the Atlantic—the storm that seemed in its fury, as it was experienced, to sum up in itself all that a storm can be, complete in itself, standing out because marked out from what went before and what came after" (p. 36 op. cit.).

The closing words of the long quotation, the reference to "marked out from what went on before and what came after," are well suited to provide a characterization of the whole series of incidents which Dewey is bringing up in this instance.

Dewey is marking here the incidental as the prevailing factor in experience.

He is marking off the incidental against the intrusion of non-incidental factors, in the stated connection.

In what follows, Dewey continues on the road of disqualification of the kind of experience he is extolling.

The qualification of what he calls *an* experience as incidental is much too specific for Dewey's taste.

The incidental, after all, can be distinguished from the non-incidental.

Were the incidental to be regarded as the qualifying factor of what he calls *an* experience, Dewey is well aware, the kind of experience he is extolling could retain an identifiable mark.

To preclude such a contingency, Dewey embarks on the task of disqualification of the rather tenuous qualification of what he calls *an* experience.

"An experience has a unity," he declares, "that gives it its name, that meal, that storm, that rupture of friendship" (p. 37 op. cit.).

He then goes on to state that "the existence of this unity is constituted by a single *quality* that pervades the entire experience in spite of the variation of its constituent parts" (p. 37 op. cit.).

Though he insists on quality in the stated connection, he has no intention to substantiate his claim, as the very next sentence indicates.

"This unity," he says, "is neither emotional, practical, nor intellectual, for these terms name distinctions that reflection can make within it" (p. 37 op. cit.).

With the just quoted sentence Dewey discounts the very conceivability of comprehending quality as quality with reference to the kind of experience he is extolling.

He amplifies his disqualification of the factor or quality in the statements which follow.

"In discourse *about* experience," he relates, "we must make use of these adjectives of interpretation" (p. 37 op. cit.).

With the stated sentence he is driving for the disqualification of the very comprehension of the kind of experience he is extolling, as a distinct and distinguishable factor.

To illustrate what the comprehension of the kind of experience he is extolling *does not* involve, he cites that "in going over an experience in mind *after* its occurrence, we may find that one property rather than another was sufficiently dominant so that it characterizes the expression as a whole" (p. 37 op. cit.).

The just cited quotation stresses with sufficient clarity that the state of consciousness or, better said, semi-consciousness which fits the experiencing of the kind of experience Dewey extolls, does not characterize a phase of comprehension in which conceptual or perceptual provisions by virtue of which a property or a quality can be distinguished as such are applicable.

Dewey's subsequent statement to the effect that "there are absorbing inquiries and speculations which a scientific man and philosopher will recall as 'experiences' in the emphatic sense" (p. 37 op. cit.) draws a distinct line between the experiences—put in quotation marks by Dewey—to which a specifiable property or quality can be attributed and the kind of experiences to which no specifiable property or quality can be attributed—which is the kind of experience to which Dewey wants to refer without quotation marks.

Those experiences, the reference to which is put by Dewey in quotation marks in order to indicate that they are not experiences in the sense in which he is treating *an* experience, are referred to by him when he concludes that "in their final import they are intellectual" (p. 37 op. cit.), and then qualifies his conclusion with a reminder that "in their actual occurrence they (the experiences which are not the kind of experiences which he extolls, P.C.) were emotional as well; they were purposive and volitional" (p. 37 op. cit.).

The just cited statements are meant to stress that the kind of experience which he, Dewey, wants to have set apart from the kind of experience he is extolling is to refer, not only to the reflection which follows the experience by virtue of which a distinctive property or quality is being ascertained, but to the comprehension of the experience in its initial phases as well.

All the factors of cognition and perception, intellectual, emotional, purposive, volitional, which can be marshalled to make the distinctiveness of the experience comprehensible, are ruled out by Dewey as factors by which his kind of experience can be assayed.

In the statement which follows, Dewey makes an attempt to subvert the kind of experience which can be comprehended in a distinctive form in all its phases to the kind of experience which cannot be comprehended in any distinctive form in any of its stages.

"Yet," he asserts, "the experience (the kind which can be comprehended in a distinctive form in any of its stages, P.C.) was not a sum of these different characters; they were lost in it," he insists, "as distinctive traits" (p. 37 op. cit.).

The just quoted statement makes it abundantly clear that it is the loss of distinctiveness in any comprehensible form which is supposed to constitute the outstanding characteristic of the kind of approach to the analysis of experience which Dewey is out to promote, in his effort to disqualify the esthetic factor in experience.

In what follows, Dewey disowns the cognitive and perceptual basis which underlies a distinctive comprehension of the kind of experience which he does not care to rate as experience proper.

"We say of an experience of thinking," he first observes, "that we reach or draw a conclusion" (p. 37 op. cit.).

Then he goes on to assert that the "theoretical formulation of the process is often made in such terms as to conceal effectually the similarity of 'conclusion' to the consummating phase of every developing integral experience" (p. 37 op. cit.).

With the just quoted statement he is trying to cast doubt on the validity of any distinctive conclusion.

He continues his underhanded attack on the distinctiveness of any conclusion, by undertaking a move to render inconclusiveness indistinguishable from conclusiveness.

"These formulations" (i.e. formulations based on conclusions, P.C.), he asserts, "apparently take their cue from the separate propositions that are premisses and the proposition that is the conclusion as they appear on the printed page" (p. 37 op. cit.).

He leaves here the impression that a specific recording of the distinguishable phases of reasoning is an undertaking which is not permissible on cognitive grounds.

His subsequent complaint that "the impression is derived that there are first two independent and ready-made entities that are then manipulated so as to give rise to a third" (p. 37, 38 op. cit.) constitutes a disclaimer of a gradual advancement of cognition.

His subsequent exclamation to the effect that "in fact, in an experience of thinking, premisses emerge only as a conclusion becomes manifest" (p. 38 op. cit.) constitutes a manifestation of cognitive undifferentiation of the premiss and the conclusion on Dewey's part.

The premiss is thus rendered as unspecifiable as the conclusion.

With elimination of premiss and conclusion as cognitive marks, reasoning as such can not take place, as Dewey well realizes.

He therefore suggests a substitute for reasoning.

"The experience, like that"—(i.e. the kind of experience which is to take the place of reasoning, P.C.)—"of watching a storm reach its height and gradually subside," he proffers an illustration, "is one of continuous movement of subject-matters" (p. 38 op. cit.).

The stated illustration demonstrates how the elimination of cognitive marks of reasoning precludes the making of any delineation, and can thus but lead to an unspecifiability of any subject-matter.

"Like the ocean in the storm," Dewey proffers a comparison, "there are a series of waves; suggestions reaching out and being broken in a clash or being carried onwards by a cooperative wave" (p. 38 op. cit.).

Suggestions which do not suggest anything which can be defined in any specifiable form are being moved here into the place which the cognitive marks of reasoning were made to vacate.

"If a conclusion is reached," Dewey follows up the introduction of non-reasoning propositions, "it is that of a movement of anticipation and cumulation, one that finally comes to completion" (p. 38 op. cit.).

The word conclusion in the stated context is not applied in the cognitive sense of reaching a conclusion by way of reasoning but in a sense in which vague anticipations come to be discounted without any accountable reason.

Dewey's subsequent declaration that "a 'conclusion' is no separate and independent thing; it is the consummation of a movement" (p. 38 op. cit.) constitutes but a reassertion of his proposition that a conclusion which is based on a specific premiss and which thus refers to something specifiable, is not a conclusion at all.

A conclusion, in the sense in which it is stated here by Dewey, in which reasoning has no distinctive role, can as such amount to no more than an unfounded guess.

At this stage of his deliberation, at which the word conclusion comes to be used as indicator of inconclusiveness and the word quality comes to be applied to indicate lack of quality, Dewey undertakes the task of confounding the esthetic and non-esthetic factors in experience.

"Hence *an* experience of thinking has its own esthetic quality" (p. 38 op. cit.), he proclaims.

Quality in the stated context refers to lack of quality.

"It differs," he then states, "from those experiences that are acknowledged to be esthetic, but only in its materials" (p. 38 op. cit.).

The stated difference refers to a difference between an esthetic experience which can be reasoned out as such and an esthetic experience which defies reasoning.

"The material of the fine arts consists of qualities" (p. 38 op. cit.), Dewey elaborates on the difference to which he had just referred.

The word qualities in the stated context refers to qualities and not to lack of qualities, it should be kept in mind.

In the amplification of what he had just stated he immediately undertakes a move, however, to have the qualities of the fine arts, which are distinguishable as such, rendered indistinguishable from the kind of qualities which are not distinguishable as such in any specifiable form.

"That of experience," he relates in his amplification of his reference to qualitatively distinguishable experience, "having intellectual conclusion are signs or symbols having no intrinsic quality of their own, but standing for things that may in another experience be qualitatively experienced" (p. 38 op. cit.).

His reference to signs and symbols in the stated connection and the qualification of those signs and symbols as intrinsic is to give the impression that the reasoned experience and the reflection based on it have no cognitive bearing, save in a way in which those symbols and signs can be made to serve as means which lead to an experience the quality of which comes to be incomprehensible in terms of quality.

"The difference is enormous" (p. 38 op. cit.), one can fully agree with Dewey at this point.

It is the difference between reasoned and non-reasoned comprehension in this case, as far as the art factor in experience is concerned.

His subsequent assertion to the effect that "it" (the difference between a reasoned and non-reasoned comprehension of the art factor in experience, P.C.) "is one reason why strictly intellectual art will never be popular as music is popular" (p. 38 op. cit.), is of a more doubtful nature.

Popular in this sense does not refer to dissemination, popular in the stated connection is based on the presupposition that the esthetic in experience is something spontaneous, something which cannot be comprehended in a reasoned form.

Music, it should be noted, is presented here as the prototype of unreasoned esthetic experience in the stated connection.

The commitment of all music experience, including the experiencing of the highly intellectualized concert music, to the fold of an experience in which the intellectual aspect is not permitted to enter in any distinctive form constitutes a highly problematical proposition, to say the least.

The aspect of the unspecifiable as far as the experiencing of the fine arts is concerned comes to be closely linked with the unspecifiable in an experience on which the arts have no bearing, in Dewey's subsequent presentation.

"The same statement," (i.e. the statement in regard to spontaneity and unspecifiability, P.C.), "holds good," Dewey protests, "of a course of action that is dominantly practical, that is, one that consists of overt doings" (p. 38 op. cit.).

"It is possible," Dewey illustrates the aspect of spontaneity, "to be efficient in action and yet not have a conscious experience" (p. 38 op. cit.).

He lays stress on the undirected, the irrelevance of the causal in action, by stating that "the activity is too automatic to permit of a sense of what it is about and where it is going" (p. 38 op. cit.).

The incomprehensibility of the action experience is brought to the fore by the statement that "it" (the activity, P.C.) "comes to an end but not to a close or consummation in consciousness" (p. 38 op. cit.).

"Obstacles are overcome by shrewd skill," he relates, "but they do not feed experience" (p. 38 op. cit.), which is to stress, once more, that the comprehension of action experience, the correlation of a preceding to a succeeding, is not to be allowed to play any specifiable role.

The subsequent statement which relates that "there are also those who are wavering in action, uncertain, and inconclusive like the shades in classic literature" (p. 38, 39 op. cit.) is, in turn, to indicate that no deliberation in regard to the question, of whether an action is to be taken or not, is to have any effect on the comprehensibility of the action experience.

"Between the poles of aimlessness and mechanical efficiency," Dewey then maintains, "there lie those courses of action in which through successive deeds there runs a sense of growing meaning conserved and accumulating toward an end that is felt as accomplishment of a process" (p. 39 op. cit.).

Though he contrasts the action experience in the comprehension of which the reason why and for what purpose is not supposed to play any role with an action experience postulated as a subjective feeling of accomplishment of a process, the stated feeling in regard to a succession of action experiences can hardly become more distinct than the comprehension of a simple action the cause of which is being withheld, as Dewey cannot be unaware.

It is with reference to the indistinctiveness of a succession of actions that Dewey makes the remark that "successful politicians and generals who turn statesmen like Caesar and Napoleon have something of the showman about them" (p. 39 op. cit.).

"This of itself," he expands his remark, "is not art, but it is, I think, a sign that interest is not exclusively, perhaps not mainly, held by the result taken by itself (as it is in the case of mere efficiency), but by it as the outcome of a process" (p. 39 op. cit.).

With this statement he clearly indicates that he is departing, as far as distinctiveness is concerned in regard to what he calls the end result of action, to which he refers as outcome of a process, as much as he had departed from specification of the factors involved in taking an action.

"There is interest," Dewey follows up, "in completing an experience" (p. 39 op. cit.).

How distinct such an interest can become is not made clear with this statement, though the very next statement disavows any specific qualification of the respective experience.

"The experience may be one that is harmful to the world and its consummation undesirable" (p. 39 op. cit.), Dewey declares, and thus disavows the distinctly qualitative.

He is not content with making the observation that "it" (the experience, P. C.) "has esthetic quality" (p. 39 op. cit.), which, in the sense in which he is applying the word quality with reference to esthetic, signifies an incomprehensible quality.

He admits that "the Greek identification of good conduct with conduct having proportion, grace, and harmony, the *kalon-agathon,* is a more obvious example of distinctive esthetic quality in moral action" (p. 39 op. cit.).

He sees in that postulation a defect, however, since, as he realizes, the Greek conception of good was as delineable as the conception of the beautiful with which the good came to be linked in Greek thought.

In defense of the indistinctiveness of his espousal of the esthetic Dewey is willing to go as far as to deny that the esthetic is strictly limited to human comprehension.

"A generalized illustration may be had," Dewey holds, "if we imagine a stone, which is rolling down hill, to have an experience" (p. 39 op. cit.).

"The activity is surely sufficiently 'practical'" (p. 39 op. cit.), he remarks.

In putting practical in quotation marks, he indicates by the stated reference that the practical does not necessarily refer to a factor in human comprehension within his frame of reference.

"The stone," he continues his exemplification, "starts from somewhere, and moves, as consistently as conditions permit, toward a place and state where it will be at rest—toward an end" (p. 39 op. cit.).

He wants to indicate by that statement, that neither the causing nor the course of the movement is of any concern in the stated connection.

He reaffirms his unconcern for a cause and effect correlation in any specific terms in the very next statement.

"Let us add, by imagination, to these external facts," he suggests, "the ideas that it looks forward with desire to the final outcome; that it is interested in the things it meets on its way, conditions that accelerate and retard its movement with respect to their bearing on the end; that it acts and feels towards them according to the hindering or helping function it attributes to them; and that the final coming to rest is related to all that went before as the culmination of a continuous movement" (p. 39 op. cit.).

The culmination of a continuous movement does not refer in this instance to either a causal or a teleological aspect, it does not even refer to a fully conscious realization of the "continuous movement" as a movement, it refers to a conception of a movement as an elemental force the generation as well as the cessation of which are rated as a force of nature the working of which is somehow predetermined.

It is to the stated kind of inexplicable predetermination to which Dewey refers when he follows up the just quoted statement with the observation that "then the stone would have an experience, and one with esthetic quality" (p. 39 op. cit.).

The aspect of an inexplicable predetermination, as far as the esthetic quality of experience is concerned, is restressed by Dewey by way of a contrasting example.

"If we turn from this imaginary case to our own experience," he states, "we shall find much of it is nearer to what happens to the actual stone than it is to anything that fulfills the conditions fancy just laid down" (p. 39, 40 op. cit.), which, in other words, means, in the stated connection, that the factor of predetermination which has been made to bear on the movement of the stone constitutes a fanciful proposition and cannot be expected to become effective in the stated case, unless it is superimposed upon the respective argumentation.

"For in much of our experience we are not concerned with the connection of one incident with what went before and what comes after" (p. 40 op. cit.), Dewey insists.

Though he outwardly refers to an absence of causal correlation, he is actually undertaking to make a contradistinction between the predetermined and the non-predetermined, as can be gathered from the very next sentence.

In his statement that "there is no interest that controls attentive rejection or selection of what shall be organized into the developing experience" (p. 40 op. cit.) the word controls refers to the controlling factor of predetermination in the stated connection.

The subsequent assertion that "things happen, but they are neither definitely included nor decisively excluded" (p. 40 op. cit.) which is accompanied by the exclamation "we drift" (p. 40 op. cit.) can well be taken as an expression which is to bring out the contrast to the definiteness, the decisiveness and the unalterability which is characteristic of the predetermined.

The subsequent reference to the effect that "there is experience, but so slack and discursive that it is not *an* experience" (p. 40 op. cit.) can definitely be taken to mean that the stated experience does not constitute an inexplicable predetermined experience.

The follow-up observation that it is "needless to say, such experiences are anesthetic" (p. 40 op. cit.) removes in unmistakable terms the esthetic in experience from the sphere of the determinable in a reasoned form to the sphere of the non-determinable in any reasoned form.

Dewey continues his quest for undifferentiation of the esthetic in experience by placing added terms within his frame of reference.

"I have emphasized the fact," he states, "that every integral experience moves toward a close, an ending, since it ceases only when the energies active in it have done their proper work" (p. 41 op. cit.).

All that the just quoted statement says in explanation of what forms an integral experience, is that it constitutes a movement which tends to spend itself.

"This closure of a circuit of energy," Dewey amplifies, "is the opposite of arrest, of *stasis*" (p. 41 op. cit.).

The just stated sentence is designed to bring out the factor of elemental force as characteristic of the movement which is involved in the integral experience.

The movement which is involved in forming of an integral experience, the just stated sentence is supposed to stress, cannot be stopped by any outside interference, it has to come to a close by itself; as such the movement which is involved in the forming of an integral experience assumes an extreme volitional character.

Dewey, on his part, is not at all anxious to have it made known that he is operating in the stated context within the cognitive range of extreme volition.

He is as anxious to draw attention away from his cognitive preconception in this case as he was in the previously referred to case of indeterminableness.

He lets the cognitive preconception of extreme volition hover in an unspecifiable manner over his subsequent elaboration of what he considers an integral experience.

His statements which immediately follow, taken by themselves, can hardly be understood, it is only in the light of the cognitive aspect of extreme volition that those statements make sense.

Take for instance the immediately following statement that "struggle and conflict may be themselves enjoyed, although they are painful when they are experienced as means of developing an experience" (p. 41 op. cit.).

The statement taken by itself is baffling.

If Dewey conducts an analysis, one is bound to ask, within a conceptual and perceptual framework in which sense reactions are accorded registration as specific factors, how could he possibly assert that painful experiences are factors of enjoyment.

Within a sensuous range of comprehension a painful experience comes to register as a painful experience, regardless of whether it ultimately contributes to another experience which is not painful; the painfulness of the painful experience cannot be disregarded as such within a sensuous range of comprehension.

It is only within an extreme volitional range of comprehension that a painful experience can be disregarded, as Dewey wants it to be.

It is only within the extreme volitional range of comprehension that a joyful experience comes to register as little as a joyful experience, as a painful experience comes to register as a painful experience, as Dewey wants it to be, since a volitional range of comprehension is essentially a range of comprehension which is predicated upon insensitiveness to either joy or pain.

Within the volitional range of comprehension obstacles do not count, nor are results of any specific significance. What counts, is movement for the sake of movement, a conception into which Dewey's postulation of integral experience can well be fitted.

The volitional range of comprehension, again without specific mention, is put to further use by Dewey.

The essential insensitiveness of the volitional range of comprehension, as far as recording of sense reactions is concerned, is being reapplied by Dewey in his effort to discount the emotional factor of what he presents as the esthetic in an experience.

"I have spoken," he states, "of the esthetic quality that rounds out an experience into completeness and unity as emotional" (p. 41 op. cit.).

"The reference," he subsequently remarks, "may cause difficulty" (p. 41 op. cit.).

He then enters a disclaimer. "Joy, sorrow, hope, fear, anger, curiosity, are treated as if each in itself were a sort of entity that enters full-made upon the scene," he declares, "an entity that may last a long time or a short time, but whose duration, whose growth and career, is irrelevant to its nature" (p. 41 op. cit.).

The just stated sentence constitutes a first move towards the disclaiming of the comprehension of emotions as emotions.

Dewey is on his way to instituting a comprehension of emotion in terms other than emotion.

"In fact," he contends, "emotions are qualities, when they are *significant*, of a complex experience that moves and changes" (p. 41 op. cit.).

The reference to emotions as qualities significant of complex experience that moves and changes is intended to have the conception of emotion as emotion submerged in a welter of factors which are not considered to be emotional.

His exclamation with which he follows up the just cited quotation, his contention that "I say, when they are *significant*, for otherwise they are but the outbreaks and eruptions of a disturbed infant" (p. 41 op. cit.) is intended to divert attention from the factor that emotions as such have ceased to play any role within the range of his, Dewey's, comprehension.

He is just not prepared, from now on, to mark off emotions as emotions, before he is trying to determine their significance.

Though he continues to use the word emotion, he does not

speak of emotions as emotions any more, but of something which might be significant or insignificant, but has no direct relation to emotions comprehended as emotions.

His reference in the just quoted exclamation to insignificant emotions as outbreaks and eruptions of a disturbed infant presents but a distorted version of his slurring over of emotions as emotions; within the range of comprehension to which he subscribes in this instance, no emotion has any place as such.

In what follows, Dewey is trying to explain away emotions.

"All emotions," he contends, "are qualifications of a drama and they change as the drama develops" (p. 41 op. cit.).

Since emotions are qualifications of something which they are not, and that something is in a constant flux, the just stated quotation makes reference to something unascertainable.

"Persons are sometimes said to fall in love at first sight" (p. 41 op. cit.), he relates.

"But," he insists, "what they fall into is not a thing of that instant" (p. 41 op. cit.).

With the but he has in mind to refer the question of what the emotion of love involves, from one instant to another, and still to another, and so on ad infinitum, as his very next sentence reveals.

"What would love be," he exclaims, "were it compressed into a moment in which there is no room for cherishing and for solicitude?" (p. 41, 42 op. cit.).

The explanation of the emotion of falling in love, the stated exclamation reveals, is to be deferred until such time as any number of instances can be cited which have but the remotest, if any connection, with either falling in love or not falling in love or, for that matter, falling out of love.

"The intimate nature of emotions"—Dewey tries another delaying action game—"is manifested in the experience of one watching a play on the stage or reading a novel" (p. 42 op. cit.).

"It attends the development of a plot," he cites, "and a plot requires a stage, a space, wherein to develop and time in which to unfold" (p. 42 op. cit.), it requires innumerable other factors which, in turn, require innumerable other factors and so forth ad infinitum, it should be added here for Dewey.

His concluding statement in the stated connection that "experience is emotional but there are no separate things called emotions in it" (p. 42 op. cit.) constitutes but an inadvertent admission on his part that within the range of the volitional comprehension to which he secretly subscribes, emotions are not specifiable as such.

In the light of what had just been stated, Dewey's subsequent references to emotion have an empty sound.

His insistence that "emotion is the moving and cementing force. It selects what is congruous and dyes what is selected with its color, thereby giving qualitative unity to materials externally disparate and dissimilar" (p. 42 op. cit.) cannot be rated as more than a declamation since he has removed emotion as emotion from his cognitive range.

His subsequent assertion that "it (emotion, P.C.) thus provides unity in and through the varied parts of an experience" (p. 42 op. cit.) can well be parried by a retort that, if such is the case, Dewey has made it impossible to ascertain it, since there is no place for an emotion as emotion within the range of his comprehension.

With emotion unascertainable as such there is, in turn, no way of ascertaining what constitutes unity in the stated connection.

Unity becomes, of logical necessity, as ephemeral a factor as the ephemeral emotion which is supposed to bring it about.

Dewey's concluding statement to the effect that "when the unity is of the sort already described, the experience has esthetic character even though it is not, dominantly, an esthetic experience" (p. 42 op. cit.) lacks any meaning since the conditioning factor of "unity of the sort already described" constitutes something which is indeterminable within Dewey's frame of reference.

Dewey has arrived here at a point at which he has made it impossible for himself to determine what is esthetic in experience by the use of any of the terms which he himself had introduced for the ostensible purpose of a discerning of the sense of beauty.

He has succeeded with his terminological fence-riding to

erect a formidable cognitive stumbling block to the answering of the question, what is, and what is not beautiful in human experience.

In place of the conception and perception of the sense of beauty, Dewey's presentation of the subject-matter of *art as experience* leaves a vacuum.

C — INSTEAD OF EDUCATION

Chapter Seven

THE SUSPENSION OF LEARNING AND TEACHING.

The feat of deconceptualization which Dewey performed in an effort to make the place which art occupies in human life indeterminable, is fully matched by him in his attempt to render the role of education in human living undetectable.

As far as his procedure is concerned, he is wholly consistent, he is applying one principal disqualification device.

He is having the conception of qualified experience submerge in the conception of unqualified experience. Just as he has made the qualified conception of an esthetic experience lose itself in the conception of an esthetically unqualified experience, he is undertaking to have the qualified conception of an educational experience lose itself in an educationally unqualified experience.

Dewey's cognitive disqualification move as applied to education constitutes a crowning of his entire disqualification drive.

Dewey's cognitive disqualification of the factor of education in experience presents a rounding out of his philosophical profession, it presents a placing of a sphere of his writing which had attracted the most attention into the general cognitive stream of undifferentiation which took him a lifetime to perfect and present in his *"Logic, the Theory of Inquiry."*

Dewey's innumerable writings on education, it should be noticed, had not been placed in a definitive cognitive frame until he had come out at the close of his literary career with the exposition of *"Experience and Education."*

He starts out his cognitive disqualification drive as far as education is concerned, by declaring that "the belief that all genuine education comes about through experience does not mean that all experiences are genuinely or equally educative," (*"Experience and Education,"* page 13).

"For some experiences," he proclaims, "are miseducative" (p. 13 op. cit.).

"Any experience is miseducative," he amplifies, "that has the effect of arresting or distorting the growth of further experience" (p. 13 op. cit.).

Within the cognitive frame of extreme relativism to which Dewey subscribes in his *"Logic, the Theory of Inquiry,"* the just stated reference is to be interpreted as meaning that any qualification of one kind of experience which marks it off as a conception of growth, is to be interpreted as a reference to a conception of experience which does not recognize a conceptual distinction between a qualified and an unqualified experience.

Within the cognitive framework of extreme relativism, the conception of growth, to which Dewey refers as a criterion for the distinguishing between the educative and miseducative experience, is cognitively prevented from performing the role of such a criterion.

Within the cognitive framework of extreme relativism, the reference to growth in regard to the conception of experience can only indicate a growth in the sense of an indistinct relation of any number of indistinct experiences to each other.

In the statement which follows Dewey, without directly mentioning it, attempts to demonstrate that a qualitative specification of an experience is incompatible with his cognitive position of extreme relativism.

"A given experience," he observes, "may increase a person's automatic skill in a particular direction and yet tend to land him in a groove or rut; the effect . . . is to narrow the field of further experience" (p. 13 op. cit.).

The objection raised in the just quoted sentence constitutes an objection to having a given experience specified as such as far as its character—such as a person's automatic skill—or its bearing—such as a particular direction—is concerned, since such specification is not compatible with a range of unqualified experience.

That is the sense in which Dewey uses here the word narrow; "to narrow the field of further experience" means to qualify the field of further experience in Dewey's cognitive context.

Without again mentioning it, Dewey demands a strict application of cognitive relativism when he observes that "experiences may be so disconnected from one another that, while each is agreeable or even exciting in itself, they are not linked cumulatively to one another" (p. 14 op. cit.).

He brings into bold relief with the stated quotation the cognitive incongruity of the aspect "in itself," meaning the distinctiveness of an experience and the factor of the "disconnected," the "not linked," in an effort to demonstrate that the cognition of an experience in any specifiable form violates the cognitive proposition according to which an experience is to be conceived as a running device for which no mark offs are permitted.

Dewey's subsequent observation to the effect that "it is a great mistake to suppose, even tacitly, that the traditional schoolroom was not a place in which pupils had experiences" (p. 14 op. cit.), is intended to underscore the difference between a distinctive and an indistinctive experience as his followup assertion clearly indicates.

In stating that "this" (the admissibility that an experience can be gained in a traditional schoolroom, P.C.) "is tacitly assumed when progressive education as a plan of learning by experience is placed in sharp opposition to the old" (p. 14 op. cit.) Dewey tries to make a case for a recognition of two kinds of experience which can be gained in a classroom.

He moves to have one kind of experience to be gained in a classroom disqualified as improper when he subsequently relates that "the proper line of attack is that the experiences which were had, by pupils and teachers alike, were largely of a wrong kind" (p. 15 op. cit.).

Dewey moves here for having the kind of experience which

is being gained in traditional schools indicted as a wrong kind of experience, since, aside from its effects, it has to be recognized as a distinct experience.

Dewey, though, is shy in placing the emphasis in this instance on the real grounds for his objection to the kind of experience which is being gained in the traditional schools, he prefers to have the cognitive basis for his opposition to the kind of experience which is being gained in traditional schools implied in this case; he chooses not to stress in regard to the stated case that he is not willing to admit any experience as being proper, unless such experience is regarded as cognitively undifferentiated from any experience which is being gained outside the schools.

Instead of clearly admitting that his cognitive pre-supposition of undifferentiation rules out the cognitive distinctiveness of any experience, including the kind of experience which is being gained in the traditional schools, Dewey chooses to go on record as decrying effects of the kind of experience which is being gained in traditional schools.

His subsequent outcries against some ill effects of the kind of experience which is being gained in traditional schools, are not, however, outcries against the maladministration of the kind of experience which is being gained in the traditional schools,— as they are made to appear by Dewey—they are, in effect, but outcries against the registering of a school experience as a specific and specifiable kind of experience, as Dewey himself subsequently admits.

His outcry "how many students, for example, were rendered callous to ideas, and how many lost the impetus to learn because of the way in which learning was experienced by them?" (p. 15 op. cit.) is really meant to have ideas banned from the school room since he considers it inconceivable to deny that the teaching and learning of ideas constitutes a specific and specifiable experience, a kind of experience in education which he, Dewey, wants to be regarded as improper.

His outburst in which he cries out "how many acquired special skills by means of automatic drill so that their power of judgment and capacity to act intelligently in new situations was limited?" (p. 15 op. cit.) is really meant to have skills eliminated from the classroom schedule, since he, Dewey, considers it inconceivable to refute that the teaching and learning of skills constitutes a specific and specifiable experience, the kind of experience in education which he, Dewey, wants to be viewed as improper.

His indignant expression, "how many came to associate books with dull drudgery, so that they were 'conditioned' to all but flashy reading matter?" (p. 15 op. cit.) is really meant to have books removed from the classroom, since he, Dewey, considers it inconceivable to dispute that the teaching and learning from books constitutes a specific and specifiable experience, the kind of experience in education which he, Dewey, is not willing to recognize as proper.

His subsequent admission that "the trouble is not the absence of experiences" (in the traditional schools, P.C.) "but their defective and wrong character—*wrong and defective from the standpoint of connection with further experience*" (p. 15, 16 op. cit.) (italics mine, P.C.) constitutes a reaffirmation of the kind of interpretation which had just been offered here by this writer in regard to the maleffects of education in traditional schools which Dewey had chosen to castigate in the preceding pointed questions.

In the just quoted citation Dewey testifies to the irreconcilability of his cognitive proposition which conceives of experience as an undifferentiable chain reaction without any specifiable cause and specifiable effect and the cognitive proposition which does permit a differentiation of experience and a specifiable identification of cause and effect relation in regard to experience.

Dewey himself is helpful in this instance in assisting to remove any doubts that he is opposed to having the cause and effect relation in regard to experience conceived in any specific form.

"Everything," he declares, "depends upon the *quality* of the experience which is had" (p. 16 op. cit.).

The word quality, as the readers of previous chapters of this volume are surely aware of by now, has an ominous ring, when Dewey pronounces it.

In Dewey's vocabulary, as can be gathered from passages in Part A and Part B of this exposition, the word quality stands for lack of quality.

Yet, Dewey does not care to depend on cross references in this instance, he is quite willing to offer another variant of disqualification of the factor of quality in his promotion of the conception of an unqualified experience in regard to the experience in education.

"The quality of an experience," he proclaims, "has two aspects. There is an immediate aspect of agreeableness or disagreeableness, and there is its influence upon later experiences" (p. 16 op. cit.).

It is characteristic in this instance that Dewey does not allow for more than a fleeting effect, as far as the immediate influence of the experience is concerned.

Agreeableness or disagreeableness refer but to surface impressions, to spontaneous sense reaction; agreeableness or disagreeableness relate but a manifestation in which neither the cause nor the effect is granted any reasoned form.

When Dewey subsequently states that "the first" (the immediate aspect of agreeableness and disagreeableness, P.C.) "is obvious and easy to judge" (p. 16 op. cit.) he indicates his intention to rest the case of the specifiability of the immediacy of cause and effect relation in regard to experience in general and experience in education in particular with the intimation of agreeableness and disagreeableness.

The just stated statement is meant to disavow any intention on Dewey's part to probe below the surface manifestation of immediate sense reactions as far as the immediate aspect of experience in general, and experience in education in particular, is concerned.

With the just quoted citation Dewey leaves the factor of cause and effect relation, as far as the actual experience in education is concerned, hanging, so to speak, in the air.

As far as the actual experience in education is concerned, Dewey refuses with the said quotation to assess either its cause or effect in any reasoned terms.

Dewey's refusal to conceive of any cause and effect relation, as far as the actual experience in education is concerned, in any reasoned manner, does not, of course, present an oversight on his part, it constitutes part and parcel of a well planned move, as his subsequent utterances disclose.

"The *effect* of an experience is not borne on its face" (p. 16 op. cit.), he proclaims, and he means by that proclamation that the effect of actual experience in education, the effect which he has refused to specify in any reasoned manner, is an irrelevant factor as far as what he wants to be regarded as the total effect of that kind of experience.

In having the effect of the actual experience in education submerge in what he calls the total effect of the actual experience in education, Dewey is sure he can have the answering of the question of what specifically constitutes the effect of the actual experience in education delayed at *Kalendas Graecas*, as his subsequent deliberation clearly shows.

"It" (the effect of the actual experience in education which is not supposed to be appraised in any reasoned manner, P.C.), Dewey relates, "sets a problem to the educator. It is his business to arrange for the kind of experiences which, while they do not repel the student, but rather engage his activities are, nevertheless, more than immediately enjoyable since they promote having desirable future experiences" (p. 16 op. cit.).

The just quoted statement provides no indication for the specifiability of the "desirable future experience," and intentionally so, it can be safely assumed, since the just quoted statement is meant to realign the unspecifiability of the immediate effect of the actual experience in education with the unspecifiability of its more remote effects.

While one could be inclined to agree with Dewey's subsequent statement in which he relates that "the central problem of an education based upon experience is to select the kind of present experiences that live fruitfully and creatively in subsequent experiences" (p. 16, 17 op. cit.), one cannot help reminding him, that his refusal of having the more immediate as well as the more remote effects of the actual experience in

181

education conceived in any reasoned form leaves him without any cognitive basis for providing a criterion by which "to select the kind of present experiences that live fruitfully and creatively in subsequent experiences."

In what follows, Dewey introduces a number of cognitive propositions which are to make sure that the kind of experience in education which he is out to promote can ever be specified as such.

Dewey wants cognitive propositions which are to insure the cognitive undifferentiation of the kind of experience in education which he considers proper to be known by the name "criteria of experience."

Criteria of experience those cognitive propositions can be regarded only in the sense that they furnish criteria for setting a distinct educational experience, the kind of experience in education which has been had in the traditional schools apart from the indistinct experience which the non-traditional schools of the variety favored by Dewey were supposed to effect, as Dewey himself admits it.

Dewey confirms the just offered interpretation in reintroducing his paramount principle of undifferentiation.

In making reference to the "category of continuity, or the experiential continuum" he states that "this principle is involved . . . in every attempt to discriminate between experiences that are worthwhile educationally and those which are not" (p. 24 op. cit.), which, put into more precise language, means that he is bent on having his principle of continuum reapplied in the sphere of education as means of placing the specifiable experience which is being gained in traditional schools beyond the cognitive range which he devises for the comprehension of experience in the kind of non-traditional schools which he has set out to defend in his little volume on *"Experience and Education."*

It is the just stated sense in which Dewey refers back to the principle of experience "as a criterion of discrimination" (p. 26 op. cit.).

Subsequently Dewey proceeds to reapply the chain of his cognitive undifferentiation principles.

He is in particular concerned in the stated connection with having the principle of continuum, which forms his major cognitive undifferentiation device, confirmed as the factor of cognitive undifferentiation with which all his other cognitive undifferentiation devices are linked.

"At bottom," he states, "this principle" (the principle of continuum, P.C.) "rests upon the fact of habit, when *habit* is interpreted biologically" (p. 26 op. cit.).

He thus reintroduces the evasive organismic comprehension of habit to which he had given expression in his *"Logic, the Theory of Inquiry,"* reference to which is to be found in the second chapter of this volume.

"The basic characteristic of habit," Dewey reintroduces a refrain which should have become familiar by now to the readers of the present critical exposition, "is that every experience enacted and undergone modifies the one who acts and undergoes, while this modification affects, whether we wish it or not, the quality of subsequent experiences" (p. 26 op. cit.).

For the benefit of those who might still be at a loss to understand what is involved in the just quoted statement, it should be considered proper to point out that Dewey is trying, all over again, to play up the aspect of undifferentiation of object and subject in the stated connection.

The undifferentiation of object and subject, via the route of his odd conception of habit, constitutes for Dewey a path which makes it feasible for him to advance a conception of compounded undifferentiation, as the very next statement indicates.

"From this point of view," he confidently relates, "the principle of continuity of experience means that every experience both takes up something from those which have gone before and modifies in some way the quality of those which come after" (p. 27 op. cit.).

Spelled out, the just quoted statement refers to the principle of continuity as a cognitive means of correlating any

183

number of experiences which are rendered indistinguishable as far as the subject and the object of experience is concerned.

Dewey's principle of continuum, taken by itself, can be regarded as an espousal of extreme formalistic relativism; it can be viewed as a cognitive means by which a something is to be related to another something and still to another something and so on and so forth, ad infinitum, in an effort to disqualify the somethings as specific entities.

Applied in conjunction with Dewey's conception of habit, the stated disqualification procedure is enhanced, since the principle of continuum can be put to use in this case by having any number of instances related to one another which do not stand for either a something in the sense of an object, or for a something in the sense of a subject.

The reduction of an entity to a nonentity which a ceaseless application of the principle of continuity without assistance of the principle of "habit" can be made to effect, can *with* the assistance of the principle of "habit" be attained ahead of the very first correlation in the stated series.

The application of the principle of continuity when it bases ittself on the principle of "habit" starts out with a nonentity.

The compounding of cognitive undifferentiation which Dewey attains by combining the application of the principle of "continuum" with the principle of "habit" amounts to an attempt to relate one nonentity to another, and still another, and so ad infinitum, in an effort to demonstrate the irrelevance of the question of the identifiability of the subject and the object of correlation, or, to state it more directly, to demonstrate the irrelevance of the question of who correlates what in a race towards cognitive undifferentiation.

By obstructing the identification of the subject and object of correlation and thus rendering the question of who correlates what unanswerable, Dewey makes it cognitively possible for himself to narrow his comprehension of continuity to a range in which it refers to *nothing else* but a relation of a relation of a relation and so on and so forth ad infinitum.

Relativism in extremis comes into full bloom again with the stated comprehension of continuity which, at this turn, is applied as a means to obstruct a reasoned analysis of the educational experience whch is to be had in non-traditional schools.

Dewey's insistence that "the principle of habit so understood obviously goes deeper than the ordinary conception of *a* habit as a more or less fixed way of doing things, although it includes the latter as one of its special cases" (p. 27 op. cit.) can be well taken as meaning that his conception of habit takes in everything and nothing.

His subsequent assertion that his conception of habit "covers the formation of attitudes, attitudes that are emotional and intellectual; it covers our basic sensitivities and ways of meeting and responding to all the conditions which we meet in living" (p. 27 op. cit.) can only be explained as a reaffirmation of his determination not to have habit cover anything particular.

Habit, as the just quoted citation candidly states, is supposed to cover "our basic sensitivities and ways of meeting and responding to conditions which we meet in living" which within the cognitive range of the undifferentiated into which Dewey places the relation of the organism to environment means that habit is supposed to cover nothing which can conceivably be specified.

Dewey, it should be recalled at this instance, does not allow for a cognition of the organism as such and the environment as such, to him, as has been demonstrated in chapter one of this critical exposition, organism does not present a factor which can be distinguished from environment and vice versa.

Organism *is* environment and environment *is*, by the same token, organism in Dewey's conception of the two factors.

The undifferentiation of organism and environment precludes in turn the conception of a sense reaction in any distinct form on the part of Dewey, as has also been demonstrated in the first chapter of this critical exposition.

Dewey himself, as the relevant passages of his *"Logic, the Theory of Inquiry"* cited in the first chapter of this critical exposition clearly indicate, does not legitimize any comprehension of a sense reaction which lies beyond the cognitive range of animal reflexes.

In the just stated context his reference to "the formation of attitudes, attitudes that are emotional and intellecual," which he cites in connection with his formulation of habit, as has been just quoted here, comes to be utterly meaningless for the very reason that the conception of attitudes lies beyond the cognitive range which he himself has drawn for the comprehension of sense reaction.

The conception of attitudes, Dewey could hardly deny, cannot be properly placed within a cognitive range which has been deliberately narrowed to an extent which does not permit any manifestation of sense reaction to be registered, which does not constitute a mere animal reflex.

In referring to "the formation of attitudes, attitudes that are emotional and intellectual" in the cited quotation he is in fact doing nothing else but bringing the conception of attitudes in line with the cognitive undifferentiation of habit.

Neither the formation of attitudes which constitutes a preliminary stage of habit formation as far as the general use of the two terms is concerned, nor the formation of habit which constitutes the succeeding stage with regard to formation of attitudes, are granted any specifiability within Dewey's cognitive range.

In making an all out effort to bring the cognitive factor of undifferentiation to bear on the experience in education, Dewey does not let the opportunity pass at this turn to deny the specifiability of the conception of growth which, more than any other conception, was intended to characterize the experience in education to be gained in the non-traditional schools which he, Dewey, favors.

As in the instance of the conception of habit, he does not care to rely on cross-references at this turn, in dealing with the conception of growth.

"Growth, or growing as developing, not only physically, but

intellectually and morally," he proudly declares, "is one exemplification of the principle of continuity" (p. 28 op. cit.).

The stated quotation places the conception of growth squarely within the cognitive range of extreme relativism, and thus confirms the implication to which attention has been called by this writer at the beginning of the present chapter.

In relating the criticism which has been voiced against his conception of growth, Dewey observes that "the objection made is that growth might take many different directions: a man for example who starts out on a career of burglary may grow in that direction, and by practice may grow into a highly expert burglar" (p. 28 op. cit.).

"Hence it is argued,"—he continues in his relation of the criticism voiced against the comprehension of growth—"that 'growth' is not enough: we must also specify the direction in which growth takes place, the end towards which it tends" (p. 28 op. cit.).

He then cautions his critics by declaring that "before . . . we decide that the objection is conclusive, we must analyze the case a little further" (p. 28 op. cit.).

He then engages in what is supposed to be a rebuttal of the criticism of his comprehension of growth of which he had taken cognizance in the cited quotation.

He starts out his rebuttal with admitting "that a man may grow in efficiency as a burglar, as a gangster or as a corrupt politician cannot be doubted" (p. 28 op. cit.).

"But" he insists, "from the standpoint of growth as education and education as growth the question is whether growth in this direction promotes or retards growth in general" (p. 29 op. cit.), and thus confounds the issues of growth which is relatable to experience in education and growth which is not directly relatable to experience in education.

By referring, as indistinguishable factors, to growth as education, which is obviously to mean a growth which is *not* a growth which can be directly ascribed to an experience gained in schools, and to education as growth, which is apparently to mean growth which *can* be directly ascribed to an experience gained in schools, he is attempting to evade the question of what accounts for growth in either the schools or outside the schools.

Dewey's evasiveness is being heightened, in the stated instance, by the proposal to have the "direction" of the indistinguishable factors of "growth as education" and "education as growth" detemrined by way of ascertaining whether the direction "promotes or retards growth in general" (p. 29 op. cit.).

The stated proposal amounts to a suggestion to relate the direction of one indeterminable factor to another.

Direction, in the stated context, constitutes but another word for relation, and direction of something indistinguishable means nothing else in the stated connection than a relation of something indistinguishable.

Thus Dewey has safely landed his conception of growth within the relativistic cognitive framework within which he had placed his conception of habit, thus achieving a goal which he, Dewey, has obviously set for himself to attain.

When he subsequently poses the question, "does this form of growth create conditions for further growth, or does it set up conditions that shut off the person who has grown in this particular direction from the occasions, stimuli, and opportunities for continuing growth in new directions?" (p. 29 op. cit.) he can hardly fail to realize that, within his range of comprehension of growth, he is unable to provide any relevant answer. Since he has deprived himself of the cognitive means to determine fhat accounts for a direction, he is obviously unable to determine what accounts for a change in the direction without a change in his cognitive position, which he apparently has no intention to make.

The subsequent question which relates "what is the effect of growth in a special direction upon the attitudes and habits which alone open up avenues for development in other lines?" (p. 29 op. cit.) is revealing in regard to another aspect.

Since attitude and habit refer to no more than animal reflexes, as has been previously pointed out in this chapter, the question which pertains to the effect of growth upon attitudes and habits can well be interpreted as an indirect admission, on Dewey's part, that he is determined to keep the comprehension of the entire problem-complex of growth on the cognitive level of an animal reflex.

Such admission can, in turn, not be divorced from a realization on the part of Dewey that a conception of growth which is strictly limited to the range of comprehension of animal reflexes creates insurmountable conceptual difficulties in the path of any conceivable attempt to tell what is a direction.

Within a comprehension of growth which is reduced to the cognitive level of the comprehension of animal reflexes, a conception of a direction cannot be had, since a conception of direction is predicated upon the cognitive ability to conceive something which is being sustained, a cognitive ability which is not provided by a comprehension which is strictly limited to the cognition of animal reflexes.

An animal reflex comes and goes without leaving any lasting impression and is thus not linkable as such to any sustained move which can be conceived as direction.

Dewey's self-administered cognitive inability to comprehend a direction, it should be noticed, leaves him in turn without any cognitive means to distinguish between a direction and a misdirection; a cognitive framework which has no provisions for a comprehension of a direction has, by the same token, no provisions for a comprehension of a misdirection.

In what follows, Dewey proceeds with his quest for undifferentiation by making a determined attempt to commit the subjective as well as the objective factors which have a bearing on the conception of experience in education, to the relativistic frame.

"It is possible," Dewey declares, "to frame schemes of education that pretty systematically subordinate objective conditions to those which reside in the individuals being educated" (p. 36 op. cit.).

"This happens," he observes, "whenever the place and function of the teacher, of books, of apparatus and equipment, of everything which represents the products of the more mature experience of elders, is systematically subordinated to the immediate inclinations and feelings of the young" (p. 36, 37 op. cit.).

In contradistinction he relates that "every theory which assumes that importance can be attached to these objective factors only at the expense of imposing external control and of limiting the freedom of individuals rests finally upon the notion that experience is truly experience only when objective conditions are subordinated to what goes on within the individuals having the experience" (p. 37 op. cit.).

He then goes on to state that in citing of the two contrasting positions in regard to the subjective and objective factors with regard to the conception of experience in education with disapproval, he did "not mean that it is supposed that objective conditions can be shut out" (p. 37 op. cit.).

He then proceeds to play up the objectivists against the subjectivists and, in turn, the subjectivists against the objectivists, in regard to experience in education.

"It is recognized," he observes, "that they (the objective conditions, P.C.) must enter in: so much concession is made to the inescapable fact that we live in a world of things and persons" (p. 37 op. cit.).

"But I think," he qualifies the just cited statement, "that observation of what goes on in some families and some schools would disclose that some parents and some teachers are acting upon the idea of *subordinating* objective conditions to internal ones" (p. 37 op. cit.).

"In that case," he amplifies, "it is assumed not only that the latter (the internal, subjective factors, P.C.) are primary, which in one sense they are, but that just as they temporarily exist they fix the whole educational process" (p. 37 op. cit.).

In the just cited quotation Dewey takes a stand against the extreme objectivists as well as the extreme subjectivists in the formulation of a conception of experience in education.

He proceeds to illustrate his stand against the extremes of subjectivism and objectivism in regard to a conception of experience in education by citing "the case of an infant" (p. 37 op. cit.).

"The needs of a baby for food, rest and activity," he observes, "are certainly primary and decisive in one respect" (p. 37, 38 op. cit.).

"Nourishment must be provided," he amplifies, "provision must be made for comfortable sleep" (p. 38 op. cit.).

"But these facts," he qualifies, "do not mean that a parent shall feed the baby at any time when the baby is cross or irritable, that there shall not be a program of regular hours of feeding and sleeping, etc." (p. 38 op. cit.).

"The wise mother," he qualifies the qualification, "takes account of the needs of the infant but not in a way which dispenses with her own responsibility for regulating the objective conditions under which the needs are satisfied" (p. 38 op. cit.).

"And if she is a wise mother in this respect," he further qualifies the qualification, "she draws upon past experiences of experts as well as her own for the light that these shed upon what experiences are in general most conducive to the normal development of infants" (p. 38 op. cit.).

"Instead of these conditions being subordinated to the immediate internal conditions of the baby"—and then follows the disqualification—"they are definitely ordered so that in a particular kind of *interaction* with these immediate internal states may be brought about" (p. 38 op. cit.).

For the benefit of those who are not versed in all the intricacies of his undifferentiation technique Dewey explains that "the word 'interaction,' which has just been used, expresses the second chief principle (read undifferentiation principle, P.C.) for interpreting an experience in its educational function and force" (p. 38 op. cit.)

"It"—the interaction in the sense of an undifferentiation principle—he amplifies, "assigns equal rights to both factors in experience—objective and internal conditions" (p. 38 op. cit.).

"Any normal experience"—he states in the way of further amplification—"is an interplay of these two sets of conditions" (p. 39 op. cit.).

The word interplay is but another word for interaction in the stated conditions, both interplay and interaction, though ostensibly used as indicators of conditioning factors of experience in education, are, in the general cognitive framework of undifferentiation into which Dewey places all his reasoning, merely applicable as means by which an identification of either the subjective or objective factors of conditions of experience in education is made cognitively unfeasible.

Within Dewey's all pervasive cognitive stricture of indeterminableness, the conceptions of interplay and interaction cannot be made to refer to anything specific.

His cognitive stricture of indeterminableness logically requires of Dewey—and he does not voice any objection to this requirement in the stated connection—to restrict his comprehension of interplay and interaction to a range in which neither subjective nor objective factors can be identified as such.

His all pervasive cognitive stricture of indeterminableness makes it incumbent upon Dewey—and he does not state anything to the contrary in the stated connection—to limit his comprehension of interplay and interaction to a range in which it indicates merely an indeterminable chain reaction.

Within the cognitive stricture of indeterminableness, as has been demonstrated in this exposition by references to Dewey's "Logic, the Theory of Inquiry," interplay and interaction can be made to mean no more than a reference to innumerable interplays or innumerable interactions.

Dewey's cognitive range of indeterminableness is predicated upon a range of comprehension from which the cognition of the factors which account for interplay and interaction is excluded.

The cognitive range of indeterminableness, within which Dewey operates, forces him to reduce any conditioning factors to such indistinctiveness that interplay and interaction in regard to experience in education can be interpreted in no other way than a correlation of unknowable factors.

In the just stated sense—in the sense of the conditioning factors in regard to education as experience as an unknowable proposition—interplay and interaction revert to the general relativistic interpretation according to which interplay and interaction are explainable in no other terms than in the terms of interplay and interaction.

An interplay and interaction to which Dewey denies any qualification which is specifiable in any other terms than in the terms of interplay and interaction—as his treatment of the subjective and the objective factors in regard to experience in education clearly indicates—cannot be interpreted as referring to something which is not mere interplay and interaction.

The question of what is interplay or interaction can only be answered within Dewey's just stated cognitive frame by stating that it is an interplay, or that it is an interaction, and has as such no recognizable connection with anything which cannot be comprehended as interplay and interaction.

Dewey's subsequent reference to the effect that "taken together,"—i.e., objective and internal conditions, P.C.—"or in their interaction, they form what we call a *situation*" (p. 39 op. cit.) does not in any way change the situation as far as the extreme relativism of his conception of interaction is concerned.

Just the opposite, it but reinforces the aspect of indeterminableness in regard to the factors of either objective or internal conditions.

Situation, as Dewey had made it abundantly clear in his *"Logic, the Theory of Inquiry,"* refers in his comprehension to a situation which is not qualified by anything which is not a situation.

As such, a situation comes to rate no more than a relation, or, for that matter, an interaction which is not qualified by anything which is not a relation or an interaction.

One situation can be as little distinguished from another situation as one relation or, for that matter, one interaction from another relation or another interaction, within Dewey's range of comprehension.

Situation comes to count but as another reference to the unspecifiable in Dewey's vocabulary.

Dewey is not askance in elaborating on the aspect of indeterminableness of his comprehension of situation in his dealing with what he terms experience in education.

"The statement that individuals live in a world means, in the concrete," he proclaims, "that they live in a *series* (italics mine, P.C.) of situations" (p. 41 op. cit.).

Series, Dewey should not mind being reminded in the stated connection, constitutes but another terminological vehicle by which he pursues his cognitive undifferentiation, as can be seen in the first chapter of this volume.

Series, in Dewey's comprehension, means a numberless series, it refers to a series in which one series cannot be distinguished from another, it points to a series of series for which neither a beginning nor an end can be determined.

One series is as indistinguishable from another as one situation from another, one series flows into another series as one situation into another, in Dewey's comprehension.

Taken within the range of Dewey's comprehension, a reference to "series" adds little as far as concreteness is concerned, as compared with his reference to "situation," despite Dewey's indication to the contrary in the just quoted citation; a break and a subsequent marking off of one series from another is as impermissible as a break and a subsequent marking off of one situation from another, within Dewey's cognitive range.

In what follows, Dewey is giving renewed prominence to the aspect of indeterminableness, as far as his reference to situation is concerned.

"And," he elaborates, "when it is said that they live *in* these situations, the meaning of the word 'in' is different from its meaning when it is said that pennies are 'in' a pocket or paint is 'in' a can" (p. 41 op. cit.).

"It means, once more," he continues his elaboration, "that *interaction* (italics mine, P.C.) is going on between an individual and objects and other persons" (p. 41 op. cit.).

With the latter statement Dewey but restresses that his conception of situation is firmly rooted within the cognitive range of undifferentiation within the range of which neither an individual, nor objects, nor other persons are distinguishable as such.

His subsequent contention to the effect that "the conceptions of *situation* and of *interaction* are inseparable from each other"

(p. 41 op. cit.) can mean only within Dewey's cognitive frame of reference that the conceptions of situation and interaction are inseparably linked with one another, in the sense that they are slated to serve as cognitive undifferentiation devices.

Dewey's paramount concern with cognitive undifferentiation is highlighted by his comparative evaluation in the stated connection of the respective assessment of objective and subjective factors in the educational experience of traditional and non-traditional schools.

"The trouble with traditional education," he states, "was not that it emphasized the external conditions that enter into the control of the experiences but that it paid so little attention to the internal factors which also decide what kind of experience is had" (p. 39 op. cit.).

"It violated the principle of interaction from one side" (p. 39 op. cit.), Dewey resolves *which, within the cognitive range of undifferentiation in which he applies the device of interaction, constitutes a rebuke of the traditional school not for non-recognition of the subjective factors in the conditioning of an educational experience but for a specific recognition of objective factors in the conditioning of an educational experience.*

When he then turns to the non-traditional school and declares that "this violation (i.e., the violation of the recognition of the objective factors in the educational experience, P.C.) is no reason why the new education should violate the principle from the other side—except upon the basis of the extreme *Either-Or* educational philosophy which has been mentioned" (p. 38 op. cit.), *he voices an objection to the non-traditional school within his cognitive range of undifferentiation, not for a non-recognition of objective factors in the conditioning of an educational experience but for the specific recognition of the subjective factors in the conditioning of an educational experience.*

Within the range of cognitive undifferentiation, to which Dewey is wholly committed, neither objective nor subjective factors can be permitted to retain any specifiable role in the conditioning of an educational experience.

Dewey, on his part, sees in the confounding of objective and subjective factors in the conditioning of an experience in education the crucial test for the kind of experience in education which he advocates.

"Continuity and interaction" (i.e., compounded cognitive undifferentiation, P.C.) "in their active union with each other," he insists, "provide the measure of the educative significance and value of an experience" (p. 43 op. cit.).

"The immediate and direct concern of an educator is then," he asserts, "with the situations (situations which cannot be distinguished from one another, P.C.) in which interaction takes place." (p. 43 op. cit.).

"The individual," he then states, "who enters as a factor into it" (i.e., into a situation which is indistinguishable from any other situation, P.C.) "is what he is at a given time" (p. 43 op. cit.), implying with that statement, that the individualistic characteristics of a person who enters an unspecifiable situation cannot be made to count much as such.

With the stated implication Dewey is trying to discount some subjective factors which condition experience in education by having them cognitively submerged in an undifferentiated situation.

He then proceeds to claim that "it is the other factor, that of objective conditions, which lies to some extent within the possibility of regulation by the educator" (p. 43 op. cit.).

Though he refers to objective conditions in the just cited quotation, his subsequent remark makes it clear that he is bent on having his reference to objective conditions in the stated context cover objective as well as non-objective conditions.

"The phrase 'objective conditions,'" he subsequently remarks, "covers a wide range." (p. 43 op. cit.).

The very placing of the words objective conditions in quotation marks provides a sufficient indication that Dewey is bent on having those words refer to non-objective conditions as well.

His determination to have non-objective conditions included in his reference to objective conditions in the stated instance is fully revealed in what he considers as ranging under the topic of objective conditions.

"It (i.e., his, Dewey's, range of objective conditions, P.C.) includes what is done by the educator and the way in which it is done, not only words spoken, but the tone of voice in which they are spoken" (p. 43, 44 op. cit.).

The inclusion of the tone of voice in his listing of objective conditions provides a clear-cut demonstration that he is bent on overextending the range of objective conditions to an extent at which a cognitive distinction between objective and subjective conditions becomes unfeasible.

Dewey's bid for an overextension of the range of objective conditions becomes even more apparent in his further listing of what he wants to be included under the topic of objective conditions.

"It (i.e., his range of objective conditions, P.C.) includes," Dewey asserts, "equipment, books, apparatus, toys, games played. It includes the materials with which an individual interacts, and most important of all, the total *social* set-up of the situations in which a person is engaged" (p. 44 op. cit.).

His insistence on the inclusion of the total social set-up within the range of objective conditions constitutes nothing less than a plea for the inclusion of everything and anything in the range of objective conditions.

Social, it should be remembered in the stated connection, is indistinguishable from the non-social in Dewey's comprehension, as the second chapter of the present critical exposition has brought out.

Dewey's underlining of the word social in the just cited quotation can be well taken as having the same meaning as the putting of the word social in quotation marks by him, and can serve as an added indication that he is using the word social in a sense which does not provide for a distinction between the social and the non-social.

The reference to "interacts" in the just cited quotation is in turn meant to have the effect of undifferentiating the everything and anything to which the words total social-setup are made to refer.

That a device for a cognitive undifferentiation of everything and anything constitutes by the same token a device for a cognitive undifferentiation of anything and nothing, Dewey could not have been unaware.

Though, as far as the keeping of his superabstraction of total social setup from assuming any degree of concreteness is concerned, it should make little difference whether Dewey's range of objective conditions refers to an undifferentiated anything and everything or an undifferentiated anything and nothing.

The overextension and subsequent undifferentiation of the range of objective factors in the conditioning of experience in education is not an end in itself for Dewey, as can be surmised, it constitutes merely a preliminary device to him for the obstructing of the conception of directed teaching and learning.

In what follows, Dewey uses his superabstract comprehension of objective conditions as a device by applying of which he can indulge in the propagation of the overconcrete.

His superabstraction of objective conditions has been so far removed from any conceivable range of concreteness, Dewey can feel reasonably sure, that no concrete objective factor could ever come to be cognitively linked with his superabstract comprehension of objective factors.

By virtue of the overextension of the range of the generalization of the factor of objective conditions, Dewey is justified to contend his general conception of objective factors is cognitively prevented from playing the role of a criterion by which any concrete evidence of objective conditions can be judged.

By having overextended the range of his general comprehension of objective conditions, Dewey can well pride himself, he has erected cognitive obstacles to the very comprehension of concreteness, as far as objective factors are concerned.

A concrete has to be linkable to an abstract in order to rate as a meaningful concrete.

A concrete which is linkable only to a concrete in the cognitive sense can signify only a reference to an array of meaningless incidents, and that is exactly what Dewey's expounding of the overconcrete presents, as the following should make it clear.

In starting out on the road of overconcretization, Dewey proffers a declaration to the effect that "responsibility for selecting objective conditions carries with it, then, the responsibility for understanding the needs and capacities of the individuals who are learning at a given time" (p. 45 op. cit.).

The emphasis in the stated declaration is to be placed on the words "at a given time," in the sense that anything that refers to "a given time" presents a factor of supreme uniqueness, a factor which is so peculiar as to defy any attempts to connect it with anything reoccurring, with anything which could conceivably be generalized.

The just stated consideration is being restressed by Dewey when he in the very next sentence proclaims that "it is not enough that certain materials and methods have proved effective with other individuals at other times" (p. 45 op. cit.), which carries the factor of individualization to the extreme.

Dewey's followup statement, in the stated connection, his insistence that "there must be a reason for thinking that they will function in generating an experience that has educative quality with particular individuals at a particular time" (p. 45 op. cit.) makes it clear that Dewey is prepared to dismiss all past experience in education and the generalizations which have been drawn upon that experience, as means of validation of his conception of educational experience, on the ground that none of the past experience and none of the generalizations which have been based upon that experience can be squared with some odd peculiarities of the educational experience of "particular individuals at a particular time."

His subsequent declaration that "there is no such thing as educational value in the abstract" (p. 46 op. cit.) constitutes but a reaffirmation of his refusal to link odd peculiarities of the educational experience of an individual at a given time with any educational experience other individuals had at some other time and the generalizations or abstractions which were warranted by the educational experience that such other individuals had at some other time.

His subsequent remark to the effect that "the notion that some subjects and methods and that acquaintance with certain facts and truths possess educational value in and of themselves is the reason why traditional education reduced the material of education so largely to a diet of pre-digested materials" (p. 46 op. cit.) is to be taken as a rebuke to traditional education for having made use of past experience in education in a generalized form.

The words "diet of pre-digested experience," there can be little doubt, constitute but substitute words for the words past experience in education in a generalized form, in the just cited quotation.

When he subsequently states that "according to this notion, it was enough to regulate the quantity and difficulty of the material provided, in a scheme of quantitative grading from month to month and from year to year" (p. 46 op. cit.), he but expresses his contempt for any delineation of the subject-matter as such, as well as his disrespect of any ordered sequential presentation of subject-matter.

Though he gives the impression in the last cited quotation and the quotation which was listed before the just cited quotation, that he objects to what he calls a diet of pre-digested material of education on the ground that it neglects to pay attention to the reaction of the individual learner to the administration of what he, Dewey, calls, the diet of pre-digested material of education, he has no intention of providing a lead as to how the pre-digested material is to be so administered as to make allowances for the peculiarities of the individual learner.

He has introduced the aspect of odd peculiarities of the educational experience of the individual, his subsequent references make it clear, as but a diversionary device; he uses that device in order to disqualify the aspect of the generalized or as he calls it "the diet of pre-digested material" in the effectuation of an educational experience of the individual.

After having attained the desired disqualification of the role of generalizations which have been drawn from past experience in education in the course of his deliberation Dewey considers himself at liberty to proceed with the disqualification of the non-generalized, the concrete factor as far as an educational experience of the learner is concerned.

Though Dewey complains that "a pupil was expected to take it" (subject-matter based on generalized experience, P.C.) "in the doses that were prescribed from without" (p. 46 op. cit.), he, Dewey, does not show any sign that he is willing to offer any clue which could possibly lead to a specific understanding of the internal or subjective conditions on the strength of which the pupil reacts.

Though he cites with disapproval that "if the pupil left it" (the subject-matter based on generalized experience, P.C.), "instead of taking it, if he engaged in physical truancy, or in the mental truancy of mind-wandering and finally built up an emotional revulsion against the subject, he was held at fault" (p. 46 op. cit.), he, Dewey, does not make any move which could posesibly relieve the stated condition.

His subsequent insistence to the effect that "no question was raised as to whether the trouble might not lie in the subject-matter or in the way in which it was offered" (p. 46 op. cit.) presages, on the contrary, his, Dewey's, determination to render the concrete, the individual experience in education in a given time, as incomprehensible as he had made the generalized in the experience in the education of any time.

When he bluntly asserts that "the principle of interaction makes it clear that failure of adaptation of material to needs and capacities of individuals may cause an experience to be non-educative quite as much as failure of an individual to adapt himself to the material" (p. 45, 46 op. cit.), he but clearly states that he is determined not to advance beyond the range of un-differentiation which is predicated upon the proper application of his, Dewey's, cognitive strictures.

By moving of the terms "interaction" and "adaptation" into position in the stated connection Dewey but once more demonstrates that he is not concerned with providing any clues for a grounded understanding of specifiable conditions as they affect an educational experience, regardless of whether those conditions are objective or subjective, regardless, moreover, whether those conditions are expressed in an abstract or in a concrete form. His sole concern is to have any of the conditioning factors relegated to a level of comprehension within the range of which nothing else can be determined than the realization that all the stated conditioning—the material as well as the needs and capacities of individuals as stated in the just cited quotation— constitutes nothing more than a compounding of an interaction, of an interaction, of an interaction, and so on, and so forth ad infinitum with an adaptation of an adaptation, of an adaptation, and so forth, and so on, ad infinitum.

(Those who might be inclined to question whether Dewey's conception of adaptation can be properly classed as one of his ultra-relativistic devices are invited to consult chapter two of this critical exposition)

Non-educative comes to mean in Dewey's characterization of educational experience neither an educational experience in which objective conditions and generalized factors based on past educational experience are given recognition, nor an educational experience in which subjective conditions or concrete factors of a singular educational experience are recognized as such.

Educative, by the same token, signifies in Dewey's characterization an educational experience in which objective conditions are indistinguishable from subjective conditions and abstractions derived from reoccurring past experience are, in turn, indistinguishable from concrete manifestations of a single experience.

In suggesting a reliance on interaction and adaptation in the last cited quotation as guide for a proper appraisal of an educational experience, Dewey clearly indicates that it is his deliberate aim to offer nothing which could clarify the issues involved in the gaining and providing of an educational experience.

The application of the stated relativistic device of interaction and adaptation with regard to material, as well as with regard to the needs and capacities of individuals, can have but a cognitive effect of making it unfeasible for an educator to differentiate the material and the needs and capacities of the individual, since effectuation of the stated relativistic cognitive strictures is bound to render both the conception of material as well as the conception of need and capacity of an individual equally indistinct.

In what follows, Dewey proceeds to claim that "the principle of continuity in its educational application means, nevertheless, that the future has to be taken into account at every stage of the educational process" (p. 47 op. cit.).

"This idea," he then states, "is easily misunderstood and is badly distorted in traditional education" (p. 47 op. cit.).

"Its" (the traditional education's, P.C.) "assumption is, that by acquiring certain skills and by learning certain subjects which would be needed later (perhaps in college or perhaps in adult life) pupils are as a matter of course made ready for the needs and circumstances of the future" (p. 47 op. cit.).

After having made these general observations as regard to the pertinence of the future with reference to the gaining and providing of an educational experience, Dewey moves to have the future disqualified as a specific and specifiable factor in relation to the gaining and providing of an educational experience.

He starts his disqualification move in the stated connection, by insisting that "' preparation' is a treacherous idea" (p. 47 op. cit.).

The very placing of the word preparation in quotation marks clearly indicates that from now on he is determined to use the word preparation in the context of his deliberation in a sense in which that word is not being commonly used.

"In a certain sense," he subsequently declares, "every experience should do something to prepare a person for later experiences of a deeper and more expansive quality" (p. 47 op. cit.). He sees that kind of preparation as constituting "the very meaning of growth, continuity, reconstruction of experience" (p. 47 op. cit.).

In citing growth and continuity as signifying factors of preparation, Dewey moves in the just quoted citations for a discounting of any comprehension of preparation in any specifiable form.

He then claims that "it is a mistake to suppose that the mere acquisition of a certain amount of arithmetic, geography, history, etc., which is taught and studied because it may be useful at some time in the future, has this effect, and it is a mistake to suppose that acquisition of skills in reading and figuring will automatically constitute preparation for their right and effective use under conditions very unlike those in which they were acquired" (p. 47, 48 op. cit.).

Though in his objection in this case he is on record in attacking what he considers the maleffects of teaching and learning of arithmetic, geography, history and other subject-matter with regard to the applicability of the taught and learned in these subject-matters in the future experience of the learner, Dewey's subsequent remarks make it quite clear that he regards it not only as useless but even as harmful to have arithmetic, geography, history and other subject-matter taught and learned as subject-matter.

It is but logical for Dewey to be opposed to any teaching and learning in terms of subject-matter which constitutes a way of teaching and learning which is predicated upon a principle of distinctive differentiation of areas of instruction, a principle which constitutes the very opposite of his, Dewey's, overriding cognitive principle of undifferentiation.

With his subsequent relation that "almost everyone has had occasion to look back upon his school days and wonder what has become of the knowledge he was supposed to have amassed during his years of schooling, and why it is that the technical skills he acquired have to be learned over again in changed form in order to stand him in good stead" (p. 48 op. cit.) Dewey provides but another angle for his attack on the teaching and learning in terms of subject-matter.

"Oone trouble," he observes in commenting on the just quoted citation, "is that the subject-matter in question was learned in isolation; it was put, as it were, in a water-tight compartment" (p. 48 op. cit.).

In uttering the word isolation in the stated connection, Dewey but reaffirms his position of cognitive undifferentiation.

In the either/or proposition of Dewey, any phenomenon falls either within the cognitive range of unqualified discontinuity or unqualified continuity, either the phenomenon is unrelated to anything else, or it is related to anything else.

Dewey does not concede a cognitive position which makes it feasible to relate a phenomenon to a restricted number of other phenomena, such procedure, on which the establishment of specifiable areas of inquiry is predicated, is alien to Dewey's bid for undifferentiation.

In charging the teaching and learning of traditional subject-matter with isolation and using the word isolation in the sense of undifferentiation, he charges the teaching and learning of traditional subject-matter with a cognitive either/or position to which he, but not the defenders of traditional subject-matter adhere.

The defenders of traditional subject-matter might be accused of drawing too narrow a range within which they deal with the problems of subject-matter, but to charge the defenders of traditional subject-matter, as Dewey does, with expounding the principle of undifferentiation, or i.e. "complete isolation" of the subject-matter from any factors related with it, constitutes a gross overstatement of the case which Dewey is trying to make.

The overstatement which is contained in the charge of "complete isolation" which Dewey hurls at the defenders of the teaching and learning in terms of subject-matter constitutes but a means of rationalization by Dewey of his cognitive either/or position of unqualified discontinuity as against unqualified continuity; as such the charging of the defenders of teaching and learning in terms of traditional subject-matter with subscribing to the principle of extreme unqualified discontinuity provides Dewey with an excuse to suggest the referring of the problem of teaching and learning of subject-matter to the opposite cognitive extreme—the principle of unqualified continuity.

That the factors which are directly related to teaching and learning of traditional subject-matter cannot become apparent and thus are unspecifiable as such within either the range of unqualified continuity or the range of unqualified discontinuity, goes without saying.

The either/or of Dewey's cognitive position, as applied to the stated case, constitutes a device for sidetracking the discussion of what is and what is not involved in the teaching and learning in terms of traditional subject-matter.

After having rendered the debate on the subject of subject-matter meaningless in his discourse, Dewey proceeds to ask the question "what, then, is the true meaning of preparation in the educational scheme?" (p. 50 op. cit.).

"In the first place," he answers, "it means that a person, young or old, gets out of his present experience all that there is in it for him at the time in which he has it" (p. 50 op. cit.).

He makes a move in the just related answer to his question to have the aspect of the present overemphasized.

His subsequent statement in which he makes the observation that "when preparation is made the controlling end, then the potentialities of the present are sacrificed to a supposititious future" (p. 51 op. cit.) is, in turn, meant to have the aspect of the future unduly deemphasized.

His subsequent assertion to the effect that "we always live at the time we live and not at some other time, and only by extracting at each present time the full meaning of each present experience are we prepared for doing the same thing in the future" (p. 51 op. cit.) is predicated upon the cognitive proposition of continuity within the range of which any specific and specifiable connection between distinctive factors of time sequence is inconceivable.

In ruling out a specifiable connection between the present and the future, Dewey renders the word preparation meaningless, and thus makes himself bear the logical consequences of having rendered the subject of subject-matter meaningless.

Dewey has arrived at this turn at a stage in which he has disallowed any specifiable connection between either the present and the future, or the past and the future in regard to the respective relation of these time factors to the providing and gaining of an educational experience.

He has thus reached a point at which he has deprived himself of cognitive means by which he can relate past, present and future, as fas as an educational experience is concerned.

His overemphasis on the present constitutes within his cognitive range but an overemphasis of an unspecifiable present; an unspecifiable present does, in turn, not differ, as far as the aspect of distinctiveness is concerned, from an unspecifiable past or future, in which Dewey's deemphasis of the past and the future in the stated connection was supposed to result.

With subject-matter rendered meaningless and the time factor reduced to the range of the incomprehensible, Dewey is groping in the dark as far as the signification of an educational experience is concerned.

Chapter Eight

THE EXCLUSION OF SCHOOLS

The previous chapter should have made sufficiently clear that Dewey succeeded in no less a feat than the removal of an educational content from the educational experience he has undertaken to espouse.

He is left at this turn with but a fragmentary shell as far as an educational experience is concerned.

He has nothing left but the cognitive framework of undifferentiation within which an educational experience constitutes but a relation of a relation, of a relation, and so on, and so forth ad infinitum.

The question of what is being related to what, just is not answerable within the cognitive range of continuity and interaction.

The ultra-formalistic stand on educational experience at which Dewey has arrived in his *"Experience and Education,"* is of course, not accidental.

It constitutes part and parcel of his plan to discount the value of systematic education, the kind of education for which schools have been provided.

With regard to the dissolute cognitive frame of continuity and interaction, within which he has placed the factor of educational experience, Dewey well realizes, it makes hardly any cognitive difference, whether he refers to an educational experience gained in schools or outside of schools.

In taking advantage of the cognitive indistinctiveness of his position, in making use of the ultra-formalism of his stand as regard to the factor of educational experience, Dewey unobtrusively switches from the range of experience which is had in schools to the range of experience which is not had in schools.

Dewey has, it should be understood, no intention whatsoever to renounce or even relax his extreme relativistic position in relating what he wants to be rated as educational experience which is to be gained and provided at the exclusion of systematic schooling.

Just the opposite is the case, he is as determined as ever to make the undifferentiation principles of continuity and interaction bear as heavily on the kind of educational experience which is to be had at the exclusion of the school as a specific and specifiable social institution.

"It is often well,"—Dewey declares in the stated connection—"in considering educational problems to get a start by temporarily ignoring the school and thinking of other human institutions" (*"Experience and Education"* p. 54).

Though he suggests but a temporary ignoring of the school, he has no intention to revert the range of argumentation to the school as such, to the school as a specific and specifiable social institution, as his subsequent deliberation discloses.

"I take it," he amplifies the just quoted declaration, "that no one would deny that the ordinary good citizen is as a matter of fact subject to a great deal of social control and that a considerable part of this control is not felt to involve restriction of personal freedom" (p. 54, 55 op. cit.).

The meaning of the last cited quotation is predicated upon the emphasis on the words not felt, such emphasis provides in turn a clear indication that Dewey is setting out on the road of equating social control and freedom via a subjectivistic route—an indication which the very next sentence tends to confirm.

"Even the theoretical anarchist, whose philosophy commits him to the idea that state or government control is an unmitigated evil," Dewey contends, "believes that with abolition of the political state other forms of social control would operate: indeed, his opposition to governmental regulation springs from his belief that other and to him more normal modes of control would operate with abolition of the state" (p. 55 op. cit.).

This contention is aimed at subverting the objective conceptions on which the philosophy of anarchism is based by making that philosophy appear as an array of personal feelings.

The subjectivistic angle is further emphasized by Dewey when he proposes to "note some examples of social control that operate in everyday life, and then look for the principle underlying them" (p. 55 op. cit.).

"Let us begin," he amplifies the just stated proposal, "with the young people themselves" (p. 55 op. cit.).

"Children at recess or after school" (note the factor of recess and after school, P.C.) "play games, from tag and one-old-cat to baseball and football" (p. 55 op. cit.), Dewey relates.

"The games," he argues, "involve rules, and these rules order their conduct" (p. 55 op. cit.).

"The games," he further amplifies, "do not go on haphazardly or by a succession of improvisations" (p. 55 op. cit.).

"Without rules," he is willing to concede, "there is no game" (p. 55 op. cit.).

"If disputes arise," he adds an observation, "there is an umpire to appeal to, or discussion and a kind of arbitration are means to a decision; otherwise the game is broken up and comes to an end" (p. 55 op. cit.).

Then he offers his interpretation.

"There are certain fairly obvious controlling features of such situations to which I want to call attention" (p. 56 op. cit.), he alerts his readers.

"The first," he argues, "is that the rules are a part of the game" (p. 56 op. cit.).

"They are not outside of it" (the game, P.C.) (p. 56 op. cit.), he insists.

The stated insistence is supposed to draw attention away from the factor that the playing group is not usually engaged in the setting of the rules of the game and that the playing group is therefore confronted with the proposition of adhering to rules which have been set outside of that group.

In equating the factor of adherence to rules of the game with the factor of setting of rules of the game, Dewey is enabling himself to ignore the objective existence of rules, as such, and have the adherence to the rules pictured as a merely subjective proposition.

"As long as the game goes on with reasonable smoothness," he argues to the just stated effect, "the players *do not feel* (italics mine, P.C.) that they are submitting to external imposition but that they are playing the game" (p. 56 op. cit.).

What counts is the *do not feel* in the stated quotation.

The stated quotation provides for a dismissal of the conception of the existence of rules, as such, as an effective factor in playing the game.

The game within the stated conception is being played *as if* there were no rules, as such, which are governing the game.

"An individual may at times *feel*" (italics mine, P.C.), Dewey continues to harp on the subjectivistic angle, "that a decision isn't fair and he may even *get angry*" (italics mine, P.C.) (p. 56 op. cit.).

Dewey, it should be noted, with reference to the stated quotation, does not insist here that the subjective reaction of the individual is actually based on the acknowledgement on the part of the individual of the existence of set rules.

To the contrary, Dewey asserts, "he" (the individual, P.C.) "is not objecting to a rule but to what *he claims* (italics mine, P.C.) is a violation of it, to some one-sided and unfair action" (p. 56 op. cit.), which, to complete Dewey's sentence for Dewey, does not have to have any reference to any really existing rule.

When he subsequently declares in the stated context that "the rules, and hence the conduct of the game, are fairly standardized" (p. 56 op. cit.), he can mean nothing else by standardized than the standardization of a subjectivistic discounting of the entering of the rules of the game as an objective factor in the playing of the game.

Dewey's subjectivistic conception of a playing of a game is being fully squared by him with his ultra-relativistic conception of educational experience.

"Control of individual actions," he candidly admits, "is effected by the whole situation in which individuals are involved, in which they share and of which they are co-operative or interacting parts" (p. 57 op. cit.).

His reference to the "whole situation" and "interacting parts" in the just cited quotation is meant to demonstrate that his, Dewey's, subjectivistic notion of control in regard to the playing of a game, or, i.e., a subjectivistic notion of control as it affects a specific area of activity, is predicated upon his ultra-relativistic cognitive position.

In his subsequent assertion in which he declares that "for even in a competitive game there is a certain kind of participation, of sharing in a common experience" (p. 57 op. cit.), the words "common experience" mean an indeterminable common experience within his cognitive framework, and, taken in that sense, his reference to common experience in the just quoted citation constitutes but a reaffirmation on the part of Dewey of his admission that his cognitive indeterminableness constitutes an overriding factor in his subjectivistic conception of control as he applies it to the comprehension of the game.

Though he finds it necessary to make a follow-up statement to the effect that "it may seem to be putting too heavy a load upon a single case to argue that this instance" (the instance of a subjectivistic notion of a conception of a game, P.C.) "illustrates the general principle of social control of individuals without the violation of freedom" (p. 57, 58 op. cit.), he nonetheless argues, "if the matter were followed out through a number of cases, I think the conclusion that this particular instance does illustrate a general principle would be justified" (p. 58 op. cit.).

"Games are generally competitive" (p. 58 op. cit.), he observes.

"If we took instances of co-operative activities in which all members of a group take part, as for example in well ordered family life in which there is mutual confidence," he suggests, "the point would be even clearer" (p. 58 op. cit.).

"In all such cases," he contends, "it is not the will or desire of any one person which establishes order but the moving spirit of the whole group" (p. 58 op. cit.), and thus imputes the subjectivistic conception of group activity not solely to the subjective notions of individuals which constitute the group but to the subjectivistic notion of the group itself.

The reference to "will" or "desire" of any one person in the just cited quotation constitutes as subjectivistic a conception as the "moving spirit" of the whole group.

Dewey but adds another and wider range of subjectivistic conception by referring to the "moving spirit" of the whole group in addition to his reference to the "will or desire" of any person.

Since however each of the two ranges of subjectivistic conceptions, the individualistic range stated in terms of will or desire of any person and the collectivistic range stated in terms of moving spirit of the whole group, are to have no other meaning than to serve as two correlatives of undifferentiation, the cognitive result, in the sense of an ultimate indeterminableness, comes to be the same as the one in which the subjectivistic notion has been made to express itself but in the single range of individual desires and wishes.

Whether a subjectivistic notion of a single range is presented in a form of a relation, of a relation, of a relation and so forth, and so on ad infinitum, or whether subjective notions of two ranges are presented in the form of a correlation of a correlation, of a correlation and so on, and so forth ad infinitum, of the two ranges, the net effect, as far as indeterminableness is concerned, will not differ in any way.

Dewey's assertion that "the control is social, but individuals are part of a community, not outside of it" (p. 58 op. cit.), which proffers the correlation of individualistic and collectivistic ranges of his, Dewey's, subjectivistic conception of activity as the ultimate explanation of social control, does not explain anything which pertains either to external or internal factors involved in societal control.

With the just cited quotation Dewey perfects a shuttle device which is supposed to render the unexplained objective factor of social control inexplicable by having it refer for signification to a correlation of subjectivistic factors the very incomprehensibility of which precludes any reasoned explanation.

There can be little doubt that Dewey has attained a cognitive undifferentiation of the factor of social control at this turn, in that sense it can be said he has accomplished half of a task to which he has committed himself by setting out on the road to equate social control and freedom.

When he subsequently proclaims that "I want to say something about the other side of the problem of social control, namely, the nature of freedom" (p. 69 op. cit.), he but announces his determination to have the factor of freedom rendered as indeterminable as the factor of social control.

His very next sentence in which he states that "the only freedom that is of enduring importance is freedom of intelligence, that is to say, freedom of observation and of judgment exercised in behalf of purposes that are intrinsically worthwhile" (p. 69 op. cit.) provides a clear indication that he intends to duplicate the cognitive undifferentiation procedure which he had applied to the factor of social control by resorting to subjectivistic devices.

The words "purposes that are intrinsically worth while" in the just quoted citation place Dewey clearly on record in favor of having the factor of freedom submerged in a welter of meaningless subjectivistic notions.

In proceeding to execute his predetermined task of subjectivization of the conception of freedom, Dewey first declares that "the commonest mistake made about freedom is, I think, to identify it with freedom of movement, or with the external or physical side of activity" (p. 69 op. cit.).

He then claims that "this external and physical side of activity cannot be separated from the internal side of activity; from freedom of thought, desire, and purpose" (p. 69 op. cit.), thus reasserting his determination to give outstanding prominence to the subjectivistic angle in the evolvement of his conception of freedom.

His subsequent assertion that "an increased measure of freedom of outer movement is a *means,* not an end" (p. 70 op. cit.) constitutes, in the cognitive framework in which Dewey operates, but a plea for a subordination of the objective aspect of freedom to its subjective aspect.

The companion statement which proclaims that "there can

be no greater mistake . . . than to treat such freedom" (external freedom, in the objective sense, P.C.) "as an end in itself. It then tends to be destructive of the shared co-operative activities which are the normal source of order" (p. 73, 4 op. cit.) constitutes, in turn, but an indirect reaffirmation on the part of Dewey that, no matter what allowance he is willing to make in the cognitive sense as far as the recognition of the objective aspect of freedom is concerned, his ultimate conception of freedom, the just cited quotation makes it clear, will not be allowed to escape the ultra-relativistic cognitive range of indeterminable interaction.

In undertaking to subject the conception of freedom to cognitive undifferentiation, via the route of subjective submergence of the factor of freedom, Dewey proffers an elaboration of his previously stated contention on the aspects of means and ends in regard to freedom, to the effect that "freedom from restriction . . . is to be prized only as a means to a freedom which is power: power to frame purposes, to judge wisely, to evaluate desires by the consequences which will result from acting upon them; power to select and order means to carry chosen ends into operation" (p. 74 op. cit.).

The stated elaboration constitutes an advance on the road of subjectivization of the conception of freedom; the objective side of freedom, the side which in the just cited quotation is referred to as "freedom from restriction" is being enveloped in a mesh of subjective factors framed in terms of individualistic evaluation.

The subjectivization of the objective factor of outer freedom from restriction has the effect of making the objective side of freedom imperceptible and thus renders any cognitive distinction between objective and subjective factors of freedom unfeasible in the stated context.

While in his initial statement on means and ends of freedom, as had been demonstrated here at that turn, he used the word means with reference to the identification of the objective aspect of freedom and referred only to the end of freedom in the subjective sense, in the just cited elaboration means as well as ends of freedom are made to fall into the subjectivistic fold.

In his subsequent elaboration Dewey undertakes to demonstrate the applicability of his subjectified conception of means of freedom.

"Natural impulses and desires," he relates, "constitute in any case the starting point" (p. 74 op. cit.).

"But," he remarks, "there is no intellectual growth without some reconstruction, some remaking, of impulses and desires in the form in which they first show themselves" (p. 74 op. cit.).

The reappearance of the word "growth" in the just cited quotation can be taken as a clear sign that Dewey is determined to have the "reconstruction and remaking of impulses and desires," to which he, Dewey, refers in the stated connection, rendered as indeterminable as the impulses and desires in the form in which they first show themselves, and reference to which is made in the preceding quotation which has been cited here.

His subsequent contention that it is "a sound instinct which identifies freedom with power to frame purposes and to execute or carry into effect purposes so framed" (p. 77 op. cit.) constitutes a candid admission on the part of Dewey that the range to which he confines the comprehension of his relation of subjectified means to subjectified ends of freedom does not extend beyond the scope of the instinctive, in the sense of the unreasoned.

Placed alongside the just cited quotation, his subsequent declaration to the effect that "such freedom is in turn identical with self-control" (p. 77 op. cit.), can only mean instinctive self-control or-to use the more common wording for instinctive self-control—instinctive reflex.

In this connection it is well to remember that Dewey's comprehension of the thinking process, which he has advanced in his "Logic, the Theory of Inquiry" in connection with his treatment of the factors of organism and environment, does not provide for a comprehension which extends beyond the range of a mere animal reflex and that his dealing with reflection in that connection is mainly designed to have reflection subordinated to animal reflexes.

(Readers are invited to consult chapter one of this critical exposition for confirmation of the just stated.)

In the just mentioned sense, Dewey is consistent, as far as his placing of the comprehension which "identifies freedom with power to frame purposes and to execute or carry into effect purposes so framed" (p. 77 op. cit.) within the range of the instinctive is concerned.

Though he subsequently insists that "the formation of purposes and the organization of means to execute them are the work of intelligence" (p. 77 op. cit.), he does not follow up that assertion by having the work of intelligence in the formation of purposes and the organization of means to execute them explained in any specifiable form.

He continues to apply the device of subjectivization when he insists that "a genuine purpose always starts with an impulse" (p. 78 op. cit.).

He continues in the subjectivistic vein when he subsequently asserts that "obstruction of the immediate execution of an impulse converts it into a desire" (p. 78 op. cit.).

He is about to turn to cognitive ultra-relativism when he follows up the two just cited subjectivistic statements with a contention that "nevertheless neither impulse nor desire is itself a purpose" (p. 78 op. cit.).

Though he subsequently declares that "a purpose is an end-view" (p. 78 op. cit.) and then proceeds with the elaboration: "that is, it involves foresight of the consequences which will result from acting upon impulse" (p. 78 op. cit.), which he expands by stating that "foresight of consequences involves the operation of intelligence. It demands, in the first place, observation of objective conditions and circumstances" (p. 78 op. cit), he nonetheless is determined to invoke his supreme cognitive undifferentiation device to render all the factors to which the stated elaborations refer, indeterminable, as his very next sentence clearly shows.

In his follow-up statement: "for impulse and desire produce consequences not by themselves alone but through their *inter-*

action" (italics mine, P.C.) "or co-operation with surrounding conditions" (p. 78 op. cit.) Dewey falls back on his supreme relativistic device.

With the reintroduction of the factor of interaction which Dewey is consistently applying as a supreme device for cognitive undifferentiation he makes it sure that the "surrounding conditions" remain as unspecifiable as the impulse and desire within the context of the last cited quotation.

In his subsequent elaboration in which he states that "the impulse for such a simple action as walking is executed only in active conjunction with the ground on which one stands" (p. 78 op. cit.), he is replacing the word interaction with the words "active conjunction."

Walking, in the stated context, becomes an activity for which no objective reason can be advanced and for which no discernible purpose can be detected.

Dewey's follow-up assertion in which he relates that "under ordinary circumstances, we do not have to pay much attention to the ground" (p. 78, 79 op. cit.) constitutes but a reassertion of his discounting of objective conditions, as objective conditions, as a basis for normal activity.

Though he issues a warning that "in a ticklish situation we have to observe very carefully just what the conditions are, as in climbing a steep and rough mountain where no trail has been laid out" (p. 79 op. cit.), he does not show any sign that he is willing to relax his dictum of cognitive undifferentiation in regard to the careful observations of which he cautions in the stated text.

In his subsequent exclamation to the effect that "exercise of observation is, then, one condition of transformation of impulse into a purpose" (p. 79 op. cit.), the words "exercise of observation" can mean only exercise of undifferentiation within the cognitive framework in which Dewey operates in this instance.

His subsequent insistence that "observation alone is not enough" (p. 79 op. cit.), which is followed by a plea that "we have to understand the *significance* of what we see, hear and touch" (p. 79 op. cit.), is meant to make provision for but another undifferentiation device.

In entering the factor of signification in the stated context, Dewey is providing for the establishment of an unbridgeable gap between the comprehension of *what is* and what merely *appears to be,* or, to present the just stated cognitive incongruity in a more elaborate form—between what is really occurring and what can be objectively confirmed through the marshalling of empirical evidence, and what is but taking place in an individual's imagination without any verifiable reference to any empirical evidence.

Significance, in the stated connection, refers to the unverifiable and thus to the unsignifiable.

When Dewey subsequently relates that "this significance consists of the consequences that will result when what is seen is acted upon" (p. 79 op. cit.) he refers to consequences which cannot be properly assayed, and thus to consequences which cannot be signified as such within the cognitive range of ultra-subjectivism and ultra-relativism, within the scope of which he forces himself to reason.

Dewey's subsequent proclamation that "the crucial educational problem is that of procuring the postponement of immediate action upon desire until observation and judgment have intervened" (p. 81 op. cit.) but calls attention to the sequence of his cognitive designification devices.

His reference to desire in the just quoted sentence constitutes a reference to his subjectivization device, the reference to observation and judgment, in turn, constitutes but a reference to his relativistic undifferentiation design.

Desire in the sense of cognitive subjectivization comes first, observation and judgment in the cognitive sense of relativistic undifferentiation is made to follow by Dewey in the realization of his quest for escaping into the indeterminable.

His follow-up declaration that "overemphasis upon activity as an end, instead of upon *intelligent* activity, leads to identification of freedom with immediate execution of impulses and desires" (p. 81 op. cit.) is meant to be a reproach to those who have placed emphasis on the subjective factor in an educational experience and have tried to account for that subjective factor in a specific form, instead of turning their analytical back on the subjective side of the educational experience, by rendering the individual's experience in education, be though the experience of a learner or a teacher, incomprehensible, through invocation of the ultra-relativistic undifferentiation device.

Intelligent activity, in the stated cognitive context, refers to an activity which has to be indefinitely delayed in view of the cognitive fragmentation of the observation and judgment, on the basis of which that activity is to be undertaken.

Intelligent activity, in the just stated sense, comes to refer to *inactivity*.

Cognitively, it should be realized in the stated connection, ultra-relativism is a step backward, as far as a specifiable comprehension is concerned, as compared with subjectivism; impulse and desire are at least identifiable as such within a subjectivistic cognitive range—within the relativistic mode of cognition, impulse and desire become unspecifiable as such; within the cognitive framework which recognizes nothing but a relation to a relation, to a relation, to a relation and so on, and so forth, it becomes wholly irrelevant whether an impulse or desire are being related to each other, or whether anything else is being related instead, since the factor of what is being related does not have to be disclosed and is, for that matter, not disclosable within an ultra-relativistic cognitive framework.

Within the ultra-relativistic cognitive framework it does not make any difference whether anything or nothing is involved in the attempted correlation.

Dewey's subsequent declaration that "traditional education tended to ignore the importance of impulse and desire as moving springs" (p. 83 op. cit.) tends to slur over the cognitive position which had been taken by the proponents of the traditional school.

Representative proponents of the traditional school did recognize, Dewey forgets to mention, the existence of subjective and objective cognitive stands.

Though it can be said with a certain justification that the proponents of the traditional school placed, by and large, a greater emphasis on the objective factor in regard to education, they did not, and do not deny that a subjective form of comprehension with reference to education is cognitively feasible and merits attention as such.

The proponents of traditional education could not have conceived of a preponderant objectivistic stand in their comprehension of education, had they not recognized by contradistinction the conceivability of a subjectivistic comprehension of education.

It, therefore, constitutes an ignoring of the respective cognitive positions of the proponents of the traditional school to state, as Dewey does, without any further qualification, that traditional education "tended to ignore the importance of personal impulse as moving strings" (p. 83 op. cit.).

The misleading presentation which Dewey proffers of the respective cognitive position which had been taken and is still being taken by the proponents of the traditional school, is matched by his misleading presentation of the respective cognitive stand to which representative proponents of the progressive schools have come to adhere.

He follows up his indictment of the alleged ignoring of the subjective factor in education by the proponents of traditional education, by claiming that "this is no reason why progressive education should identify impulse and desire with purpose and thereby pass lightly over the need for careful observation, for wide range of information, and for judgment if students are to share in the formation of the purposes which activate them" (p. 83 op. cit.).

The stated claim with reference to progressive education, constitutes an indictment on the part of Dewey of progressive education to which there is no actual reason for the adherents of progressive education to plead guilty.

When Dewey talks about "passing lightly over the need of careful observation, for wide range of information ,and for judgment" in the just stated connection, he is but referring to the passing over lightly of the *cognitive factor of undifferentiation* as applied to the "need for careful observation, for wide range of information, and for judgment," it should be realized.

The proponents of progressive education could be rightly accused of overemphasizing a subjectivistic stand in regard to education, their stand does not justify, however, an accusation that they have not attempted to take a position against the cognitive undifferentiation in regard to education; the proponents and adherents of progressive education, as it has come to be practiced, cannot be accused of passing over lightly the factor of application of ultra-relativism in regard to educational experience, since they had to realize that the very existence of progressive schools, as schools, is predicated upon their firm opposition to the effectuation of the ultra-relativistic undifferentiation principle in regard to educational theory and practice.

Dewey, it should be remembered, is pressing in the stated connection for the non-recognition of schools as a specific and specifiable social institution with reference to an educational experience, and it is within that range of argumentation that he is trying to discredit by misrepresentation the cognitive position of the proponents of any school education, regardless of whether the education is to be had in traditional or progressive schools.

When Dewey subsequently states that "in an *educational* scheme, the occurrence of a desire and impulse is not the final end" (p. 83 op. cit.), he means by final end the aim to attain cognitive undifferentiation.

In underlining the word educational in the just cited quote, Dewey, moreover, emphasizes that he considers the effectuation of cognitive undifferentiation a major factor in the predication of an educational plan.

An educational scheme or plan, in the stated cognitive context, can become but a plan for planlessness.

His subsequent assertion, that the occurrence of a desire and impulse "is an occasion and a demand for the formation of a plan and method of activity" (p. 83, 84 op. cit.) and that it is "the teacher's business . . . to see that the occasion is taken advantage of" (p. 84 op. cit.), constitutes, in the cognitive context in which it is offered, but an invitation to the teacher to abandon his role as orientor, and assume, instead, the role of a medium of disorientation, it constitutes an admonishment of the teacher, to accept planlessness and inactivity as educational goals.

In the amplification in which Dewey states that "since freedom resides in the operations of intelligent observation and judgment by which a purpose is developed, guidance given by the teacher to the exercise of the pupil's intelligence is an aid to freedom, not a restriction upon it" (p. 84 op. cit.) intelligent observation and judgment, it should be kept in mind, refer to a kind of observation and a kind of judgment, the function of which is to lead to a disordered comprehension, since the respective observation and judgment are supposed to be confined to the cognitive range of indeterminableness.

Guidance, in the stated connection, refers thus to a guidance which is based on something disordered and undirectable.

Within the exclusive cognitive range of the disordered and undirectable, neither freedom nor restriction can be conceived as such.

Freedom and restriction can assume meaning only when they are placed within a cognitive range which permits a contradistinction of the disordered and undirectable with the ordered and directable.

It is therefore plain verbosity on the part of Dewey to refer to a guidance on the part of the teacher in the just quoted citation as "an aid to freedom, not a restriction upon it," since the words freedom and restriction have become empty sounds within his cognitive range in which the disordered and undirectable are supposed to circumscribe the educational goals.

Dewey's subsequent remark in which he states that "sometimes teachers seem to be afraid even to make suggestions to the members of a group as to what they should do" (p. 84 op. cit.)

constitutes, in the light of his just stated cognitive position in regard to freedom and restriction, but a chiding of teachers for their unwillingness to lend themselves to the role in which, following Dewey's precepts, they would have to encourage contempt for direction and serve as promoters in the creation of disorder.

Dewey's subsequent insistence that "the way is, first, for the teacher to be intelligently aware of the capacities, needs, and past experiences of those under instruction, and, secondly, to allow the suggestion made to develop into a plan and project by means of the further suggestions contributed and organized into a whole by the members of the group" (p. 85 op. cit.) constitutes but an assertion on the part of Dewey that it is incumbent upon the teacher to consider it as his task to keep his awareness of the "needs and past experiences of those under instruction" within such cognitive bounds, as to allow that awareness to serve as a basis for a suggestion, the cognitive level of which would not permit to advance a cognitive distinction between plan and planlessness, between projection and a misprojection, between means and ends, and, moreover, between a further suggestion which is, in turn, to be held on a cognitive level which is to make it cognitively unfeasible to differentiate between what constitutes an organized and a disorganized whole.

(Parts and whole, it should be remembered in this connection, cannot be distinguished as such within Dewey's cognitive frame, as has been made clear in the respective treatment of that aspect in Part A of this critical exposition.)

In its net effect, the just stated proposition is meant to serve as an admonition to the teacher on the part of Dewey to restrict his awareness "of the capacities, needs, and past experiences of those under instruction" to a level of comprehension in which such awareness could lead to no more than the making of a vague suggestion of something unspecified and unspecifiable, which in turn is not to lead to anything more than another vague suggestion of something unspecific and unspecifiable.

In the follow-up proposition which states that "the plan, in other words, is a co-operative enterprise" (p. 85 op. cit.) the word co-operative stands for inter-active, in the stated cognitive context, and the just quoted sentence thus refers to a plan which is an enterprise in interaction, which in turn, means that the plan is not to be permitted to refer to anything else but to a relation of a relation, of a relation and so on, and so forth, ad infinitum.

The undifferentiation of the conceptions of freedom and social control on the part of Dewey, it should be realized, leaves him without an organizing principle for the molding of educational experience and thus equips him for the providing of a scheme for the progressive disorganization of the subject of education.

The subject of education, it should be noted, refers to a different range than the subject-matter of education.

The subject of education refers to what Dewey calls, life experience.

"Anything which can be called a study," Dewey declares in the stated connection, "whether arithmetic, history, geography or one of the natural sciences, must be derived from materials which at the outset fall within the scope of ordinary life-experience" (p. 86, 87 op. cit.).

"In this respect," he then states, "the newer education contrasts sharply with procedures which start with facts and truths that are outside the range of the experience of those taught, and which, therefore, have the problem of discovering ways and means of bringing them within experience" (p. 87 op. cit.).

With the just cited statement, Dewey provides a clear indication that he continues to adhere to his previously stated determination, not to recognize educational subject-matter, as such, and that he is bent on pursuance of that determination to have the entire subject of education, whether it refers to an educational experience to be had outside or inside schools, weighted down by an undifferentiated non-formalized life experience.

The words "facts and truths that are outside the range of the experience of those taught" in the just cited quote constitute a reference to formalized subject-matter which is provided in schools, while the citation of "the problems of discovering ways and means of bringing them within experience" constitutes a reference to the unformalized undifferentiation of the subject of education which is provided outside of schools, in the sense in which Dewey uses the respective wording, there can be little doubt, in the light of his preceding treatment of the matter, as well as in the light of the succeeding deliberations on the subject.

"But finding the material for learning within experience," Dewey makes a follow-up statement, "is only the first step" (p. 87 op. cit.).

"The next step," he relates, "is the progressive development of what is already experienced into a fuller and richer and more organized form, a form that gradually approximates that in which subject-matter is presented to the skilled, mature person" (p. 87 op. cit.).

The two just cited statements are merely declaratory in character, their real meaning is provided by the statement which follows in which Dewey relates "that this change (i.e., the progressive development of what is already experienced in a fuller and richer and more organized form, P.C.) is possible without departing from the organic connection of education with experience is shown by the fact that this change takes place outside of the school and apart from formal education" (p. 87 op. cit.).

The just cited statement places Dewey clearly on record in refusing to extend the range of the subject of education beyond the scope of a comprehension of an educational experience in which formalized subject-matter and schools have no part.

He amplifies his stand on having the subject of education confined to a range of educational experience in which neither formalized subject-matter, nor schools have any part, by the elaboration which follows.

"It is a cardinal precept of the newer school of education that the beginning of instruction shall be made with the experience learners already have; that this experience and the capacities that have been developed during its course provide the starting point for all further learning" (p. 88 op. cit.) he first relates, in the stated connection, and thus reasserts his determination to have all educational experience routed via the route which by-passes formalized subject-matter and schools.

"I am not sure," he ostensibly remarks in the stated connection, "that the other condition, that of orderly development toward expansion and organization of subject-matter through growth of experience, receives as much attention" (p. 89 op. cit.).

"Yet," and then he turns to what he is really after in the stated context, "the principle of *continuity* (italics mine, P.C.) of educative experience requires that equal thought and attention be given to solution of this aspect of the educational problem" (p. 89 op. cit.).

With the reintroduction of his conception of continuity as a principle for the fashioning of what he terms the "orderly development towards expansion and organization of subject-matter through growth of experience" Dewey but reaffirms his determination not to let the subject of education with reference to the educational experience which is to be had apart from formalized subject-matter and schools escape the stricture of cognitive undifferentiation.

Dewey keeps within the scope of the respective comprehension which he had set for himself, when he posits the subject of education versus subject-matter in education and sets in turn the range of educational experience to be had in schools against the range of educational experience to be had outside of schools, when he advances the claim that "because the studies of the traditional school consisted of subject-matter that was selected and arranged on the basis of judgment of adults as to what would be useful for the young sometime in the future, the material to be learned was settled upon outside the present life-experience of the learner" (p. 92 op. cit.).

When he subsequently declares that "in consequence, it had to do with the past; it was such as had proved useful to men in past ages" (p. 92 op. cit.) the "it" is meant to refer only to the specification of the past in reference to subject-matter and educational experience to be had in traditional schools, but he is implicitly attempting to voice with the stated declaration his opposition to have the past specified, as such, in reference to subject-matter, as such, and the delineability of school experience, as such.

The subsequent declaration to the effect that "the achievements of the past provide the only means at command for understanding the present" (p. 93 op. cit.) constitutes a preparatory move on the part of Dewey to have the past subjected to his cognitive undifferentiation device along with the present, as far as the respective bearing of a specifiable time sequence in regard to the subject of education which is not formalized subject-matter and the educational experience which is not a school experience are concerned.

The cognitive undifferentiation of the past and the present as specifiable aspects of time sequence is meant to be effected by Dewey's follow-up statement in which he declares that "just as the individual has to draw in memory upon his own past to understand the conditions in which he individually finds himself, so the issues and problems of present *social* life are in such *intimate and direct connection* (italics mine, P.C.) with the past that students cannot be prepared to understand either these problems or the best way of dealing with them without delving into their roots in the past" (p. 93 op. cit.).

Intimate and direct connection constitute but a varied wording for the principle of continuum in the just quoted statement and, as such, the reference to intimate and direct connection in the stated context constitutes nothing less than an invitation to render the present in reference to issues and problems of social life, in terms of the subject of education which is to be had outside the schools, as indiscernible as the past, in reference to problems in terms of a subject of education which is not formalized subject-matter of education.

The subsequent follow-up statement in which Dewey declares that "in other words, the sound principle that the objectives of learning are in the future and its immediate materials are in present experience can be carried into effect only in the degree that present experience is stretched, as it were, backward" (p. 93 op. cit.), is meant to complete the application of the cognitive undifferentiation device in regard to the specific and specifiable aspects of time sequence by having the future included in the respective undifferentiation drive.

The suggestion of having the present of educational experience as far as it refers to its immediate materials—which in the stated context means subject of education which is not to be had in schools—"stretched, as it were, backward" constitutes a reaffirmation of the invitation to render the present cognitively indistinguishable from the past in regard to the stated context.

The linking in turn of the future with regard to the objectives of learning—which in the stated context means learning without benefit of any specific and specifiable educational plan—with a present and a past, which are rendered indiscernible with reference to any educational experience, can have but the effect of leading to a cognitive undifferentiation of the future with reference to the stated context.

Dewey's subsequent insistence that "it" (the present educational experience outside the school, P.C.) "can expand into the future only as it is also enlarged to take in the past" (p. 93 op. cit.) constitutes but a reaffirmation of Dewey's stand on having the undifferentiation of the present and the past include the future as well.

That the rendering of the future as an unspecifiable factor in regard to an educational experience is cognitively fully compatible with the conception of a planless education, goes without saying.

The undifferentiation of the specific aspects of time sequence with regard to the educational experience which is to be had outside of schools and without the benefit of a delineated subject-matter is followed up by Dewey by an undifferentiation of the conception of a cause-effect relation in regard to the stated kind of educational experience.

"When education is based in theory and practice upon experience"—Dewey opens his undifferentiation drive on the cause-effect conception by restating his previously taken stand—"it goes without saying that the organized subject-matter of the adult and the specialist cannot provide the starting point" (p. 103 op. cit.).

"Nevertheless," he then ostensibly reassures, "it" (the organized subject-matter of the adult, P.C.) "represents the goal toward which education should continuously move" (p. 103 op. cit.).

"It is hardly necessary to say," he then concedes, "that one of the most fundamental principles of scientific organization of knowledge is the principle of cause-and-effect" (p. 103, 104 op. cit.).

He then makes the observation that "the way in which this principle is grasped and formulated by the scientific specialist is certainly very different from the way in which it can be approached in the experience of the young" (p. 104 op. cit.).

"But," he asserts, "neither the relation nor grasp of its meaning is foreign to the experience of even the young child" (p. 104 op. cit.).

"When a child two or three years of age," he relates, "learns not to approach a flame too closely and yet to draw near enough a stove to get its warmth he is grasping and using the causal relation" (p. 104 op. cit.).

In the just cited observation, Dewey, it should be noted, fails to make a clear distinction between imputation, in terms of a subjectivistic projection, and causation, in terms of an objectified projection.

The objectified projection of causation, which Dewey does not care to have mentioned, is predicated upon the recognition of attributes as a constituent part of objects without any direct reference to a subjective reaction to such attributes.

Dewey tries to slur over the conception of objectified projection of causation by insisting in his subsequent statement that "there is no intelligent activity that does not conform to the requirements of the relation (read causal relation, P.C.) and it is intelligent in the degree in which it is not only conformed to but consciously borne in mind" (p. 104 op. cit.).

The reference to "consciously borne in mind" in the just cited quotation is meant to have the subjectified projection of causation serve as the sole signifying factor of the causal relation.

When he subsequently relates that "in the earlier forms of experience the causal relation does not offer itself in the abstract but in the form of the relation of means employed to ends attained; of the relation of means and consequences" (p. 104 op. cit.) he continues to withhold the factor of the cognition of an objectified attribute as a constituent part of an object.

The distinction which he offers in the just cited quotation refers to a distinction between a subjectivistic projection of causation as applied to a concrete situation and a correlation of a number or for that matter, of any number of subjective projections of causation.

To identify the correlation of a number of subjective projections or, for that matter, of any number of subjective projections he uses the word abstract in the stated connection.

His subsequent insistence that "the trouble with education is not the absence of situations in which the causal relation is exemplified in the relation of means and consequences," coupled with the assertion that "failure to utilize the situations so as to lead the learner on to grasp *the relation* (italics mine, P.C.) in the given cases of experience is, however, only too common" (p. 105 op. cit.) is meant to emphasize that the deficiency, as far as the comprehension of cause and effect relation in educational experience is concerned, is to be ascribed to the lag in the correlation of any number of subjective cause and effect projections with each other in a numberless series.

When he subsequently remarks in the stated connection that "the logician gives the names 'analysis and synthesis' to the operations by which means are selected and organized in relation to a purpose" (p. 105 op. cit) he but reaffirms that he is determined to keep the range of an analysis and synthesis within the scope of his subjectivistic comprehension of cause and effect relation.

The reference to means as well as the reference to purpose in the just cited quotation is kept within a subjectivistic frame.

The putting of the words analysis and synthesis in the just quoted sentence in quotation marks provides a sufficiently clear indication that Dewey is conscious of proposing a use of the logical devices of analysis and synthesis not in a way in which those two logical methods have been generally conceived by logicians who were cognizant that the restriction of the application of analysis and synthesis by the purpose of an intended correlation of subjectivistic projections constitutes an unwarranted attempt to narrow and to cripple cognition.

In what follows, Dewey does not mind demonstrating the effects of a loose application of the logical devices of analysis and synthesis.

He first reaffirms his subjectivistic stricture by stating "that the more immature the learner is, the simpler must be the ends held in view and the more rudimentary the means employed, is obvious" (p. 106 op. cit.).

Subjective conception of means and ends are here presented as a comparatively lower and undeveloped form of comprehension.

The comparatively higher, the more developed form of comprehension is being presented as the one, in which even a subjectivistic comprehension in the counterposing of cause and effect in terms of means and ends comes to be discarded.

"With increased maturity," Dewey asserts, "the problem of interrelation of means becomes more urgent" (p. 106 op. cit.).

He thus moves for having the factor of ends, the factor of cause in a subjective form, eliminated as a subject of comprehension.

A further move to remove the factor of ends is being undertaken by Dewey in the very next sentence.

"The final justification of shops, kitchens, and so on in the school is not just that they provide opportunity for activity," Dewey asserts, "but that they provide opportunity for the *kind* of activity or for the acquisition of mechanical skills which leads students to attend to the relation of means and ends, and then to consideration of the way things *interact* (italics mine, P.C.) with one another to produce definite effects." (p. 106 op. cit.).

In the just stated sentence Dewey reapplies the succession of his designification moves.

He first removes the factor of activity, which in the stated connection refers to activity engendered through education, from objective educational means and ends, which in the stated connection refers to educational means and ends provided in schools; he places activity—the kind of educational activity which he expounds—within the subjectivistic framework of means and ends relation, in which the means and ends of school education have no cognitive place; he caps his exclusion of means and ends of school education from the cognitive range of the kind of activity—which is the kind of educational experience which he expounds—by insisting through reintroduction of his ultra-relativistic conception of interaction (he uses the verb interacts in the just stated quotation), that nothing more can be made knowable about activity than the factor that it is an effect.

The effect of what is not supposed to be asked in the stated connection; with the dismissal of the factor of cause as a subject for comprehension nothing more comes to be knowable of the kind of activity or the kind of educational experience which Dewey expounds than the realization that the activity is an activity—or, to use Dewey's substitute word for activity in the stated connection, that a definite result is a definite result. Whether the result is positive or negative does not matter within Dewey's cognitive frame.

His subsequent relation that "it is the same in principle as the ground for laboratories in scientific research" (p. 106-7 op. cit.) places Dewey on record for a removal of the activity, or more specific the educational experience which is provided in the higher, the scientific educational institutions to the range of comprehension of the kind of activity, or, more specific, the kind of educational experience which he, Dewey, expounds.

The kind of comprehension in which the specific educational experience, whether it is to be had in higher or lower educational institutions, rates as applicable knowledge is discarded by Dewey in favor of a comprehension of educational experience which comes to rate as an experience in which any knowledge which could have been conceivably attained through systematic schooling comes to register in no other way than in scattered fragments.

Fittingly, Dewey closes his essay on *"Experience and Education"* by devising the slogan *"Experience—the means and goal of education"* (p. 113 op. cit.), which, in the light of what he had stated before, can only be interpreted as an appeal for the ridding of the comprehension of educational experience from all the factors which make it feasible to distinguish between what accounts for education and what does not account for education; he thus sounds off his espousal of a philosophy of education by issuing a plea—in full accord with his ultra-relativistic cognitive stand and its subjectivistic counterpart—that the educative, the mis-educative and the non-educative factors in human experience be denied any specification as such.

The educative, the mis-educative and the non-educative factors, Dewey wants to make it particularly sure, are not to rate as distinct and distinguishable elements in the kind of experience which he, Dewey, wants to be regarded as education.

BIBLIOGRAPHICAL NOTE

PART A—*In Place of Science* (Chapters one, two and three) constitutes in the main a critical evaluation of Dewey's mode of conceptualization—or, more adequately stated, mode of deconceptualization—in the sphere of Philosophy of Science as is had been advanced by Dewey in his most mature work on Logic: *Logic, the Theory of Inquiry* (Henry Holt and Company, New York. 1938)

PART B—*In Lieu of Art* (Chapters four, five and six) presents mainly a critical appraisal of Dewey's mode of concept formation—or, more properly called, Dewey's mode of deformation of concepts—in the sphere of Philosophy of Art as it had found expression in Dewey's most systematic work on Art: *Art as Experience*, (Minton Balch & Co., New York, 1934.)

PART C—*Instead of Education* (Chapters seven and eight) contains in the main a critical examination of Dewey's mode of conceptualization—or, more correctly stated, mode of deconceptualization—in the sphere of Philosophy of Education as it had been given expression by Dewey in his conceptually most rounded work on Education: *Experience and Education*, (MacMillan Company, New York, 1938.)

Other works of John Dewey, this author has ascertained, contain either fragments of restatements of the conceptions which have been dealt with in this critical exposition or refer to matter which is extraneous to Dewey's overriding cognitive proposition of *Extreme Relativism*.

INDEX

Adaptation, 11, 74, 132, 201, 202
Alogical, 93, 97
Analysis, 232, 233
Anarchism, 210
Aristotle, Aristotelian, 42, 43, 84, 85

Balance, 7, 132
Belief, 21, 23

Causation, Causelessness, 7, 13, 19, 31, 44, 126, 152, 154, 163, 164, 180, 183, 229, 230, 231, 232
Change, 9, 11, 14, 26
Common Sense, 75, 76, 77, 78, 81, 83, 87
Communication, 48, 49
Consciousness, 33, 34, 36, 136, 138, 139, 147, 157
Continuity, 3, 4, 5, 118, 183, 184
Continuum, 6, 8, 36, 46, 183, 229
Control, 210, 213, 214, 215, 226

Death, 143
Descartes, R., X
Direction, 22, 162, 188, 189, 224
Disorder, 224, 225
Doubt, 21, 23, 24

Empirical, 34, 35
Emotions, 125, 135, 136, 168, 169
Ends of education, 233, 234
Environment, 23, 24, 29, 36, 130, 145, 185
Equilibrium, 133, 147
Experience, Educational, 175, 177, 199, 207, 209, 212, 226, 227, 228, 234
Experience, Esthetic, 98, 121, 124, 127, 143, 148, 151, 155, 160, 167, 169, 171
Existential, 51
Experimentation, Experiments, 27, 29

Fact, 32, 34
Fictitious, 73, 146
Freedom, 210, 215, 216, 217, 224, 226
Form, 143

Game, Rules of the, 211, 212
Growth, 176, 186, 217

Habit, 18, 20, 183, 184, 185
Harmony, 133, 136, 145
Hypothesis, 4, 61, 63

Ideas, 21, 23
Inactivity, 221
Indefiniteness, 14, 32, 99, 134
Indeterminableness, 4, 9, 21, 24, 28, 30, 32, 33, 98, 166, 192, 213, 214, 218
Indistinctiveness, 45, 53
Individual, 199, 200, 202
Inference, 32, 47, 71, 72
Integration, 24, 25
Intellect, Intellectual, 46, 136, 137, 139, 140
Intelligence, Intelligent, 218, 221
Interaction, 10, 24, 25, 26, 141, 201, 202, 210, 216, 233
Instinctive, 28, 40, 148
Instinctive Reflex, 150, 218
Intuitive, 28, 31

Judgment, 27, 220, 224

Language, 48, 49, 53, 54, 57, 58, 64, 66
Learning and Teaching, 204, 205, 206
Locke, John, X

Meaning, 51, 52, 56, 61, 63, 64, 65, 70, 131, 170
Meaninglessness, 51, 63, 65, 72, 86, 91, 129, 132, 140, 206
Means of Education, 233, 234
Mill, John Stuart, X

Nihilistic Devices, 3
Noncultural, 43, 44
Nonreasoned, 35, 36, 48, 135, 161
Nonreasoning, 135, 159, 180
Nonreflective, 36, 89, 101
Nonrhythmical, 133, 142
Nothingness, 3

Object, 27, 88, 137, 183, 184, 211
Objective, 64, 76, 82, 88, 195, 196
Ogden, C. K., 65
Organism, 5, 10, 12, 21, 23, 24, 27, 36, 130, 145, 185

Plan, Planlessness, 31, 223, 224, 225, 230
Plato, 108
Premise, Premiss, 123, 160
Progressive Education, 222, 223
Psychology, 87, 88

Quality, 21, 83, 86, 141, 156, 160, 168, 180

Rational, 34, 36, 55, 76
Reasoned, Reasoning, 36, 48, 93, 133, 135, 146, 159, 161, 180
Reflex Reactions, 40, 188, 217
Reid, T., 78
Relativism, Relativistic, 21, 23, 86, 176, 184, 185, 187, 210, 212, 216, 218, 220, 221, 223, 235
Rhythmical, 133, 142
Richards, I. A., 65
Rignano, 9

School, 195, 210, 221, 223, 228
Serial, 29, 30, 32
Series, 12, 145, 194
Significance, 168, 220
Situation, 29, 193
Spinoza, B., VIII
Stewart, D., 78
Subject, 21, 183, 184, 226, 227
Subject Matter, 21, 32, 39, 73, 86, 204, 205, 206, 227, 228, 229
Subjective, 46, 76, 82, 152, 162, 195, 196, 201, 202, 212, 216, 222
Subjectivism, 21, 220, 221
Subjectivistic, 21, 33, 211, 213, 214, 218, 235
Symbol Constellation, 48, 49, 64, 65, 66, 67
Symbols, 52, 59, 62, 63, 65, 68, 70, 72, 111, 141
Synthesis, 232, 233
System, 54

Teaching and Learning, 204, 205, 206
Time, 24, 146, 206, 207

Understanding, 101, 102, 126, 201
Undifferentiated, 51, 134, 175, 182, 184, 201, 204, 209, 215, 218, 219, 220, 223, 229
Undifferentiation, 6, 41, 49, 76, 122, 123, 129, 131, 132, 143, 151

Volition, Volitional, 166, 167, 168, 170

Whole, 225